MANAGING PROJECT RISK

Business risk management for project leaders

YEN YEE CHONG ● EVELYN MAY BROWN

London · New York · San Francisco · Toronto · Sydney
Tokyo · Singapore · Hong Kong · Cape Town · Madrid
Paris · Milan · Munich · Amsterdam

PEARSON EDUCATION LIMITED

Head Office:
Edinburgh Gate
Harlow CM20 2JE
Tel: +44 (0)1279 623623
Fax: +44 (0)1279 431059

London Office:
128 Long Acre, London WC2E 9AN
Tel: +44 (0)207 447 2000
Fax: +44 (0)207 240 5771
Website: www.business-minds.com

First published in Great Britain in 2000

ISBN 0 273 63929 3

British Library Cataloguing in Publication Data
A CIP catalogue record for this book can be obtained from the British Library.

10 9 8 7 6 5 4 3 2 1

Typeset by Northern Phototypesetting Co. Ltd, Bolton
Printed and bound in Great Britain by Biddles Ltd, Guildford and King's Lynn

The Publishers' policy is to use paper manufactured from sustainable forests.

About the authors

Yen Yee Chong is actively involved with the aspects of project management for DSL Consultants Ltd, covering projects in the UK, Russia and Greece. He has lived and worked in the Baltic and Russian region for over three years, and worked for George Soros's Civic Education Project at universities in the Baltics, especially Estonia. His previous book for Financial Times Publications was *Risk Management in Russia and the Baltic States*, October 1997. He specializes in the markets of Greece, Russia and the Baltic States for DSL Consultants Ltd.

Evelyn May Brown is at executive level with DSL Consultants Ltd and is involved with various levels of project assessment activities within the UK, Greece and Egypt. She previously worked for the Australian government situated in the UK, also for British government departments including the Department of Trade and Industry and Value Added Tax headquarters. Part of her duties entailed enforcement of liquidation, insolvency and bankruptcy for various companies, partnerships and sole-proprietors.

Since its creation in 1981 DSL expertise has been in designing office information systems, and office environments. Our independent service is to evaluate and install the most suitable systems for the client – DSL does not stock or sell equipment. This process brings DSL into all stages of project management, from systems analysis and design to implementation (production) of office systems.

Analysis covers the user's needs, system requirements, feasibility, access, council planning, company authorization and operating licences, etc., as well as estimation of budget, schedule and manpower with ergonomic considerations. Design involves creating user specifications and blueprints for system construction to satisfy user needs, capacity and safety features (mechanical aspects, heating, ventilation, air conditioning, electricity circuits, cabling, etc.). We then combine the user's system requirements with IT and telecommunications technology to design the 'best fit' and ensure compatibility of specialized applications in banking and trading software platforms, especially with existing systems. But our involvement does not stop there – we continue to expand or upgrade the client's system for additional and future needs.

DSL has to assess all the above factors in a project, such as constructing a bank's dealing room. There are also the various issues of personnel management, and linking with all the parties involved in the project. These include the customer, end-users, regulatory authorities, contractor, sub-contractors et al. One of the main tasks is obtaining supplies and systems from sub-contractors, and getting the best deal for the customer during the invitation to tender (ITT). This is complicated partly because of the client's lack of knowledge about the systems and technology on the market, and partly because of contractors' performance. Hiring a contractor who under-performs can have such an impact that we help in framing the ITT process.

This process exists to sift out those contractors who are unlikely to deliver the suitable service or product for the customer. There is also the possibility that a bidding contractor may be bribing one of the client's employees to make the hiring process unreliable. DSL comes in as an independent arbitrator to determine who and what will provide the best deal for the customer, thereby cutting down the selection risk. The downside risk of hiring the wrong firm or taking on unsuitable equipment for the job is too great. The customer may be king, but he still can make the wrong choice in picking the wrong product or contractor.

Contents

Acknowledgements

Writing a book is a considerable project that encompasses a variety of tasks that are never thanked in full. We would first wish to express our gratitude to those kind enough to write a book foreword or to review the earlier versions. In alphabetical order:

Dr. Mamdouh Barakat, MB Risk Management, London
John Barclay, Credit Suisse First Boston, London
Dr. Lev Borodovsky, Credit Suisse First Boston, New York and Global Association of Risk Professionals (GARP)
Simon Card, BT Global Finance, London
Tony Carter, Halliburton, Brown & Root, UK
Air Marshall Sir John Curtiss, Pathfinders, London
Jim Godwin, Moscow-Narodny Bank, London and Moscow
Simon LaMoon, AON Group Insurance, London
Giles Pallister, Royal Academy of Arts, London
Prof. Charles E. Scott, Loyola College, USA
Prof. Dr. M. Peter van der Hoek, Erasmus University, Netherlands
Klaus Winkler, Telepassport GmBH, Frankfurt.

In addition, we thank:

Mahmoud Awaad (DSL Consultants) for his sterling efforts in project management.
George Littlejohn, Emerging Markets Forum, London
Hana Bishop and Paul Casterton, London
Det. Supt. Ken Farrow, City of London Police
Mike Kolker, USA
Andrew Blythe, Hanscomb, Moscow
Alex K., Athens (shipping)
Thomas Tow and Melanie Francis (architects), Tow-Francis, Singapore
Chu Mei-Peng, Malaysia
Tomas Gilså, Stockholm

Also, our thanks to the banking consultants. In particular:
Steve Peachey, London

Wolfgang Berg, Munich
Marinus Piek, Netherlands

Our thanks also to the team at FT Prentice Hall who devoted their efforts to this book: Richard Stagg, Amelia Lakin, Valerie Roberts, Linda Dhondy, Iain Campbell and others who were kind and patient enough to help us. Our FT Prentice Hall editors Vivienne Church and Elizabeth Truran helped considerably in reading earlier proofs and being diligent wading through reams of paper – seemingly a thankless task at times and one for which we are very grateful to them.

Finally, we would like to express our thanks to those we have omitted or who wished to collaborate but had to keep their names confidential.

Yen Y. Chong
Evelyn Brown
DSL Consultants Ltd.
2 London Wall Buildings
London EC2M 5UU
Tel: 0171 448 5000
Fax: 0171 448 5222
Email: DSL@BTinternet.com

Foreword

Risk management encompasses a wide variety of different types of risk in any financial institution – market, credit, liquidity, event and operational. Until fairly recently, operational risk was something of a Cinderella – never quite invited to the ball attended by the big players in market risk and their brethren in the other fields. It lacked the perceived thrill of the eternal 'poachers and gamekeepers' struggle between risk managers and financial engineers. Identifying and managing operational risk seemed little more than sound common sense, a vital but rather pedestrian back-office function.

Two developments have changed that – an awareness amongst senior management that operational risk deserves to be taken seriously in an increasingly risky world; and the attempt to incorporate all forms of risk in the next generation of enterprise risk management systems.

Five key forces are changing the way that senior managers in major institutions round the world view their future – new technologies, globalization, non-bank competition, deregulation and the opening up of previously protected markets. Cross-border activity always heightens risk, and the trend towards globalization amongst the big banks' customers means that they must follow the trend, go global and thus have to cope with a rapidly-growing set of risks.

Increased competition, partly in the wake of liberalization, always puts pressure on profits, at least in the short term. So corners may be cut and ever-bigger risks may be taken to maintain bottom lines.

At BT Global Finance, we work closely with our customers in the biggest financial institutions worldwide to help them cope with all forms of risk. Cooperating with them in building enterprise-wide risk management systems is as much part of the job as installing a phone line.

So my colleagues and I welcome Yen Yee Chong and Evelyn Brown's distinguished contribution to the field of operational risk. They, and others in the industry, have finally managed to get it its long-overdue invitation to the ball.

Simon Card OBE
Senior Marketing Manager
BT Global Finance Sector

Introduction

There are business projects that run smoothly and according to plan, but many do not. There is no such thing as a risk-free project. Running a project requires a lot of planning and some occasional gut-wrenching decisions when the unexpected happens. A mark of a good project manager is that he understands the risks and can meet them. It is not possible to foresee and to know how to handle each risk beforehand, but a successful manager knows how to change plans to meet risks. Adapt or die!

Gambling, risk and risk management

A business project has a life of its own; it can enliven or terrorize the faint-hearted. Part of the thrill of the project lies in the project owner's appetite for risk. The fine dividing line between adventure and folly rests on the understanding of the potential losses arising from the project, and the definition of acceptable risk for the project owner and all collaborating parties. There are many factors operating against your project, and there are people who would be happy to see your project fail. Handling risk entails putting your money where your mouth is. Business sometimes works on a winner-takes-all basis.

Looking at the real world, what do these have in common?

- NASA space shuttle
- Piper Alpha oil platform
- LTCM hedge fund
- Barings bank derivatives trading
- Royal Opera House
- European Monetary Union
- Millennium Bug.

These were, or are, major events, or high-profile projects. Such projects were created to take on changes in the marketplace – they carried a multitude of risks in various forms. Many organizations and people undertook them; some projects were adjudged successes, others failures. The major failures in this list also provide us with lessons to be learned; that is, if we want to learn from them at all. We have to accept that risk crops up in our everyday lives. Business is part of this wide picture, only with more complicated investments and bets laid on the outcome. *'Life is a gamble at terrible odds. If it was a bet, you wouldn't take it.'*[1]

This book does not assume that the reader has deep project risk management experience, rather, it aims to be a practitioner's handbook on risk management. Theory is fine, but practice is better. Proper exercise of risk management in real life does not only lower the potential damage to your project, it may well help you reap more profit.

Lady luck

Business managers are sometimes quoted in the media blaming the fate of their company or project on unforeseen events outside their control. Can they be right? We will show that in many cases they were able to lead the business better when they had risk-managed the project properly. Proper project risk management reduces the likelihood of poor business results that are commonly attributed to 'bad luck'. There's bad luck and there's improper project management. Businesses operate in situations where there is an element of uncertainty, therefore, a factor of risk. As Caesar, that great project manager, said of his fate determined by casting a die: *'Alea iacta est.'* (See *Gambling With Your Life*, p. 9.)

> Our modern business instincts were honed by the early gambling habits of the ancient Chinese and the classical Greeks.

Our modern business instincts were honed by the early gambling habits of the Pharaohs, ancient Chinese and the classical Greeks. Peter Bernstein wrote of risk, riches and gambling: *'The prospect of getting rich is highly motivating, and few people get rich without taking a gamble.'*[2]

Classical Greeks and Romans were not unknown to have 'doctored' gambling instruments or to have openly cheated. Such issues are examined in *Insiders and Corruption*, p. 127. Project success is not all luck by any means. We will show that this 'pro-active' business stance is part of effective risk management. Risk management also involves the accurate evaluation of probabilities and risks; some of the

> The notable difference between a business investor and a gambler is that the latter exercises very little control over his destiny.

theory was born on the outcome of dice cast. Taking risks can always appear profitable to the business-minded person – it is all part of business. The world's greatest central banker, US Federal Reserve Chairman Alan Greenspan, said: *'Risk-taking is a necessary condition for wealth creation.'*[3] Place your bets! The notable difference between a business investor and a gambler is that the latter exercises very little control over his destiny. This book turns the focus away from gambling towards those who manage business projects. Therefore, by skill and good project management we can stack the business odds in our favour. Successful project managers can be influenced and fashioned – it is not just down to genetic abilities or fate.

We must work on business skills just like reading the current form of horses before a race. True, unexpected events do crop up along the way, but running a business is partly surprise management; there are often no nice surprises. We would like to think that business people think and operate rationally with great levels of intelligence and that they conduct thorough market research. Few who do good market research end up poor. We will prove that some business activities are little more than a game of mere chance, and take on too much risk. You will see that a lot of profits, expected or promised, are misleading. Take the risk out of your business – get your profit expectations on track.

> " Few who do good market research end up poor. "

Our goals on risk

All projects have goals. We set ourselves the goal of delivering something a bit different and more useful than the large range of project management books available. This is designed to be a book for practice. It does not assume a prior knowledge of managing major business projects, nor a significant background in mathematics. Our explicit objective from Financial Times Prentice Hall was to be practical, and to display knowledge in a simple format which can be put into practice easily. Our contacts in various industries indicated that our book could fill a niche in the market. It is not a recipe book to meet all types of risk in all types of enterprise. Take the parts you need for your project risk management knowledge, tailor them, then put them into practice.

We look at various aspects of risk and the approaches that a project manager must take. SMEs (small and medium size enterprises) figure too because they comprise a growing part of our economy. We assume little advanced mathematical knowledge on your side – project management is not full of equations from nuclear science. On the engineering/operations research side, this is not a book focussed on critical path method, scheduling or budgeting. All these issues crop up, and are examined, although not in great detail. Such standard techniques, if somewhat mechanistic, are left to the operations management textbooks. We do not focus solely on one profession or industry; we have taken cross-sections from many fields and experiences. Hopefully, such variety will be beneficial. Nevertheless, the focus of the book is on the project management practitioner. It is a case of not just knowing, but doing. This book is a whistle-stop tour of project risk management. It may go at break-neck speed at times, but hopefully there will be stations along the way that you may wish to revisit.

How to use this book

You do not have to be a high-powered financier or a high-falutin mathematician to use this book. You will note the intention to omit complicated mathematics and equations; we designed it to be understood, not to blind the user. Perfectly responsible and successful business people run their enterprises without using overly complex mathematical calculations. Every business person is running one or more projects, and proper project management should involve adequate risk management. Thus, many people in business who do not consider themselves project managers are, in fact, managing important business projects. You have to be a risk manager somewhere whether you like it or not.

We used numerous scenarios from our real-life experience, or outlined semi-fictional case studies to illustrate the major points in a readily understandable manner. Important messages are highlighted in the form of bullet action points. This makes it possible to refer back to the book quickly and easily on a day-to-day basis during the implementation of risk management in a project. Risk management is not easy, but it is applicable if you set your mind on it. *Project risk management is* not *rocket science!* We will revisit this theme constantly.

Finally, some work examples have been included at the end of the book to give the reader the chance to explore more in depth. We pose questions which allow the reader to test his/her understanding and practise some risk skills. Take the material and tailor as necessary for your specific project.

Managing project risk: opening to endgame

Running a project is like a game of chess in some ways – you have to plan your moves at the outset.

The start of the project reflects planning, or chess opening, as presented in the analytical sections of Chapters 1, 2 and 3. The middle game is often more akin to trench warfare, where you have to look over the battle-ground to see how your troops are coping. A lot of project risk management is rather mundane, just like warfare, except that you deal with the 'enemy' through meetings, phone calls and documentation. The roles of your troops in the risk management process are dealt with in Chapters 4, 5, 6, 7, 8 and 9. The end game is the culmination of successful planning and adept project man-oeuvring, putting you into a tactical position of advantage to execute the *coup de grâce*. One again, these are rather bureaucratic moves because the modern manager has to cope with regulations, national standards, EMU, project management toolkits, etc. The finale approaches and the end game preparations continue apace in Chapters 10, 11 and 12.

Notes and references

1   Stoppard, T., *Rosencrantz and Guildenstern are Dead*, Act 3.
2   Bernstein, P. (1998) *Against the Gods*, Wiley, p. 21.
3   *Financial Times*, 2 October 1998, Lex, p. 14.

1

Objectives

❝ The easiest way to double your money is to fold your cash in half. **❞**

Groucho Marx

In this first chapter, we seek to establish the context and focus for the book and to give the reader some pointers on how to get the best out of it. The best way to manage risk is to get the most out of your projects, more money or other reward. That's business. The business context is one with which we are all familiar. The marketplace today is increasingly volatile, and subject to swift changes with potentially major impact. In every business sector we see an increasing number of emerging products, services and new ventures, exhibiting ever-increasing technical and technological complexity.

Business risk springs up where the products or services are manufactured/ processed, offered or purchased. There can be many outcomes for enterprises: continuation, bankruptcy, natural disaster or a transition to another form of enterprise. *Project risk* comes within the phase from the finite series of business activities that are defined at the project start to the project end to meet specified goals. A business is generally a series of projects; often the organization runs a collection or portfolio of interdependent projects simultaneously. This is also known as a *programme*, not to be confused with program – US English for a computer software module. The programme is sometimes called, confusingly, a project. The *project* is an enterprise or activity planned to use a combination of resources, notably capital, land, labour and time, towards achieving a *goal* or a set of goals. The project control brings in two traditional project tools: an estimated or fixed *budget* and a set *schedule* or time period to reach these goals.

In the meantime, the concept of the 'community enterprise' is no longer finding favour; the opportunities, investment and jobs go to the places of highest likely profit in a global trading environment. Lenders still want the high investment returns, but they also fear worse outcomes, so they can be increasingly risk-averse in various situations. There will be returns that are not monetary, but these will still have to be factored into the project equation. Some organizations will set their goals as being defined by non-numerical values, or to gain a benefit that is not a monetary profit. Today's leaders want the best compromise to balance the *risk-return ratio*. It will be shown in successive chapters that the traditional measures of investment return – internal rate or return, discounted cash flow, net present value, pay-back, etc. – are inadequate because they fail to take account of the *cost of risks* during the project life.

Risk in context

We live in a time of social and political uncertainty. Globalization is a major factor for businesses. The business environment is no longer limited to the country in which our company is based. Far Eastern and ex-Communist Bloc economies interact with the west and the emerging markets in a complex network. Competition for today's businesses can come as easily from across the globe as it can from the next town. Today's management teams need to be better, faster, leaner and quicker on their feet than ever before. The pace of technological change suggests that this is likely to continue well beyond the foreseeable future and it is clear that standing still is not an option. Only those organizations that adapt well will prosper; change management becomes both a business necessity and an art. The true measure of a business's success is the rate at which it can improve its range of products/services, and the way it produces and delivers them.

The reason why risk is so difficult to determine is mainly because of the varied and uncertain extent to which project players act to influence the final outcome of the project. The normal project situation is one of a project team collaborating within the corporate structure. This is the conventional or 'hard' view of the project life. The reality is much broader and more complicated. Many people and parties exert influence on the project, either seen or unseen (see Fig. 1.1). Your project is at the centre – the pressures and strains make it 'piggy in the middle'. The wider view is often termed the soft system view, or one that has a fuzzy logic. There is something of Heisenberg's uncertainty principle here. You can never be completely sure of the speed or direction of your project because of the various influences of people and parties on your progress. Others, e.g. Checkland, have discussed this soft system view in great detail.[1]

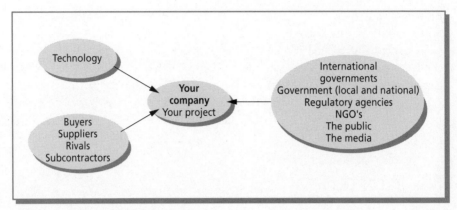

Fig 1.1 ● The universal set of project players

Threat management

Risk management is seen by many business people as the answer for developing our ability to anticipate the unexpected. We can identify and analyze project risks and then use our ability to manage them. There are plenty of rewards for those who can capitalize on the threats, those who can be cleverest at 'threat management'. Conversely, there are potentially great profits for those who can assess risk better than their rivals; they can see investment conditions much more clearly. This is a case of 'opportunity management'.

Risk management should not be seen as yet another task for today's business player to fit into an already overcrowded business schedule. Risk managers have to adopt ways of prioritizing the working day and deploying people and capital most productively. They need to succeed through accepting that life is far from predictable, but they also realize that things do not work out exactly as planned. Risk management can help to ensure that they reach the successful goal eventually. The important issue is to focus on the uncertainties of tomorrow and to be able to identify and handle them.

First we have to undertake accurate project selection with the resources available to us, that is to say, the best portfolio of projects that give the highest rate of profit under *acceptable risk conditions*. This means that we will accumulate the projects which we have concluded give us the optimum risk-return. In order to reach this stage, we have to avoid two kinds of potential error:

● Type I – we end up accepting a project that we discover is too costly or too risky. This would result in lower-than-expected profits, or worse, net loss or damage. Eurotunnel is often cited as one such business example (see the Channel Tunnel case study, p. 83. Another is the Ford Edsel, a car that failed despite favourable initial market research. Henry Ford liked it so much that he named it after his son; he also regretted its astonishingly low sales. Pharmaceutical cases, such as the Thalidomide disaster which left babies with deformed limbs, generally force us to exercise caution against accepting medicines that may involve us in Type I errors.

● Type II – we rejected a project that not only posed an acceptable level of risk but also made exceptionally high profits. This is particularly embarrassing or damaging as we usually discover this fact because a business rival has taken up the initial costs and risks to run a very profitable project. The examples are many: The Full Monty, the British hit movie rejected by many and eventually funded by Fox, is one; or Dell computer stock rising in value by 30 times in ten years. K'NEX, the $100 million-sales-per-year rival to Lego toys, is another example. K'NEX was rejected by all major toy producers until Hasbro picked it up for launch in 1992.

We then need to concentrate on outcomes that have the greatest potential to prevent business success through causing project damage or loss, i.e. to 'ring fence' them once they are operational. The achievement of a profitable project that runs itself is, perhaps, the ultimate joy for risk management acolytes. Risk-free projects in real life – paradise postponed, you might say?

Risk attitude and perspective

Business success depends partly upon the risk perception. We each have our own attitude towards or way of dealing with risk; we choose to define four.

1 Risk-averse are those who are inherently conservative investors, e.g. putting money in UK gilt government securities/US Treasury bills (zero risk of default), working in secure pensionable employment, and protected by appropriate health insurance. '*I want to work in a secure nine-to-five job.*' We see this attitude in percentage football, where clubs may play safe defensive formations, but dull games. Tennis players also generally adopt this attitude on the second serve by hitting the ball more slowly so as not to commit a double fault.

2 Risk-seekers are those who invest their savings in the market, take more open or vulnerable investment positions, and are fatalistic about the future. They want to operate knowing there is a considerable chance of experiencing a 'downside'. '*I want $100 on Brazil to win the 2002 World Cup.*' Or: '*I could make a million on the next bet.*' Or: '*These penny stocks could double overnight – I don't want blue-chip stocks.*' It is a moot point whether some of the top sports people are really risk-seekers as such; they have no choice on many occasions – it's all part of their job. Grand Prix motor racing embodies this spirit. The 1998 racing season demonstrated the intense rivalry and huge sums at stake in this multi-million dollar business. The on-track and off-track rivalry between the McLaren-Mercedes and the Ferrari teams showed the need to take (calculated) risks on every turn of the race-course (see Formula 1 Grand Prix racing case study, p. 119).

It is also often pointed out that cigarette-smokers are quintessential risk-seekers. We do not see cigarette-smoking as a project, we prefer to classify it as a lifestyle and one that carries a foreseeable risk. Insurance companies are inclined to do the same and thus charge higher life premiums for smokers. Each puff of a cigarette is shown by scientific research to shorten the life expectancy of the individual smoker. The government warning on a packet of cigarettes does not seem to influence the intake significantly. It is estimated that over 100,000 people in the UK die each year from smoking-related diseases and illnesses.[2] An even greater number require healthcare for smoking-induced ill-health. This medical care has to be paid for, as do the liability claims against tobacco manufacturers that have touched $250 billion over ten years throughout a number of US states. Liability and risk are issues that crop up in modern life.

Some business leaders see the warnings but take their businesses into commercial territory that is unduly risky. This book would have to say 'Tough!' to those who read warnings but ignore them. Risk management is about heeding the warnings, mapping out the risks and trying to avoid or lessen their impact.

3 Risk-aware project-players and investors are those who try to see the uncertainties of life for what they are and take appropriate action. These people adopt a consistent risk analytical and risk management procedure (implicitly or otherwise) to select the best course of action. Insurance companies personify the type of people whose job it is to enumerate the likelihood of the risk hazards and to offer suitable options. But there is a variety of role-players who go into the market and are seen to be risk managers in some form, including bank credit officers, international fund managers, industrial health & safety workers, mechanical testing engineers, architects, airline pilots, etc. (see Business Roles, Chapter 6).

4 Risk-ignorant are those blissful in an intentional or unintentional lack of knowledge about their exposure. '*We can't do much. This is a risky business anyway.' 'You can't guess the future.' 'You can't judge from the past.' 'It's a fool-proof business.' 'Every project is different – we can't predict much either way.*'

The Japanese banking industry is quite possibly included in this category. The Japanese spent a lot of the 1990s denying there was a crisis. Then the house of cards began to fold. Yamaichi, Nomura, Daiwa and others either stopped trading abroad or were taken over. The 'no problem' syndrome culminated in the government take-over of the bankrupt Long Term Credit Bank (LTCB) in October 1998; the party was over.

You may care to believe that you are risk-averse rather than risk-seeking by nature; most business people do not care much to be viewed by their peers as risk-seeking. Yet developing a greater awareness of risk represents a better business strategy and it will lead to improved performance. A more realistic understanding of the uncertainties and potential outcomes will benefit business. It can mean less investment in unnecessary insurance, protection and safeguards. It can also give you the freedom of operation to see a good business opportunity which others shun as too risky. Even for the few truly committed risk-takers, a proper understanding and healthy respect for the risks involved is a sound philosophy. If investors are really prepared in this way, they are less likely to suffer the pain of failure or disaster. Forewarned is fore-armed.

Acceptable risk

The essence of risk is that it crops up in everyday life in some form. Just to complicate matters, people are wont to give us advice, and sometimes it may be of rather dubious quality. It may be peppered with phrases like: *It's a piece of cake.' 'Don't worry. It's not dangerous.' 'Are you scared? There's nothing to be frightened of.' 'The likely profits seem good.' 'This is a good investment.'* The worry about the risk is increased when one has to pay for this spurious advice.

The ancient Greeks attempted to divine the future by consulting the Oracle at Delphi. The priestess would prophesize the future based on the interpretation of various signs or portents. These days, we enlist experts in a specific field and amalgamate them into a Delphi group to advise us. The project risks would be ranked by a Delphic group of experts according to likelihood, e.g. A) very probable (75 per cent), B) possible (25 per cent), C) improbable (1 per cent or lower). The risk impact would then be tagged for these Delphic scenarios on, for example, interest payments or total project costs of A) $12 million, B) $15 million, C) $25 million+. But you still need to cut down the risk of planning errors because of the fundamental opacity of the market (nobody can divine the future for certain), plus the possibility of your Delphi group being biased or inexperienced. If you want to see how we can improve on the basic Delphic forecasts, read on.

The question of risk-return is distilled into a pertinent project question: What is an acceptable risk? This issue brings together economic, business, political, technological and environmental factors. Risk-benefit analysis comes in to help us make a decision. One approach is that of: formulation, analysis and interpretation.[3]

1 Formulate and identify scope of anticipated risks, e.g. through brainstorming, teamwork or Delphi.
2 Analyze and model risk.
3 Interpret results; select options, plan and implement for the chosen options.

Acceptable risk is not a factor that is defined by one variable; it is a more complex issue. We can, for example, take five categories for Consequence (impact):

1 Disastrous
2 Severe
3 Substantial
4 Marginal
5 Negligible.

Six grades of Likelihood (probability of event):

1 Highly likely
2 Likely
3 Fairly likely
4 Unlikely
5 Very unlikely
6 Extremely unlikely.

Source: extracted from RAMP[4]

You may wish to list the events yourself according to the designated probability groups, with appropriate weightings for the resultant effect. The project actions will be partly based upon your risk appetite – how much you wish to risk (win or lose) in a probabilistic game. The subjective judgement of your acceptable risk can be a source of great dispute when running projects. Where the risk impact for your project has been initially evaluated, the next step is to decide how to act:

Risk impact	Action required
Intolerable	Must eliminate or transfer risk
Undesirable	Attempt to avoid or transfer risk
Acceptable	Retain and manage risk
Negligible	Can be ignored

Source: extracted from RAMP[5]

Acceptable risk is, nevertheless, a fuzzy notion that is frequently a source of great dispute in projects.

Gambling with your life

The Royal Statistical Society of the UK outlined in 1998 its guide for assessing risk during life. The relative base of merely living on earth carries a value of zero on the scale up to ten.

Life, we are told, is ultimately lethal in the long-run. The DSL experience in emerging markets tells us that people are willing to gamble with their lives. For example, our work in Greece, Russia and Egypt shows how risky driving is, with red traffic lights and one-way signs often a matter of individual interpretation. Greece has the highest death rate per capita on EU roads.[6] More than 2000 people are killed each year, and 35 000 are badly injured. Only 37 per cent of those with serious head injuries make a full recovery. Motorcycle riders are required to wear crash helmets, but many don't. Helmets are often seen strapped on the back of bikes or hung on the handlebars. Comfort counts more than safety. The death rate among motorbike riders is about 30 times that of car drivers. Traffic jams and accidents may have an impact on the success of your project. Do these incidents influence people's attitude? Not really. But then, there seem to be real limits from our experience on how you can change people's attitudes, even when their lives are at stake.

Our understanding of mathematics and probability was built on breakthroughs in calculus by Leibnitz and Newton, with seminal work by Blaise Pascal. Recent Royal Statistical Society research sheds some light on the way in which the insurance industry views risk. The earliest insights into life risk analysis were provided by John Graunt of England in 1662. His seminal work *Natural and Political Observations Made Upon the Bill of Mortality* in 1662 set the foundations for much of the direction of insurance and actuarial analysis. This ground-breaking research built on the treatise on gambling and dice by the famous Dutch physicist Christian Huygens, *De Ratiociinis in Alae Ludo*, of 1657.[7] He helped to encourage the study of probability in England. Some of the phenomena investigated, such as unbiased or unfair judges, modelling devices or dice, still trouble investors and business to this day (see LTCM case study, p. 165).

One phenomenon that causes problems is the existence of long probability distribution tails. We can look at the example of BSE or 'mad-cow' disease.

CASE STUDY

BSE cattle infection, UK

The outbreak of bovine spongiform encephalopathy (BSE) or 'mad cow' disease created a truly political issue. The peak years of BSE were 1985–9, and the Conservative government and the regulatory health authorities were faced with essentially two choices – either to keep things under wraps ('there is no problem – official') or to inform the public and act immediately ('there is a possible problem and to contain the risk of contagion, we are culling x million cattle'). See the earlier discussion of Type I and Type II errors.

The media publicity throughout Europe was extremely negative for Britain. The beef export ban partly reflected widespread anger, and the possibility that innocent consumers in the UK had been exposed to contaminated meat and a life-threatening disease was worrying. The possibility that the government had quashed information about people being poisoned by infected food developed into a major scandal.

The distribution chart of the infected cattle took a normal bell-shape pattern. But the questions remain:

● what is the extent and risk of long probability distribution tails?
● will many more infected cattle be found after 1999?
● how can we cut down the damage?
● who will be affected?

We outline the spread of those cases in the UK which follow the normal or bell-shaped distribution. There are long or fat probability distribution tails that exist at the left and right-hand extremes of our data. We know what happened in the past, but we are unsure of the risk in the future and whether we will encounter fat probability distribution tails. This means we are faced with a mathematical possibility of another BSE outbreak. We are unable to state conclusively that the risk after 1999 is zero because of uncertainties over the incubation period of BSE before it manifests itself in human beings. Thus, the long probability distribution tail at the extreme after 1999 may even reflect an upsurge in BSE cases.

We encounter some project environments where there is a lack of information to base forecasts accurately. The average incubation period for CJD could be 20–25 years, according to an epidemiologist at the London School of Tropical Health and Hygiene. So we may be unsure about the full risk or incidence of BSE spread in the human population until about the year 2010–15. We have little certainty in extreme cases during risk modelling even though the models tell us there is a low risk.

Another way of demonstrating this analogy is to look at the past normal distribtion of height in people. We know there is a history of a low proportion of people above 2m in height based on centuries of evidence. But we are not 100 per cent sure that this will be the same in the next generation; we can say we are confident of a probability, e.g. 99.99 per cent that this trend will continue. And we can hope to be correct based on data and records spanning centuries. However, the extreme probability distribution tails for medical tests, e.g. of the impotence drug Viagra introduced in 1998, pose risks because we are not yet sure of its results on the population. The risk of side effects such as fatalities will be reflected in the extreme probability distribution tail of the time series after 1998.

We often read headlines for new products, e.g. 'Safe painkiller set to launch pharmaceuticals world war',[8] but remember, there are some side effects for all drugs. The drug Thalidomide, for example, was administered to women around the world, but its results in inducing thousands of horrendous birth defects were largely unforeseen. It was prescribed to pregnant women for curing morning sickness, but it resulted in ghastly deformities in the foetus. Now, after the Thalidomide disaster of the 1960s, we are faced with the potential prospect of helping AIDS patients by administering doses of Thalidomide, should the FDA and drug agencies approve its use.[9] Another case is that of genetically-modified (GM) foods which have caused controversy over their possible health dangers. Testing and development of new food products still

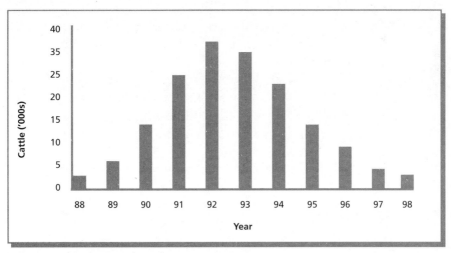

Fig 1.2 ● **BSE-infected cattle, UK**   Source: *The Economist*, 28 November 1998, p. 37

raises the fear that the benefits do not outweigh the threat of health risks. Government efforts to calm worries over these health risks have not been completely successful in the light of the BSE fiasco. Once again, we do not have a long enough time-series of data to extrapolate a probability distribution of risks with great certainty.

Risk need not necessarily have a negative impact on the individual. The likelihood or risk of winning a Western European national or American state lottery is extremely low. It is worthwhile comparing the attraction for lottery punters to those of the sophisticated investor in the market. Some of these sophisticated investors have been banks and fund managers which have lost billions of dollars in unwise schemes (see Barings and LTCM case studies, p. 60 and p. 165). The increasingly new-fangled investment instruments can carry an extremely low risk of success, and a higher risk of failure. A cynic would say one thing is certain: *'There's a sucker born every minute!'*

One would like to think we would feel happy delegating the role of assessing the risk or benefit of an investment or project to the risk and investment specialists. It may seem unlikely, but many companies do not pay fundamental attention to the risk perception of their staff, certainly in the risk management area. There are many everyday cases where risk analysis is no more than a feeling; people get the notion that they have just found a good investment. Few would openly confess to being risk-ignorant or risk-seeking in any way. But real life is more uncharitable.

1 Investment banks tend to say that their foreign currency trading operations are hedging risk, but in reality they are gambling on open positions ('bets') being worth more in the future. A perfect hedge has no profit and no loss because these cancel each other out during a hedging investment. Banks and corporations that admit to losing money on hedging operations have lost money through short-term speculation on the market (see LTCM case study, p. 165); this is a risk-seeking strategy.

2 Companies which attract staff on a short-term basis through higher and higher wages alone are similarly not risk-averse. In fact, by raising the wages in their sector, such companies are increasing the risks of staff being attracted to them for the wrong reasons, including greed. The potential downside is that loyalty to the company is shorter than the duration of the most recent pay-cheque, and staff turnover must affect the health of the project. The risks and issues of recruiting staff are discussed in more detail in Chapter 7.

3 Firms that are considered well-run are not necessarily in the habit of screening staff. Thus, key project staff who lack self-control must be exposing the company and their projects to potential damage. We have come across cases where staff who drink excessively, dabble in drugs and

prostitution, and other vices, must be viewed as risk-seeking project members. A company that has little control over its staff must be viewed as risk-ignorant.

There has been a lot of computer-based technology that comes under the risk management banner. There has been a lot of literature published about risk management. Now, the term itself invites a lot of interpretations. We can clarify two points initially:

1 technology never provided a solution on its own
2 reading a book does not solve a problem by itself; a business needs action and solutions.

It is said in American football that you get paid for results: '*You get paid for scoring points, not yardage.*' Projects need results too. The creative actions come from the project team; the same with destructive actions. Project managers who do not review the fundamental qualities of their staff are not engaging actively in staff development or staff threat management. Project managers have a duty to the company and to the success of the project; sometimes projects have to go outside the company and its limits of 9a.m. to 5p.m. working. A complete lack of staff monitoring, or an unwillingness to keep an ear out, will leave a project open to the risk of damage from its own staff. A lot of financial crimes such as fraud are 'inside' jobs. The City of London police reported a 32 per cent annual increase in fraud and forgeries.[10] You are possibly inviting a hit on yourself – protect your business.[11]

Notes and references

1 Checkland, P. and Scholes, J. (1990) *Safe Systems Methodology in Action*, John Wiley, Chichester.
2 Reinsurance, January 1996.
3 Shtub, A. et al. (1994) *Project Management Engineering, Technology and Innovation*, Prentice Hall NJ, USA, p. 133.
4 RAMP – Risk Analysis and Management of Projects (1998) Institute of Civil Engineers and Institute of Actuaries.
5 Extracted from RAMP, 1998.
6 European Commission statistics (1998) www.Europa.int
7 Institute of Actuaries & Faculty of Actuaries (1998) *Modelling the Future*.
8 *Financial Times*, 5 February 1999.
9 *The Economist*, 'Thalidomide: On probation', 13 September 1997.
10 Reuters, 13 October 1998.
11 Refer to *Fraud Strategy* (1996) City of London Police.

2

Business projects and risk

❝ Life's business being just the terrible choice. **❞**

Robert Browning

There are differing conceptions about business projects, but most would tend to agree that business involves a combination of:

- capital (money, equipment, land)
- time (schedule)
- labour (physical effort and intelligence)
- plus (quite possibly) an element of luck.

It can also be shown that consistent bad luck or good luck may be hiding something a bit more incriminating or worrying. These are combined, using a skill called management, to arrive at some goal. This goal may be monetary profit, or the creation of some service or product. There may be additional ways to define whether you have reached this goal in terms of operational performance or parameters that comprise success characteristics. These normally go in the quality assurance (Chapter 8) or project review stage.

What is a business project and what is project management?

We can set about creating a project plan once we accept that there is a good side to planning that can remove (not eliminate) much of the bad luck element in business.

Let us recap on what a project has:

- an objective (to create or achieve something)
- some resources (manpower, management, physical resource)
- a budget – the estimate of resources needed
- a schedule or time-span from identification to achievement of the objective

- milestones for monitoring at set stages
- success criteria for measuring our progress.

Let us look at the way business projects are viewed.

The business project cycle – old and new

The Waterfall model is the classical hard engineering look at the business cycle. It is roughly:

- project initiation
- analysis
- design
- testing
- production
- maintenance.

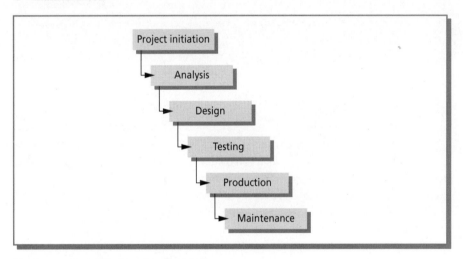

Fig 2.1 ● **Waterfall view of project cycle**

This looks something like the classical Gantt chart, with discrete blocks for tasks that have to be finished along the horizontal time axis. This traditional model has taken some more modern directions under government and private industry tutelage towards defined methodologies such as SSADM, PRINCE, etc. (see Toolkits, Chapter 10). Both were devised under the auspices of the UK's Central Computer and Telecommunications Agency (CCTA).

PRINCE 2, RAMP and SSADM are methodologies that create structures to handle project management. PRINCE 2 is an established methodology that seeks to control the project life cycle from wandering into unacceptable variation, such as poor product quality. It is a definition of logical procedures and documentation to control project direction; it does not represent an explicit risk management methodology.[1] Other methodologies and risk management products seek to control the project progress and reduce the probability or effect of business risk. SSADM (Structured Systems Analysis and Design Methodology) is different in that is limited to IT and software projects.[2]

RAMP (Risk Analysis and Management of Projects), a newer method of managing business risk, was devised by the UK Institute of Actuaries and Institute of Civil Engineers (ICE) explicitly to manage project risk. In particular, it is designed to prevent or reduce the likelihood or impact of cost overruns, a late schedule or failures in quality. The RAMP method looks to categorize all kinds of business risks, then to evaluate and control their potential impact. It operates on an analytical basis first, then imposing risk management or containment where possible for the immediate project environment. This extends from initial concept to operation and termination.

These methodologies are sometimes seen as straitjackets or bureaucratic paper-chases by those who prefer a more fluid approach to a project. Unfortunately, with millions at stake, and professional reputations on the line, ad hoc operations become a less attractive proposition. The methodologies embody best practices and procedures and checks to reduce the possibility of failure. PRINCE and RAMP seek to administer any large project such as construction or the delivery of a defined end-product; they are not industry-specific. The view taken in this book is that the methodology does not consist merely of paperwork; there are checks, controls and reminders that transcend a simple tick-list of events. The element of bureaucracy and paperwork comes in automatically to some extent, but with huge sums of money and vast manpower at stake, the methodologies are designed to avoid the high risk that things will fall between the cracks. The chance that people will forget or overlook important factors is too great without a consistent set of checks and controls.

PRINCE in particular puts these logical processes in large sequential volumes that describe the process from project initiation to close-down. These come in particularly useful when there are many people involved and we need to impose standards or continuity. Key definitions of product, service and process planning are required at the outset, while change controls and quality reviews are fundamental to ensuring that the final performance tends towards the design criteria. A documentation logging process keeps the project on track despite human, material and environmental changes. Thus, when key staff leave, are ill or are unavailable, you have to ask certain questions that might be better answered when you are operating under a structured methodology. For example:

'Jones from Accounts is off ill. We really need to get the digger onsite now.

● who is handling this order now?
● where is the order for the new digger?

- who needs to sign it?
- how much was it for?
- what were the cost justification reasons?
- what are the risks involved in getting this equipment?
- what are the issues of buying this equipment from the particular supplier?
- what is the delivery date and who arranges and pays for customs clearance?
- could we get a better price and a better product elsewhere?
- what is the status of this order?'

Spoce addresses the issue of smaller projects, where PRINCE and RAMP entail too much paperwork and too many procedures to make the project viable. Spoce has created 'Spocette' as a methodology for running these smaller enterprises. Small companies and projects could be deluged by paperwork and administration if the standard methodologies were used. And if small companies plan to undertake the full risk analysis and risk management procedure for a minor project, it might not be justified simply on cost and time factors. Part of project risk management incorporates the key questions: What are the risks? What are the effects on our project? What can we do? And: Can the risk management exercise take too long or cost too much for such a project?

Small and medium enterprises (SMEs) or firms undertaking small projects are characteristically restricted by time and budget limitations. The costs and time involved for analyzing the risks would be too great using the traditional risk management procedures which are designed for large projects or companies with the time and manpower to devote to risk issues. The use of Spocette is worth looking into as a slimmed-down methodology (among other alternatives) where controls and checks have to be introduced. The key aim is to keep the small project running with a good degree of risk protection and without being bogged down by too much paperwork and bureaucracy.

Limitations of the Classical Waterfall model

This model is a little too inflexible and too mechanical; it does not allow a very human view of the project participants. The real world has dynamic properties that promote change or exert strains on a business. There are too many social interactions and political elements in a project that are not factored within the standard, traditional hard project models. Many projects risk failure because they are potentially a political mine-field:

'In many instances, workers' and managers' perceptions of behavioural and organizational issues far outweigh the technical issues, and it is

19

precisely these issues that most often are the major cause of implementation failure.'[3]

We have seen good projects around the world that were technically excellent, fall flat in the mire of political intrigue or social insensitivity. It is often a case of good idea, but lousy execution.

There are usually many different tasks going on at the same time in a large project; we do not always get the clean-cut delineation between project phases. This constant shift blurs the distinct stages of the Classical Waterfall project model. Sometimes, the classical approaches give the false impression that projects continue in a smooth upward progression, and that they carry on to completion. This may not be the case. The same project mistakes are being repeated throughout history. Some projects should never be completed. They should never have been started in the first place, or the end product is wholly inappropriate, or the cost-benefits show the projects not to have been worthwhile. Such projects must not get off the drawing-board, or they should be killed off before they drain your company of much-needed resources (see Project Termination, Chapter 4).

The increasing complexity of uniting these project phases, coupled with the rise in the specialization of project skills needed, results in questions being raised over the traditional models. Formerly, many scheduling and budgeting exercises in projects catered for the mechanistic forecasting and control.

Table 2.1 ● A simple project initiation

1 June	Project X, 10% deposit	300 000 euros
9 June	Delivery of materials	100 000 euros
10 June	Labour, 300 man-days @ 500 euro/day	150 000 euros
	Production elapsed time 120 days	
9 November	Goods completed	
1 December	Distribution (7 days elapsed)	100 000 euros
Total cost of project		650 000 euros

Planning defects

The traditional project view assumed people had very homogenous skills; similar skills. In the old days you could hire a carpenter, now you would outsource a computer programmer. It does not seem to matter much that there are dozens of types of computers, hundreds of software languages and thousands of business applications. A computer systems analyst with 30 years' experience in manufacturing is not essentially what you need when you are building a global marine insurance system. There are a million different strokes for different folks. Many traditional projects have little slack or leeway; the assumptions are that things work out well and on time in one way or another.

There are no, or very rudimentary, risk analysis/risk management stages incorporated in these projects. Contingencies for minor hiccups are not catered for. Thus brainstorming, scenario analysis and the Delphi group are there to create contingency measures (see Chapter 5: Contingency Management).

Questions you might like to pose could be:

- what if I lost my chief engineer?
- who would replace her? How fast could I find a replacement?
- could the replacement do the job?
- how would this impact on the project?
- would I be sued?
- would my secretary quit like that?
- what would I do?
- what if my conductor resigned? (See Royal Opera House case study, p. 76)

It is difficult to incorporate the interaction of various project parties within the Classical Waterfall model. Some parties, possibly outside the project's jurisdiction, may wish to be involved in the project or to hinder the project in a destructive way. The classical approach does not easily recognize the political agenda at work during a project's life. The project has to satisfy somebody, and this is not limited to the project owner. The danger is that the finished product in large projects carried out over a long time will be out of date and irrelevant to the customer's current needs. The end-user or client may be dissatisfied. *'This is not what I wanted.' 'It's what I really wanted last year, but I can't use it now because ...'*

The process of changing user requirements is rather widespread within projects.

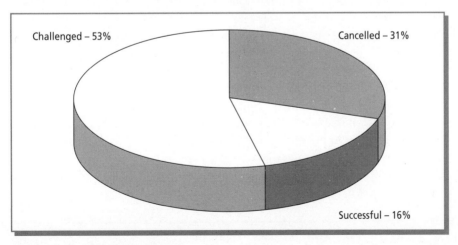

Fig 2.2 ● Overall project outcomes[4]

Projects that are in development for years before final delivery or completion are subject to this particular risk (see Change Management, Chapter 5).

> '(Projects) that no longer meet the needs of the business because the business has changed much more rapidly than the initial technology implementation. This trend will continue, with 70 per cent of applications in development not flexible enough to satisfy rapidly changing business conditions as we enter the next millennium.* It is inevitable with such long-term projects that the initial requirements will not in fact reflect the final requirements for the system.'[5]

Success means delivering what is wanted on time and on budget. What is wanted is ideally set in the user requirements document, but this does not always happen, so there is a risk of the project going out of control. Project managers would want all such requirements frozen to avoid or to limit downside risks.[6] The project risks revolve around the definition of functionality and scope – you can try to limit the dangers by a change management process to avoid the disease of requirements creep.

The downside of highly structured project management is that it may tie up the project team in paperwork and make it inflexible. There is a compromise that states that project managers should be responsive to market demands, but that they should have some structure set or they will be changing plans every day – very infuriating and rather frustrating. A harsh attitude is *sometimes* needed for the customer. *'This is what you ordered, this is what you get!'*

Prototyping

Thus, two ways around this inflexibility are to prototype or pilot. This is one of the applications of testing the water. Artifacts from the second millennium BC excavated in the Cyclades islands show imports of pottery from the Greek mainland.[7] These samples or prototypes enabled the local ceramic craftsmen to develop their own examples. Four millennia later, the Japanese imported car kits, studied them, then improved on the British Austin A40 to develop their own mighty car industry. Prototyping enables the customer or project owner to get an early glimpse of what the finished product will look like. Design errors or inadequacies can, hopefully, be spotted and rectified. Cars, ice-cream and movies, for example, are all evaluated by a control panel to test early reaction to a product launch. Even the finest wines from Burgundy have to pass the test of the connoisseurs' palate.

---

* Gartner Group, R-ITD-101. March 1996.

CASE STUDY

Producing a big-budget movie

Big companies in the film industry typify the high-cost, high-risk type of business project. The players range from the backers of Tristar, Miramax, Buena Vista and Dreamworks in Hollywood, to the smaller companies that span the European continent, to Bollywood in India. The recipe for risk comes from three main sources:

1 cost: expense of signing film stars, the whole cast, technical staff and equipment, pre-release marketing and advertising;

2 political: deep involvement of personalities and possibility of personality clashes. Possibility of contravening regulations, and attracting censorship;

3 uncertainty: high risk of not knowing what will sell to the audience. Not being able to recoup project set-up costs.

One way to try to avoid problems is to recruit backers by using a short footage of the pilot idea, then, once filming is nearly completed, release the rushes to a structured sample audience. Film previews by well-known critics can also influence the course of action. Analyze their feedback on the film; if response appears to be dire, edit the film and try to pull it together for a better audience reception. It will be too late generally to change the overall film because the crew and cast will probably have finished their contracts by the time the decisions to re-edit are taken. We can play all contingency measures that are reasonably open, such as retargeting the advertising or strengthening the video sales, or plugging for the cable TV market.

A housing complex is usually built on a prototype basis for various reasons. The architect will draw a cardboard or acetate mock-up to show the clients what the projected product will look like. This can be put into production on satisfactory approval. The buildings need not be completed at the same time; one should be completed before the rest. This will allow any design weaknesses to be revealed, or time for any customer preferences to be incorporated to suit market demands.

Then there is the need for self-financing through selling off completed buildings, or selling houses ahead of completion in order to pay for the costs incurred so far. 'Show-houses' are an essential part of real-estate selling, as they gain publicity and attract customers. There is a tradition of bringing prospective buyers to show-houses to raise publicity. Revenue comes in long before the rest of the construction is finished. It is a classic example of a bird in the hand is worth two in the bush.

Off-the-shelf versus bespoke products

Recently, other ideas have developed, but many of them have taken on the principles of prototyping. Rapid application development (RAD) is one example. This is similar to prototyping, and it incorporates its core principles. But RAD involves a stricter and more formal methodology. What has become more widespread has been the installation of packages or existing products for modification. In essence, this comprises a partly-built product, or a toolkit, that you can tailor to fit your needs.

It is often felt that these packages will be faster and cheaper to produce than trying to build the whole thing yourself in a bespoke way. This practice is prevalent in computer software systems where software packages are bought off the shelf. The apparent benefits are the ability to rise up the learning curve rapidly, without such high start-up costs as those incurred establishing the product from scratch. This will not be the result in 100 per cent of projects; there are numerous examples where buying packages and then customizing them has worked out to be more expensive than building the whole thing yourself. The summary of advantages and disadvantages of packages are:

PRO	CON
Faster	May take longer than expected
Cheaper	May be more expensive
Skills and support already exist	Dependent upon supplier
Needs less in-house labour and skills	Less understood, maybe some 'black box' techniques supplied
Easy to demonstrate prototype	May not do what you want, how you want it

| CASE STUDY |

Microsoft – how Bill Gates began

In the 1980s, the PC came on to the market. Apple machines were slugging it out with others such as the Radio Shack TRS-80. IBM muscled in on the scene with its hardware. But there was one thing IBM desperately needed: the operating system software. The smart money was on Gary Kildall's existing option, CP/M, that was being used and shown to work. IBM executives approached Kildall and CP/M but there was a hitch – he could not meet them for the business appointment IBM wanted. This window of opportunity gave Bill Gates one chance, and one chance only, to move. He promised IBM an operating system, Microsoft MS-DOS. IBM bought it.[8]

But there was one slight catch – MS-DOS did not exist. In fact, Bill Gates and his team had not even begun to write it. Gates bought an existing system, 86-DOS, for $50 000, amended it, and got that to work. The rest is history.

Fund-raising

One of the great problems or challenges in starting a project is that of raising the finance to make it happen. Venture capital is often cited as the way to do it, especially with commercial and research and development technological projects. The magnitude of this problem should not be under-estimated; countries outside the USA do not have the same degree of development in their venture capital markets. As businessman Tim Jackson, an internet entrepreneur in the UK, said: *'Finding others to share risk is a great deal harder in London than in Silicon Valley.'*[9] The main *modus operandi* is to get a patent, then show the prototype around to attract interest from financiers. This is a more challenging task when no patent or working prototype exists. The race for funds is on!

> **CASE STUDY**
>
> ## Launching the Voyager
>
> The story of how Dick Rutan and Jeana Yeager flew their aircraft 40 000km non-stop around the world is truly remarkable. The flight finished in California on 23 December 1986 without any refuelling. The aircraft is a success in terms of engineering and project devotion. It uses a pusher-puller propeller engine configuration, on a wingspan of 35m that can flex 10m up and down. The pilots flew in a horizontal position, but it was discovered during development that the noise generated by the engine was so deafening as to make sleep impossible. A sine wave sound generator was installed to deaden the noise. Yet it was not the technological or pilot skills that nearly killed the project, it was the fact that no major corporate funds were raised until the flight tests started. Millionaires such as Lee Iacocca or Ross Perot refused any funding. A Japanese firm offered financial assistance, but this was refused because of the unfavourable political ramifications of receiving Japanese resources to put an American aircraft in the air. In the end 80 per cent of the project time was spent trying to raise funds, not on building and testing the aircraft.[10] The funding task is crucial enough to make or break projects.

Implementation of a project

There are generally two ways of handling projects that inevitably introduce a new way of doing things.

Big bang

This is the most dramatic and drastic change. Everything gets changed on a specific date when the switch is flicked on. The political risks involved and reputations that depend on the success of the change mean that this is often the least-favoured option. Examples are the decimalization of the British currency from £, shillings and pence in 1971 or the switch of Swedish driving from the right-hand side of the road to the left-hand side in 1956.

Parallel running is a way in which old and new systems run at the same time, then we can flick over to the new one when we are happy with the way it runs. However, running two duplicate systems uses a lot of manpower, money, time and hardware and is extremely expensive. Big bang is also the most risky option in project management.

Phased implementation

This is the more common way to introduce change. It is often found in computer and telecoms systems because project managers can introduce a new product or service feature one element at a time. This allows the client or end-user to test and evaluate the quality of the new element in order to accept or reject it. The customer can choose to back out or roll back parts of the system, or all of it, if something wrong is detected. One advantage is that the whole company is not devoted at the same time to introducing the change, so there is less manpower constraint.

Another example is the switch-over to the euro under European Monetary Union. The conversion to the currency in Europe in 2002 will be completed only after it has been in circulation with member states' currencies for over three years. The outline of these factors is the easy part; the integration or project management of all these factors is the difficult part. The theory suggests that the project takes place in a smooth progression. We can illustrate this with an example of a traditional or hard project.

Unfortunately, real life tends to be more complicated. We will show you that the factors in action demonstrate that projects do not achieve this smooth transition from the drawing-board abstract to concrete real life because of various oversights. The factors most easily neglected are those handled by the risk analysis and risk management processes.

Our mainstream business activities are focussed on combining resources towards project expectations. But a fair number of political factors are at work within the lifespan of a project; these will have considerable influence over its eventual performance (see Fig. 2.3). An important factor is how the project is initiated or born. People must first see and understand the need for it. We take an example of an IT system in the UK examined in depth under research entitled 'conflicting perceptions of success in an information systems project':

> *'It seems that "sales hype" which took place ... early in the project raised project expectations well beyond what the project was subsequently able to deliver.'*[11]

Yet, without 'selling' the project to the client, management and end-users, there would be inadequate support for the project to succeed. Management support to overcome anti-project resistance, and their involvement/drive to maintain control over the project, were critical success factors. This enabled the project analyzed to be delivered on-time, on-budget and fulfilling most of the desired performance criteria. Still, there has to be enough of a balance between the need to stir up the client's enthusiasm for the project against the possibility that they go overboard and become 'sold' on a notion of a fantastic/superhuman system. If so, there are likely to be major eventual deviations from the expected project outcome. *'There is no such thing as a nice management surprise!'*

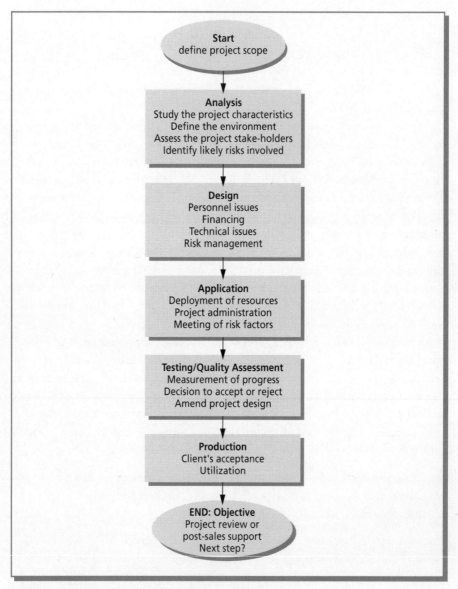

Fig 2.3 ● **Example of a project explicitly handling risk**

The project team

There are various views of a business project, but they all incorporate a web of interaction between the project parties. One such view is outlined in Fig. 2.4.

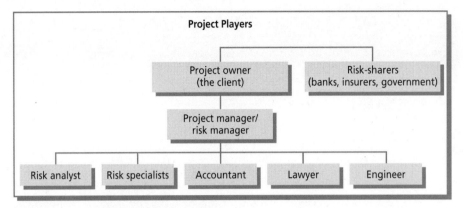

Fig 2.4 ● How the project players interact

Apart from the risk of the project being cancelled, either at the feasibility stage or mid-way, there are two fears for business project management. One risk is that the project will go over-budget; another is that the project will run over the schedule. Let's look at a prime example.

CASE STUDY

Heathrow Terminal 5, London

This is a classic example of how a project can run seriously late when it hits planning problems. The schedule of (non) progress looks something like this:

1986 British Airports Authority, the operator, decides to build new terminal
1988 Design work started in detail
1993 Environmental report submitted
1994 Planning application submitted
1995 Public inquiry begins. Scheduled for one year
1997 Inquiry still running; T5 opening forecast for 2005
1998 Inquiry delayed; T5 opening forecast for 2007

The schedule shows that big projects, with all their resources, are not immune to delays. The entire Terminal 5 project was thought to cost £2000 million. The likely legal costs of handling the whole application and inquiry are about £100 million, the bulk to be paid by BAA.[12]

The essence of project management

We look to a plan to cut down overruns. The concept of making a plan is:

1 preparing the plan: schedule, budget, resource allocation and technique;
2 checking that the plan is practicable, affordable and that it will achieve its objective;
3 implementing the plan;
4 checking the project regularly to measure actual performance against the plan;
5 revising the plan to suit actual performance along the way where needed.

A project manager needs to plan and direct the project to give it the best chances of success. He/she has to provide leadership and direction to the process. This leadership usually involves diplomatic, managerial and political skills needed to get the project done under difficult constraints. Otherwise, the project is in danger of joining the long list of those that have failed, gone over budget or over schedule.

Project inertia

Both the project owner and the project manager have to understand the type of project they are working with. Each project, and each project type, has a certain variety of project inertia. There are some which are very slow to start, very quick to finish. Some projects are the opposite; they are very fast to start, but extremely slow to complete. One of the main risks in project management is that either the project owner or the project manager is unaware of the nature of the project inertia. This can lead to them devoting too much time and resources at the project start, or at the end. An experienced project manager has to recognize the nature of the industry, and the type of project inertia involved. ˷

Business risk conditions

Risk is the likelihood that some event can happen, and often, the uncertainty of not knowing exactly where this risk is or how likely it is. The event can trigger a loss or some other event that creates damage. Sometimes the risk can be a positive outcome; e.g. a gambler also stands the risk that he/she could suddenly become very rich. Reckless business managers can be tempted to adopt the strategy known as 'gambler's ruin', where they double the bets, and double the potential losses.[13] The driving reason seems to be part greed and part pride. And pride always comes before a fall. We have seen this with a few banks – these were more like casinos, but then you would not expect the bank/casino to go bust. Nevertheless, risk is a daily part of life and business.

Business is, by definition, a risky affair – there are potential hazards everywhere. It is sometimes said that because projects allocate fixed amounts of resources, risk cannot easily be factored in without affecting quality. For example, building a power generator in an area of known thunderstorm activity has obvious risks. If the costs of the project and the schedule have already been negotiated and fixed, then the issue of performance or project quality arises. One way out is to externalize the risk of power failure during thunder by insurance policy clauses that protect the plant during such conditions. Another option is to 'de-scope' or limit the operation of the plant to non-thunder weather conditions – an obvious fall in the quality of the power generating performance. These obstacles should be identified and marked during a process of risk analysis.

Risk management organizes the way in which we can bear risks through four fundamental ways:

Table 2.2 ● Options for risk management

Four methods of risk management
1   **Avoid** – e.g. do not invest; pick another project partner, enterprise or country
2   **Mitigate** – reduce the risk by limiting our exposure or potential damage
3   **Share** – ask others to come in as partners. Form a consortium or take out insurance
4   **Absorb** – strengthen our position to bear shocks, e.g. recruit or deploy back-up staff, have alternative sites, increase profit margin, raise capital reserves

Some business people fail and others succeed; there is about a 40 per cent chance of failure for UK start-up enterprise in its first year. Risk can be a negative or positive phenomenon in itself; normally, it is seen to be a bad phenomenon. Because risk management bears a strong lineage from insurance, much of the risk revolves around an event that causes loss or creates damage. In reality, the effects of handling risk will either have an upside (gain) or downside (loss). The usual, but not the only, way of looking at risk is the likelihood that the event will happen, and the loss that this event will create to the interested party.

What risk or damage can strike you?
Risk or risk exposure = probability of event × cost of loss

Thus, a 1 per cent chance of flood that wipes out a $1 million house would have a $10 000 risk or loss-expectation, often known as the 'exposure'.

Table 2.3 ● Examples of risk exposure

Type	Cause
Natural	Flood, thunder, subsidence
Man-made	Electrical short-circuit, muggings, fraud, incompetence
Both	Drowning: failure to evacuate despite warnings Power outage: unprotected electricity supply in an area of thunderstorm activity

Instead of looking at losses, we can look at the profits. Thus, a lottery ticket-holder may have a one-in-a-billion chance or risk of winning $15 million. A business takes on a too-risky project because it is unaware of the real benefits from intended actions. We can think of a business project in terms of a linked or related series of outcomes, each with a certain profit or benefit. Most companies are running more than one project, or have a choice of several projects; they can be said to have a portfolio of projects. These projects, e.g. A-B-C-D, can be laid out in a simple matrix for analysis (see Table 2.4).

There are some conclusions from this over-simplified example which uses an investment of 20 000 euros for all projects:

A) Had a large variance of probability outcomes, relatively constant benefits, average expected reward.
B) Had a low variance of probabilities, relatively constant benefits, low to average expected reward.
C) Had a large variance of probabilities, varying benefits, high expected reward.
D) Had a large variance of probabilities, relatively constant benefits, average expected reward. This would have been viewed as a 'dead cert' investment (100 per cent sure profit) on the basis of the first event, when it seemed that we could be certain of large potential profits. This turned out to be untrue on the evidence of later events.

Just as we are told not to judge everyone prematurely, it seemed in one example that the duck became a swan. Project C, which started out with the lowest probable favourable outcome, finished up with the most expectation of benefit, and it is the most profitable project under these conditions. There are, naturally, potential hazards on the way, but the benefits of the ugly project may far outweigh those of the sexy project in quite a few cases.

Table 2.4 ● The project benefits matrix (figures in euros)

Outcome	Project A			Project B			Project C			Project D		
	Benefit	Probability	Expect	Benefit	Probability	Expect	Benefit	Probability	Expect	Benefit	Probability	Expect
1	4000	0.5	2000	6000	0.2	1200	1 000	0.1	100	2000	0.9	1800
2	5000	0.1	500	5000	0.2	1000	1 000	0.2	200	4000	0.4	1600
3	7000	0.3	2100	4000	0.2	800	5 000	0.3	1 500	6000	0.2	1200
4	4000	0.1	400	5000	0.2	1000	13 000	0.7	9 100	8000	0.1	800
Total benefit expected			5000			4000			10 900			5400

The benefits to an enterprise come from knowing which project has the best reward at an acceptable risk, then finding out how best to apply the results and by-products from this project within the business enterprise. We have used a monetary reward in this example, but there might be unquantifiable benefits, e.g. in research and development projects. Take a good look at project benefits first before you kill off a potential golden goose.

Notes and references

1 Refer to *Managing Successful Projects with PRINCE 2* (1997) CCTA.
2 'Instruction to SSADM 4+' (1997) CCTA.
3 Corbitt, G. and Norman, R. (1991) *Journal of Systems Management*, pp. 32–3, vol. 42.
4 Bishop, H. and Casterton, P. (December 1998) First Consulting Group, London.
5 Ibid.
6 Refer to ICE 'Design and Construct Conditions of Contract' (1991).
7 National Archaeological Museum, Athens, Greece.
8 Wallace, J. (1997) *Overdrive*, John Wiley, Chichester, p. 41.
9 *Financial Times*, 12 November 1998, p. 23.
10 Meredith, J. R. and Mantel, S. J. (1995) *Project Management*, John Wiley, p. 288.
11 Fowler A. and Walsh M. (1 February 1999) IPMA, vol. 17 nr, pp. 1–10.
12 The *Observer*, 11 October 1998, Business, p. 1.
13 *Financial Times* supplement, 24 October 1998, p. xxv.

3

Risk analysis

" They can't shoot straight. "

President de Gaulle of France after yet another failed assassination
attempt on him.

We would like to think that we understand and assess risk accurately. Let's look
at risk itself first.

Defining risk

There are various conventions and definitions for discussing risk:

- event or hazard –   the general threat (it could also be positive)
- risk –   the area of uncertainty surrounding this event
- probability –   likelihood of it happening
- effect –   what is the significance of the outcome?

Impact

We can also categorize and measure the likelihood of events in a matrix.

Probability	Impact
Highly likely	Large business effect
Unlikely	Small business effect
Highly likely	Small business effect
Unlikely	Large business effect

There are various forms and magnitude of the business effect or hit on your
enterprise. Let us look at them in turn.

Small business effect

There are minor or small effects that are so negligible that you may not even notice them – you suffer so little damage, or experience virtually no effect, that there is no variation to your plan or expectations. The trick is to place the events in the correct category; an incorrect definition can easily throw even the best risk-managed projects out of the window. Personnel changes that are envisaged and catered for, or minor raw materials cost increases/delays, can be easily incorporated within the project plan's contingency margin, or slack, so that the final project is delivered on time and on budget.

Large business effect

Running on ahead as normal is not an option when encountering events with a high impact. This is not possible where there has been no contingency margin or slack planned. Unforeseen events upon tight plans can easily force cost increases or delays on the dependent events, e.g. the activity is on the critical path and there is zero float, so all following activities are delayed (see Project failure: scheduling, p. 67).

There are two strands to study in risk analysis.

Risk identification

Which risks affect your project? What is their exact nature? This will involve a detailed description of the risks, writing reports about your research, examining historical documentation about the nature of the risks. There may be a technical appendix of tables, checklists, flowcharts, interviews, etc.

Risk quantification

This will involve evaluating the appropriate project risks, their probability, scope, interaction and probable results (usually this refers to project damage, but it could also include project benefits). The sources of risk, stake-holder risk tolerances, scenario analysis, cost estimations and schedule risk will be analyzed and listed. Where risk is felt to be too great, i.e. unacceptable, warning bells over the project should ring immediately. This may even result in cancelling certain events in the project train later (see Project termination, Chapter 4).

CASE STUDY

The NASA space shuttle disaster

This was one of the largest projects ever, certainly within space exploration. The vast sums of public money and NASA resources budgeted were political hot potatoes. Earlier delays and cost overruns meant that NASA administrators felt they were forced to undertake tight plans to justify their government grants if they were to continue in the future of manned space travel. *Cost-benefit analysis* (see later) had been imposed on NASA to curb earlier excesses when it had operated on a cost-plus basis of pricing parts and contracts. Naturally, contractors had been inclined to quote higher prices, in order to make potentially huge profits. Politicians on Capitol Hill were aware of the earlier excesses, and they were more inclined to examine public costs and benefits in the cost-cutting climate of the 1980s.

   This whole politically-charged project environment had the effect of committing NASA to an ambitious schedule of 24 launches per year in the Space Shuttle programme. This is not the sort of schedule you want foisted on you when the shuttle was a research and development vehicle. It was testing some untried technology at a rate that better suited a tried and trusted warhorse. Thus the shuttle was a glorified truck that had to be put into operation rapidly; plus, it had to be serviced quickly, then turned around for the next launch in the tight schedule. The shuttle programme was also 60 per cent over budget in many areas, so additional costs for testing were not deemed politically acceptable. Some things were likely to be classified as of minor importance, so as not to jeopardize the chances of the next launch being on time. Morton-Thiokol, the rocket motor company, had warnings from its engineers pointing out the dangers of using rubber 'O'-rings as seals for the propellant during cold-climate conditions.[1] The cold snap in Florida during January 1986 had the effect of freezing these seals to make them brittle, and thus liable to leak explosive rocket fuel during the launch process. The result was fatal, 73 seconds after launch on 28 January that year.

It is not always true that a company or client will welcome a risk manager. Like a pest control worker, they are resisted. Calling them in is like admitting you have a problem, and there is some social stigma. Part of risk management lies in controlling your staff, especially if they are untrained, incompetent or corrupt. Some of your staff in influential project roles could be at fault and could be putting your project success at risk. Pressure could come from higher echelons (see NASA case study above) to keep them on a risky path. Someone in your company could be making accidental project errors, or they could be passing on your confidential data, taking bribes, making secret transfers or losses. Sometimes, you just have to call in a rat-catcher. But no one really wants the public to know they have vermin in the house.

Measuring risk

There are various ways of measuring project risk. Real-life business environments tend to operate towards the right of the spectrum:

100 per cent sure	v.	100 per cent uncertain
quantifiable	v.	un-quantifiable
statistical	v.	subjective assessment.

The first essential step is to understand the business environment in depth and identify the existing risk factors that can affect your project. Events can be defined as good (beneficial) or bad (damaging or undesirable). Their probability can be described thus:

High, medium, low, zero

or in percentage terms

90 per cent, 50 per cent, 10 per cent, 3 per cent, etc.

Continuing problems exist in attempting to estimate the probabilities accurately. Risk analysis, as a professional iterative process, must have inherent features which strive to obtain the appropriate risk perception for the job. There are various means by which we can attempt to seek a more accurate risk probability estimate. We have the use of:

- our experience to hone in on more realistic assessments
- our in-house Delphi group, forming a jury to judge risk
- documentation: what happened in previous similar cases
- heuristics: rules of thumb that might be applied here
- consultants or external risk gurus that are brought in to assess likelihood
- simulation: assessing the outcomes under similar or semi-realistic conditions
- a risk analysis toolkit (usually computer-based) that can incorporate all these techniques.

There are also various probability types:

- discrete: finite outcomes – a coin has heads or tails, your horse wins or loses, an investor gives you a Yes or No decision about backing;
- predictable: e.g. $150 000 cost plus/minus $5000 or 60 days' project completion time with 3.5 days' variance with probability distribution slanted to the left or right. You also have to look at how flat or acute the curve is (leptokurtic). See the probability distribution charts listed further on;

39

- unpredictable: we have poor experience or insufficient data concerning this phenomenon or event, e.g. completely unfamiliar counter-party with unknown details or background; a bolt from the blue.

Assessments of types of business risk

Risks to a project can be classified by their negative effects, as one of three types:

1 quality or function (failure to achieve the objectives)

2 cost (failure to achieve budget)

3 time (failure to achieve project aim on schedule).

Look at risk analysis. Part of the risk analysis process involves estimation and modelling of risk. We have to go around comparing risk estimates and models, asking:

- how good is one model relative to another?
- when should we use one model instead of another?
- how practical/affordable is this risk model?
- which is the best risk model or estimate?
- what does the estimate or prediction mean to us (the impact)?
- what should we do as our prioritized actions?

Because of the different types of risk, and the uncertainty over trying to obtain an objective measurement, many projects take risk as a subjective assessment. This can be measured or evaluated, but this will include the respondent's bias.

The Delphi group

Many companies attempt to even out biases or personal errors by asking for opinions. An estimation of risk probabilities can thus be done using a 'Delphi' peer group of experts. We can take six expert opinions on a specialized aspect of risk, e.g. maritime insurance in crude-oil shipping around the Indian Ocean. The group are asked for their subjective evaluations of the risk, listed in order. It is hoped their biases will be cancelled out by other experts in the sample. Their responses can be tabulated into data that give us a picture of what we think the future cost (or schedule) is going to be. A fundamental question is to ask whether the probability distribution is skewed left or right. That is to say, do the estimates indicate that the downside risk is greater, i.e. the schedule in the worst case is likely to see a large cost overrun, or be extremely late.

Sources of risk

Risks to a project can be classified by their cause, as one of the following types:

1 External. There are the global conditions in political and regulatory areas and markets. Regulatory agencies take many forms, e.g. the Financial Services Authority in the UK, or see Formula 1 case study, p. 123. A lot of external control embraces the field of ecological regulations and compliance. This field contains a large discipline of thought, effort and legal strictures to govern the operation of companies and enterprises. The degree to which you can operate is limited before you encounter legal obstacles, or unofficial political demonstrations that can harm your project operations and reputation. The public uproar and protest against Shell Oil over the proposed sinking of the Brent Spar oil platform in the North Sea showed the potential for damage to corporate PR. The Sea Empress oil spill in February 1996 ruined 190km of Welsh coastline in a valued conservation area. The authorities showed they had teeth when they fined the Milford Haven Port Authority £4 million.[2] Damage to your project can be serious.

2 Internal, owing to the project design or the human factor. Counter-party risk, business dispute, communication failure, technology failure, can all harm the project. Human performance, skills availability, capability and motivation are essential factors that contribute to the success of the project. These are discussed in further detail in Chapter 7: Operational Risk.

You as the project leader should have the skills to exercise consistent risk management in order to keep the business project on track. It is not possible to eliminate risk; it is possible to handle risk conditions. Some types of risk are avoidable; these are within the realm of the project manager's control. The first group (environmental risk) is largely outside one's control, but we can learn to operate better where the law allows us to make our project more efficient.

> *'Ensuring that the materials you order are delivered on time, seeing to it that the items you plan to sell are produced on schedule, and getting your sales facilities in place all must be planned before that moment when the customers show up and lay their money on the counter.'*[3]

DSL experience in Russia, Greece and Egypt teaches us that regulations are subject to the interpretation of different agencies and how well you know them. Customs, tax and operating licence authorities typify this interaction. There are likely to be regulations that can be used against your project at inopportune times. But you can mitigate against regulatory damages, and take further contingency precautions such as having additional reserve funds or insurance. The project manager is encouraged to take risk management actions to try to avoid the risk, to build up reserves and to establish a network of contacts to be able to better withstand project shocks.

There are various ways in which risk analysis can be carried out. These involve a mix of:

- observation: we can experience the phenomena either directly or at a distance. We can see the destruction caused by a tornado at a safe distance; we can study the good and bad points of a business process by closely examining the current system;

- previous documentation: past experiences may be recorded on company files, reports, third-party company analytical reports or newspaper accounts on electronic or paper format;

- interviews: bringing people with the greatest direct experience of the phenomena into face-to-face sessions to determine the nature and extent of the risks;

- modelling: use of risk toolkits or simulation by computer or other aids to reflect the real thing.

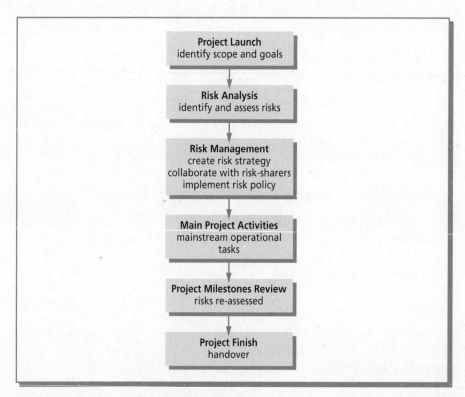

Fig 3.1 ● Project life cycle with risk handling

When the project is under way, monitoring and reporting must be undertaken constantly to detect trends and adapt where necessary. Thus, onsite visits and progress status meetings are usually scheduled every two weeks or monthly. These are backed up with correspondence and surveys or market reports to check that the direction of the project is still in line with the original aims or the changing demands of the market. We can divine the future! (Rather, we can give it a good try.)

There are various risk forms that break down into constituent types of risk. We will briefly examine some of the major types.

Political risk

The enforcement of policy changes can significantly affect the operations of a project. There are two levels of political risk; one is at the project level. The interactions of various groups and administrative agencies in the market will have effects, although, neither their actions, nor the effects, may necessarily be immediately apparent within the project. Some projects that have failed have done so because of a too narrow definition of the project team and support members. The success or failure of the entire project can rest upon key staff. These people may have been correctly identified beforehand, or left out at the project analysis or design stage. These personnel are not necessarily visible as the project team members, but their inclusion/exclusion or non-performance may have a major negative impact upon the entire project. To define a project team, it is necessary to include backup members, or those performing administrative tasks in the office or company headquarters. But this view of the project environment has to be widened to include the broader context of the fringe supporters who have significant input, which may not be immediately noticeable. Such *de facto* project members are: regulatory agencies (local and central government level), NGOs (non-governmental organizations) which can support or oppose the project, company accountants, secretaries, designers, raw material suppliers and transport/delivery staff.

The definition of these key project players is complicated by the opacity of the project arena. Then there is the tendency for other people to want to be in on the action; sometimes they will have no right (legal or otherwise) to be involved. Their demand may be entirely reasonable, perhaps to correct an earlier oversight, or it might be a request for bribes or a pay-off which may be reinforced by a threat. The reality is that members may have to be part of the project by default if the project is to run as planned. This inclusion can be achieved only after a proper evaluation of how they might benefit or damage the project. The key result is that compromises will have to be reached at some stage if the risk of damage is to be reduced; the message often relayed within a project is: 'What is important is not what you do, but who you know.'

A higher degree of political risk comes at the national and international level. We have seen some of the effects on a project cycle caused by those officially outside it, within Europe as well as in the emerging markets of the former USSR, Asian and African countries. Many key investment decisions involve a deep analysis of political risk, and the likely actions of foreign governments. The main risks include:

1 government moratorium – where a country decides to stop or postpone payments, e.g. Russian government debt in August 1998;

2 contract frustration – action taken by an overseas government which prevents the buyer from meeting the terms of the commercial contract;

3 confiscation – where assets are seized through nationalization, confiscation or some other form of government action which deprives the supplier or foreign investor of the assets, whether they are physical like goods, or financial. Let's take Egypt as an historical example. The Egyptian leader Nasser nationalized the Suez Canal Company in 1956, in opposition to Anglo-French interests. It precipitated the Suez armed conflict from which the British and French troops had to withdraw in ignominious defeat. British Prime Minister Anthony Eden resigned not long afterwards. Foreign project owners must be aware of the risks of significant changes in operating licences, up to and including sequestration of foreign assets in the emerging markets.

Our experience is that even the best experts can make decisions that ignore political risk, and their investments cannot be reasonably justified merely on common-sense grounds. The headlong rush into foreign emerging markets illustrates this in part. Skilled investors put billions into Russia and Indonesia while paying scant attention to what they themselves refer to as the fundamentals.

● Was it sensible to invest vast sums in countries which were not politically stable?

● Was it wise to place this money in Russia, where its president, Boris Yeltsin, was in ill health after a quintuple heart by-pass? Or in Indonesia, ruled by its president-for-life, 75-year-old Suharto?

CASE STUDY

Indonesia's President Suharto

Foreign companies, including many in the west, were seduced by the stunning economic growth of the Asian Tigers during the 1980s and 1990s. Indonesia was one of these tigers, and companies bought in a big way into the regime of Suharto and his cronies, even though the president was way past pensionable age. Doing business in any project, particularly in a foreign market, merits a search for viability and an explicit analysis of risk. Investors in this case were wont to forget this lesson.

However, foreign investors should have been well aware that project initiation for any significant business enterprise generally carried the overhead of a large tax levied by members of the Suharto family and their cronies. If you needed strings pulled, they came in as project facilitators or full partners. A few notable examples included rice (the staple diet), cement (an essential building material), motor cars and cigarettes. There were large energy projects under the influence of Siti Hardiyanti (Suharto's eldest daughter) while Tommy (the youngest son) controlled the monopoly in cloves. Foreigners felt they had to pay significant amounts of money to gain leverage into the Suharto-controlled industry. This had massive ramifications when President Suharto was ousted by popular protests in 1998 in favour of his protégé, B.J. Habibie. A Bank of Indonesia survey shortly afterwards, which forced 1800 firms to respond on their foreign exchange debt positions, reported that these firms owed $58 billion (while the banks owed another $78 billion). About 30 per cent of the non-bank debt (c. $17 billion) was taken by 20 of the largest Indonesian companies which were linked to Suharto's relatives or associates.

The obvious dangers exist, particularly when the country's rulers change. Let's look at some of the US energy companies who were caught out.

Table 3.1 ● Business ventures in Indonesia

US company, project	Suharto relative or associate	Status
Unocal, Sarulla	Mohammad Hassan, friend	postponed
CalEnergy, Dieng	Retired Generals Association	in arbitration
CalEnergy, Bali	Sigit, son	postponed
Enron, Pasuruan	Bambang, son	postponed
Duke Energy, Cilicap	Bambang, son	postponed
Morrison Knudsen, Serang	Martini, half-sister	postponed

Source: *Wall Street Journal*, 23 December 1998, p. 10.

Project risk management should not ignore the greatest of management assets – common sense.

Some of these political factors are brought up in Chapter 7 devoted to operational risk, and the sub-section Insiders and corruption.

Country risk

A lot of risk elements come under this umbrella. In some countries it is harder or more expensive to obtain insurance or trade finance than in others. The bond yields vary according to the issuing country, and credit rating agencies also make their assessments of the sovereign credit risk (see Credit risk, p. 57).

Certain countries issue warnings to their citizens operating overseas. The US State Department or the UK's Foreign Office occasionally issue an advisory notice, or in extreme circumstances a blacklist, covering certain geographic areas. This is backed up by intelligence feedback on the ground. A list of the world's most dangerous places in 1998 shows:[4]

Rank	Most dangerous places
1	Russia (Chechnya)
2	Afghanistan
3	Burundi
4	Somalia
5	Sierra Leone
6	Sudan
7	Lebanon
8	Kosovo
9	Sri Lanka
10	The Congo

However, the inclusion of a country in the ranking hides many anomalies and patterns. Russia, for example, encompasses a landmass covering 11 time zones, of which Chechnya, no longer administered by Russian security forces after their failure in the Chechnyan conflict, comprises only a tiny part. The area gained notoriety, particularly in the tabloid press, when the severed heads of four western businessmen who had been held hostages by separatist gunmen were found in Chechnya in December 1998 (see Granger Telecom case study, p. 127). One source in Moscow said that three of them, Britons Darren Hickey, Peter Kennedy and Rudi Petschi, had told her they were moving to Chechnya for more pay. One Briton got into a drunken rage and accused the Russian people as a whole of killing them. The source said she hoped the west did not view the whole of Russia in this appalling light.[5]

It is true that an entire population cannot be judged by the actions of some bad individuals. Furthermore, it can be down to bad luck that your project goes down the tube – being in the wrong place at the wrong time. Emerging market countries make the news because some investors have been seduced by high returns, sometimes ignoring the high risks. High risk must be balanced by high return – there is no such thing as a free lunch!

Referring again to Russia, many foreign businessmen operate in Moscow or St Petersburg with little or negligible fear for their lives, among them DSL Consultants. They simply ensure that certain reasonable precautionary measures are taken. Still, emerging markets hit the headlines occasionally because investors have ignored the high risks and had their fingers burnt.

> *'Some Wall Street bankers acknowledge that in pursuit of profits they glossed over warnings about Russia – corruption, failure to pay loans on time, accounting irregularities and tax evasion – because they were blinded by the country's natural wealth. Many bankers acknowledge that they courted Russia more eagerly, and sometimes with less discretion, than they did other darlings of the developing world.'*[6]

Russia may be easy to pick on, but it seems that investment analysts do tend to repeat their over-enthusiasm. China has eaten up an even bigger slice of foreign investment over recent years. The money cannot easily leave because it is tied up in manufacturing and hemmed in by restrictive capital flow regulations. In the past seven years, foreign companies have invested about $181 billion in China, much of it to finance long-term industrial joint-ventures or wholly-owned foreign factories.[7] They then regret it when projects fail to deliver the expected profits.

> *'More than half the multinational corporations in China are failing to make a profit according to a survey by AT Kearney.'*[8]

One example is in automobile infrastructure and manufacturing.

> *'A large highway project and a petrochemicals plant in southern China have run into difficulties on debt payments to foreign banks. A Guangdong official warned that other infrastructure projects might shortly have difficulties paying foreign debt.'*[9]

Is this blindness or irrepressible optimism? Sure enough, the risk was highlighted when GITIC (Guangdong International Trust and Investment Corporation) went belly up with debts of $4.37 billion. Creditors had been eager to lend in a burgeoning economic climate, but the chances of getting back more than half of the original debt were slim. Foreigners would not get preferential treatment.[10]

New investors coming to China were often naïve about local market conditions. Business people may have been a little surprised to hear, from even government officials, a Mandarin phrase that is best translated as: 'Come with money.' A DSL trip to China in 1997–8 revealed that there were a lot of economic and social strains not immediately apparent to foreigners. Sometimes these are found out only after the event. On a more mundane level, you have to understand that the place where you site your project will have major impact on your chances of success. Your costs of operation rise with the appropriate risk ranking if you operate only on the basis of trade credit or staff and office insurance. Pick the site or area where you stand the greatest chance of success. In the oft-said real estate mantra, it is a case of three things: 'The location, the location and finally, the location!'

CASE STUDY

Leeds versus Sheffield

You may wish to locate in the British north. Even two cities about an hour apart can have very different characteristics, such as Leeds and Sheffield. There are various risk factors that interact in these areas, and it would be best to list them in order to assess the relative risk they pose for a business project .[11]

Factor	Sheffield	Leeds
History	Industrial – steel	Industrial – cloth mills
Current industrial base	Heavy industry	Manufacturing, financial services, retailing
Local job market	Industrial	Diversified industrial, financial and retailing
Unemployment	7.2% (high)	4.8% (average)
Income relative to UK average	88%	100%
Economic growth	Negative	Positive

Market risk

The changes in the price level of the market reflect a fundamental interplay between the forces of supply and demand, which are not transparent. Investors are often pressured to read the market for when to go to quality stocks and bonds, i.e. to play safe, or when to take the plunge and go into more risky financial instruments. The fundamental changes in the market can easily surprise the unwary, and even fool the experienced player. Accurate timing is the critical factor in this game.

Thus, a person who put $30 000 (in present-day terms) into one rare type of Dutch tulip bulb in 1634 would have been a wise investor, as it would double in price the following year. Someone paying $15 000 for the same bulb in 1636 would have been a fool, as she/he would have been lucky to get one-hundredth of that sum back at the end of that year. What relevance have tulips to market risk? Maybe lots. The US Dow Jones Industrial Average rose to a new high on 23 November 1998. Why? As summed up by a financial markets trader:

> 'It was the biggest single merger day in history, and that was catalyst enough. I don't think it's sustainable, but right now it's tulip mania.'[12]

A stock market investor in September 1987 would have lost about 30 per cent in one week. Just after the drop, the markets rose sharply, so a really savvy punter could have played the peaks and troughs perfectly, though perhaps more effectively with the help of hindsight or extra sensory perception. A very good assessment of risk, luck or timing separate an unlucky fool from a genius. George Soros has shown that you can make big money out of timing your investment decisions during boom and bust conditions. Nevertheless, it is important to distance yourself from the timing of the herd while the bulls and bears run on the market.

> 'The public has learned that it pays to buy during dips to what has been an everlasting bull market. But it will take time before it discovers that the bull market does not last forever.'[13]

Timing is everything!!

We see that the real return is an inadequate indication of profit even when discounted for interest rates or inflation. We have to take into account the element of risk, which may turn the risk-adjusted return into a realistic loss (see case study below).

Internet-based stocks

There has been a love of high-tech stocks in the 1990s. Investors, eager to emulate those who made millions (or as in Bill Gates's case, billions: see Microsoft case study, p. 25) on computer stocks, have come into the market as if on a feeding frenzy. These investors often try very short-term plays on the market (day traders), buying or selling within days or during the same day. This type of behaviour is extremely short-term and risky, speculative action of a high order. Let us look at internet stocks in the USA.[14]

We have heard of Netscape, but what about the Internet auction company eBay or Onsale? These kinds of stocks have risen in price by anything up to 100 times within a year. This would take their price:earnings (P:E) ratio into hundreds too. Yet they can go into free-fall within a day. You are waiting for profits based on fundamentals that do not exist. There is a crock of gold at the rainbow's end.

Let us move from the practice of gambling and speculating into investing. There are ways in which an investor can protect against likely loss through various risk management strategies. Furthermore, good luck or bad luck are often convenient labels to disguise something that might be unacceptable or even unpalatable. Proper business projects are calculated enterprises that bring together people and interested parties in pursuit of common goals and profit – they are not reckless gambles or rip-offs. A genius investor may be genuinely brilliant, lucky or even corrupt. Nick Leeson and Ivan Boesky were hailed as extremely successful investors who cleverly parlayed large funds into even larger amounts with a high rate of profits. They were subsequently revealed to be fraudsters who either created fictitious trading profits or manipulated the market through illegal insider information.

Investors can factor risk into their returns; this will discount their nominal returns to get a more balanced picture of the project's health. Risk management seeks to protect the investor against an unfavourable change in foreign currency rates by using hedges. Similarly, a firm can try to avoid bankruptcy when faced with a downturn in demand through product or market diversification, or sharing the risk burden with partners. These measures are not elements of luck, but concerted attempts by the investor to reduce a chance shock.

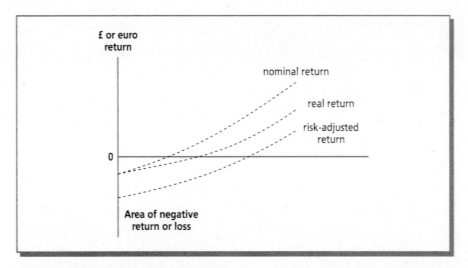

Fig 3.2● Factoring in risk: discounted returns

Discounting the nominal return gives us the real return curve. But to get the picture of risk involved we need to discount this profits curve to derive the real risk-adjusted curve.

Currency risk

This is a subset of market risk. An increasingly global trading environment creates the need to exchange goods and services in mutually acceptable forms of currency. The British Empire provided a sound foundation for the pound as a widely used currency. This position has been largely usurped by the US dollar in the 20th century as the dominant currency of trade. We await developments as to what extent this role will be taken by the euro, introduced in 1999.

> CASE STUDY

Russia's economic crisis 1998

Currency fluctuations on the foreign exchange markets is a source of risk and worry for many merchants. Thus, many emerging market countries price goods in US dollars; Russia is a prime example. Even when the exchange rate varies like a roller-coaster, merchants still price their goods in dollars, then convert to roubles at the daily prevailing rate. DSL work in Russia has always been priced in hard currency as a matter of procedure.

The rouble fluctuated madly during the summer of 1998, dropping from Rbl 6.1 to US$1, to around 17 Rbl, before being stabilized by the Central Bank. The rouble even went to 50 against the dollar on the unofficial market at one stage. But still, most people could not withdraw their deposits from the banks. The ironic, but sad, scenario was of banks going bankrupt and depositors and creditors facing significant losses. The US dollar-pricing mechanism or hedge for those holding dollars limited the potential losses *if* they had already taken this position before Russia faced this crisis.

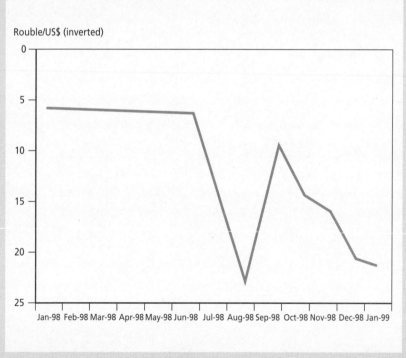

Rouble/US$ (inverted)

Fig 3.3 ● Russian rouble decline 1998–99

Source: extract of rates from Datastream, January 1999

There were, however, limits to the efficacy of such hedging strategies. The other 'if' or caveat was if the authorities did not take action which was beyond the abilities of individual companies. This turned out to be the case. Such force majeure incidents made payments and contracts ineffective for a large part of 1998. Russian Trading System stocks fell by around 80–90 per cent (in US dollar terms) that summer. Russia and Malaysia, another emerging market in crisis, introduced stringent exchange controls that meant that companies wanting to pull their money out were not able to do so at will. The Russian government called for a 90-day moratorium on its foreign debt payments. This affected the national liquidity considerably, and created such a cash-flow crisis that several enterprises were bankrupted. Negotiations to recover debt, particularly from the Russian government, were expected to take months. One example was the protracted foreign debt negotiations with western creditors known as the London Club, with payment made through Vneshekonombank.[15]

The lessons seem to be that:

- an exit strategy for investments is advised for all players
- preparations should be made to anticipate force majeure and the blocking of exit paths.

The Wall Street Journal took a pessimistic view, with this front page headline: 'No Exit: Note to investors – getting into Russia may be the easy bit. Lucrative ventures collapse in nasty legal disputes; Swedish migraines follow'.[16]

Some of the problems that come from dealing in several currencies revolve around getting a **fair price**. When using valuations and prices, it is worth getting several independent quotes. Thus, currency dealers may ask for three to four market quotes simultaneously on different telephones. This is the same principle used when buying bonds, real estate or fleets of motor vehicles. Even so, it would not be much good when the fundamentals are bad. The prospect of doing business would be poor in a country like Indonesia during 1997. The Suharto government was rife with corruption, the country hugely indebted, and the currency dropping from 6000 Rupiah to US$1, to 17 000 to US$1 in days. Risk analysis entails proper evaluation of the whole market situation.

We have mentioned hedging. One way to reduce the risk or uncertainty is to lock in at a currency rate that is known at the outset. Therefore, a trader could choose to buy a fixed amount of foreign currency at an agreed exchange rate to be delivered at a future date.

All futures contracts or forward rate agreements (FRAs) have something in common. This is the agreement to exchange or buy:

1 a certain amount of a currency for delivery …

2 on a certain date …

3 at a known exchange rate or price.

If you want to obtain a known amount of US dollars six months from now, but you want some protection from currency fluctuations, you can arrange a forward rate agreement or futures contract. Thus, in very basic terms, a rate agreement can be to get a fixed amount of currency for a pre-set price to be delivered at a known date in the future. The customer's circumstances (particularly how much they can afford, for how long, and how much they understand the complexity of the instruments) have major impact upon the effectiveness of such an agreement. Hedging is good theory, and it sounds great, but it may not be suitable for everyone.

Interest rate risk

This comes partly under market risk. Interest rates affect the success of projects significantly. A common occurrence is public discomfort when interest rates rise and mortgage-holders face increased monthly repayments. Many businesses take out loans of some form that have floating interest rates; the rate fluctuations are potentially devastating. The interest rate directly affects the net present value or the real rate of return on investments in projects. The increasing extent of world trade and the development of newer financial products mean that investors can pick a selection of interest rate derivative products to protect against an unwelcome rise in rates. See section on derivatives.

Most investors avoid short-term plays by investing in a basket of shares/bonds (diversification) over a longer term (years and months, not weeks and days). There is also the increasing availability of fixed rate loans, such as mortgages which have fixed interest rates for a limited period, e.g. two years, with maximum interest rate, e.g. 10.85 per cent after the two years are up. The benefit for the customer is that he is able to budget his limited resources to avoid fluctuations in interest rates, which cannot rise so much that they drive mortgage-holders into bankruptcy. The customer can be said to have taken a risk limitation or risk mitigation strategy.

There is a tendency to take an extrapolation of a trend, such as lower interest rates, and base a project on this assumption. This straight-line way of thinking can prove fatal. Just look at the graph for Russian rouble rates in 1998 on p. 52.

Counter-party risk

This usually comes from trade with another direct party. It can be linked with credit or non-delivery risk. It is worth avoiding complacency or too much self-confidence because these traits are dangerous; it is easy to get 'burned' by a partner regarded as trustworthy. The LTCM hedge fund fiasco showed what can happen with poor risk management or superficial counter-party analysis (see Long-Term Capital Management case study, p. 165).

There are many ways in which people handle their relationships with counter-parties. One is the due diligence or search on the trade partner. A DSL search on a prospective central European partner for a western client came up with a fairly standard trace of the company. Taking the lead from Moody's or Standard & Poors credit ratings is usually not possible; the emerging markets have a lot of newer or smaller companies which are not listed.

CASE STUDY

Due diligence – DSL searches of prospective counter-parties

DSL has found that the main western listings of companies and key staff may quickly become out of date; they may not include 'deep' local knowledge either. Our screening process depends on the client and his/her needs, as we have found in the former Soviet Union. The questions that have to be asked and the type of service required vary, depending on the sophistication and demands of the client, from a basic/general screening of the counter-party to something more detailed and specific, in a top-down process:

> **General**
> is the counter-party a former communist?
> is he a mafia member?
> is he honest?
> is he technically knowledgeable?
> is he reliable?
> overall, is he okay?

> **More detailed**
> what was his position in the Communist Party?
> how well did he do his job?
> what is his schooling?
> what academic level did he achieve?
> what academic and job backgrounds do his friends have?
> has he delivered most projects on time?
> can we trust him with the project and money?

▶

Specific

how did the counter-party obtain his position in the Communist Party?

does he know Mr X who was then in Novogorod Komsomol or Pioneers group?

do you think Mr X can help us get our project completed?

how can he do this?

how much would the counter-party's services cost?

what is the likelihood in percentage terms that we will succeed with him?

what is the likelihood that we will succeed without him?

what/who else will he need?

would you trust him with the project and $1 million?

what will the project pay-back period be, and what is the probability variance?

what are our contingency measures if he does not perform?

Fig 3.4 ● Screening of a counter-party

Thus, on-site pre-screening of counter-parties is a must; it is not a task that is easily conducted on the telephone or on the internet. A trace on a counter-party is not something that should be left to an inexperienced junior staff member. The lowest risk in many cases comes from going out and doing the search yourself.

Time limitation, and poor knowledge of the locality and contacts, means that this screening task is usually given to local contractors or consultants who can do the background research. It is worth listening to local people; some westerners make the mistake of refusing to believe 'communists' or Russians. Arrogance is not a good trait when we are searching for suitable counter-parties. Nevertheless, it is best to obtain more than one opinion where possible (see Delphi group, p. 40).

Credit or default risk

A simple way to evaluate credit risk is to think in terms of past credit worthiness. Apart from the big credit rating agencies like Moody's, Standard & Poors or Fitch-IBCA, there are the databases compiled by Equifax and CCN on people whose credit-worthiness is frequently queried by companies and banks. The project owner or leader can run a series of questions to screen the customer to see what type of credit performance they are likely to be up against. The credit screening has a standard template, with points for each factor and pass-fail decision boxes, to build up a picture of the likely credit risk. The customer may be the project owner, so sub-contractors and the project leader should check that the customer has a good credit standing to get the project finished and pay all staff on time.

A simple template might look like this for someone who wants to set up a trading account with a broker or investment bank. The weights and questions are usually re-assessed periodically, and the reports on candidates are checked to ensure that credit is given to those who deserve it.

Screening presumes that the bank or organization really wants to screen the client in the first place. There is a practice of granting illegal soft loans to designated friends or associates of the organization. This lax practice was epitomized by the granting of soft loans on too favourable terms, without adequate collateral backing or the likelihood of getting the principal amount back, in the case of BCCI (Banque de Credit et Commerce International, see case study, p. 91). At other times, the bank may not wish to ask embarrassing questions even if it is reputable. This occurred with Citibank and Raul Salinas in 1998. The brother of the former President of Mexico managed to deposit about $100 million at the bank, then wire it across to accounts in Europe. This money was widely believed to come from money-laundering. Salinas had been jailed on murder charges in 1995, so it cannot be said that he was an exemplary client. Citibank was criticized by the GAO (General Accounting Office) of the US Congress for not taking effective measures against money-laundering.

Table 3.2 ● Evaluating the customer's creditworthiness

Customer A	Yes	No	Value	Action	Points awarded
Age			55	Reject if more than 65 years	2
Occupation			Civil servant	Personal search if self-employed	4
Criminal record		x		Personal search if yes	2
Annual wages			DM80 000	Reject if less than DM30 000	5
Collateral/ net worth			DM800 000	Query if within 300–500 000 If less, reject	
Similar past investments made	x				3
Experience of trading in this country	x				2
Total investments worth			DM100 000	Query if less than DM20 000	4
Down payment	x		DM10 000	Not worthwhile if less than 5000	2
Points				Reject if less than 25	30
Overall rating					Good
Client credit	x				Yes

'Citibank, while violating only one aspect of these policies, facilitated a money managing system that disguised the origin, destination and beneficial owner of the funds involved.'[17]

Furthermore, the case showed

'a disturbing vulnerability of private banking to money-laundering.'

Organizations should want to, and try to, implement effective financial controls.

Sometimes, investors prefer to use due diligence which has been done by another party. Well-known organizations such as The European Bank for Reconstruction and Development, the International Monetary Fund, or the World Bank, will have done analyses of various organizations or countries, as will have credit rating agencies. These are often taken as *de facto* stamps of approval. But such actions do not adequately make use of the due diligence process because they rely on other data that may not be suitable for the prospective investor. Furthermore, the tendency for the investor community to enter or leave en bloc means that business players can collectively get it wrong. For example, the EBRD's shareholdings in some banks cannot always be deemed to be sound:

> 'EBRD, counting on no debt repayment, has effectively written off its Tokobank shareholding and is therefore no longer directly involved in the process of liquidation ... We consider the $20 million–$30 million invested in Tokobank as lost.'[18]

The EBRD also had a 2.28 per cent ($6.66 million) share of Inkombank which had to be regarded as similarly lost. You cannot really rely on someone else's opinion of a good investment, or mere hearsay.

Various companies and agencies provide insurance cover against this risk of non-payment. Examples of trade finance organizations that guarantee or support exports are ECGB, EXIM, COFACE, MIGA, etc. Your project can benefit from this assistance, although this sort of cover carries a price. In essence you should be able to cover your back within the project. Search for the partner who supplies the best cover for you on the most suitable terms. Sometimes we make mistakes when we search for a partner, even those who are meant to be working for us.

Operational risk

This involves a 'catch-all' for risk factors within an enterprise and we devote a whole chapter to it. Operational risk is due to inadequate internal controls, human error or failure of IT systems. The three main areas of human error are inexperience, incompetence or corruption. The deviation from the project plan, its delay or loss will vary according to:

- who these people are
- what access they eventually secured
- what they did
- when and how they acted
- whether there were adequate risk management practices in the company.

Whether a company's operating structure is tight or loose can do much to determine the impact of operational risk. Where individual staff have a great deal of leeway, a lot of damage could be done. When we have greater freedom in the work environment, we can encourage greater flexibility and creativity in employees; it is also a potentially risky way of operating a business. One area of risk is when your staff go on the take and become open to gifts from other parties. In DSL, we found that one of the most frequent times when bribes occur is when a company is at its procurement stage (see Invitation to tender, p. 153). Bribes or incentives will be offered for the decision maker (or advisers) to buy the best product or services. The competition at this stage may wish to play dirty. Such behaviour is axiomatic when the contracts at stake are high-value. Even non-profit making projects do not seem to be immune.

CASE STUDY

The Olympic Games

Controversy has always surrounded the Olympic Games because of doping, biased judges or other forms of cheating. Off field, Juan Antonio Samaranch, head of the International Olympic Committee, had to threaten to fire some members after allegations of bribery. Marc Hodler, former president of the International Ski Federation and second most senior IOC member, said agents were offering IOC votes for sale for between $500 000 and $5 million to cities bidding for the honour of hosting the games.[19] Allegations extended to the award of the 2002 Winter Olympics to Salt Lake City, Utah. This spurred the Americans to appoint former Senator George Mitchell to hold an inquiry into possible corruption. Conflict-of-interest charges against gifts and bribes were the order of the day. Six International Olympic Committee members were expelled in January 1999 for taking bribes and favours in relation to the granting of the Olympics to Salt Lake City and Sydney. There is no doubt: 'Bribery allegations have done great harm to Games.' Your project could be in line for this sort of treatment.

If a man asked you for a couple of hundred million dollars, would you lend it? Probably not. But if you had already lent him hundreds of millions of dollars, and then he asked you for a hundred million more, would you lend it? If not, you are probably not an investment banker dealing with hedge funds.

CASE STUDY

Barings Bank

Some of the aforementioned systems for trading in financial derivatives and futures have come to epitomize playing with risk. Risk management is still, in many ways, under-developed or poorly practised in certain areas of the financial sector. It may be more accurate to say that in some banks there is good risk management, whereas in others it is no more than a pretence. The examples of Barings Bank and the Nick Leeson fiasco,[20] Peter Young at Morgan Grenfell, or the trader Hamanaka at Sumitomo highlight lax control.

It is facile to say that one rogue individual brings down a bank. Leeson was meant to have contributed half of the entire bank's profits. A factor in these Barings-type trading debacles could be summed up by a glib explanation: *'I don't know how he makes all those profits, but it's great for the bank, so we'd better not disturb him. After all, we depend on him for our annual bonus.'* Therefore, the track record of trading operations and fund management in some well-known banks is an insight into how not to conduct project risk management. Nick Leeson was in charge of both trading and settlements, managing the flow of vast sums of money on various markets. He was also given responsibility for the controls and checking mechanism, the local Barings settlements and accounts division. It was a case of a rogue trader being in charge. Perceived rewards turned out to be real losses, perhaps as much as £900 million ($1.6 billion).

It is unthinkable that one trader could manage to operate unsupervised in Singapore without the top echelons of the company in London being responsible in some way. One person who gets away with fraud for a couple of weeks or months may be solely guilty. When she/he manages to evade corporate controls for years, the structure of the system must be rotten. In these cases, operational risk was not localized in one person, it pervaded the whole system because it was spread and increased by the risk-bearing attitude of top management who let it continue unchecked. It is not surprising that there is an occasional blindness in the pursuit of large-scale investment projects. According to George Soros:

> *'Institutional investors do not generally measure their performance in absolute terms but relative to each other. They operate as a herd, following the latest trend.'*[21]

The UK High Court placed banning orders on some members of the Barings management which forbade them from holding another directorship of a UK company.[22] As Nick Leeson said:

> *'I knew from my experience … that when it came down to detail, no senior managers actually wanted to get their hands dirty and investigate the numbers. They always felt that they were above that.'*[23]

Because Nick Leeson seemed to be contributing so much to the bank's profits, and these so-called profits formed the base of the managers' annual bonuses, it is not surprising that senior staff chose to be risk-ignorant.

Various possible reasons and motives have been ascribed to the downfall of Barings, now owned by ING bank of the Netherlands. The poor human performance during this fiasco can be attributed to various forms of greed, incompetence, ignorance or lack of training. The ultimate damage has many manifestations that we might choose to place in the category of operational risk. It is one of the phenomena we believe to be possibly one of the most devastating. These factors are dealt with in more detail in Chapter 7: Operational Risk Management.

Position-keeping or stock-keeping

So, is operational risk confined to investment banking? Obviously not. The Barings episode reflects a case of improper or non-existent controls in the company's organizational structure, plus a deep fundamental problem with position-keeping. This is an issue that troubles many companies and projects, whether they know it or not. It comes down to knowing how much you have spent, how much you have received, then how much you have left. Some people call it position-keeping, others know it better as balancing the books or stock-keeping. The principles are more or less the same. Businesses and projects can easily sink by neglecting the fundamentals.

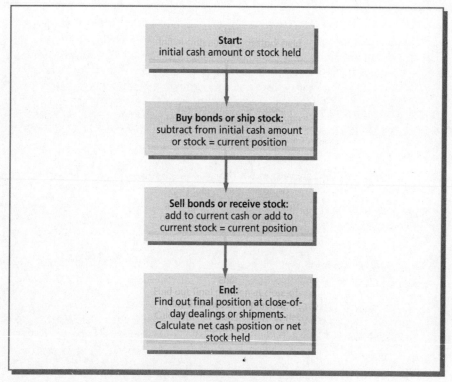

Fig 3.5 ● The fundamental principles of position-keeping

Project failure

Projects that are deemed to have failed are judged by results that indicate under-performance in one way or another. The degree of project failure can be defined by a variety of factors:

Business

This heading specifies a variety of performance characteristics that may not have been immediately apparent at the project initiation. Thus, the project inception may have defined a scope for the project that is no longer appropriate. Many corporations that are subject to take-overs or mergers find out that certain projects are not in keeping with the new business image or strategic plan. One of the key assets of any individual or company is also a wealth that is difficult to quantify. It is the asset of *reputation*. This is the public image of business skill and honesty that comprises an intangible wealth (if you have it). If you do not have it, then any business project can be doomed to failure. Let us look at what a reputation can do to your project.

CASE STUDY

Computer and IT sales manager, Greece

This is a classic example of how not to sell a project. Mr X came unprepared to sell it. He was socially inept to deal with an expensive and highly-charged project, and technically unversed to handle the customer's requirements and questions. There was no comfort factor for the customer in any way, and there was little respect shown to him. Mr X was not perceived as an honest person. Whether he was or not is immaterial, the customer *thought* he was crooked and/or incompetent. The way in which Mr X pressured the customer to sign the contract was uncouth salesmanship. He could not see that telling the customer it was a good system was not important. It was for the customer to judge whether it was a good system. Mr X could not set up the system demonstration properly, nor answer the customer's technical questions. This showed singular incompetence. He did not get on with the client. So, in terms of a beauty contest, points out of ten:

Technical	2
Managerial	3
Social	3
Total	8 points/30
Verdict	FAIL

Some fault must rest with his bosses – they recruited him and they did not detect that he could not sell. If they were friends or buddies from school or university days is irrelevant; you do not recruit key staff who are gauche and technically incompetent. Choose your project staff well or lose the deal! That is why a project that is well-structured places a series of gates or controls upon staff selection and assignment. This can be demonstrated partly by the Job description process in Chapter 7.

Budgetary

This is one of the most likely reasons for under-performance or the factor that determines project termination or failure. The British TSR2 supersonic fighter project is often cited as a technological success, but one that was judged a budgetary failure by the Wilson government. Similarly, the Channel Tunnel is an engineering triumph, but not necessarily a commercial one (see Channel Tunnel case study, p. 83). There are many incidents of projects running out of funds, or being cancelled (see Project termination). These events are not always within the control of the project manager, but are often the result of business and political decisions made by the project owner and related parties. We will look at reasons for this.

Scheduling

The occurrence of projects running over their planned schedule is one of the alarming phenomena of management science. Scheduling failures are also attributed to the growing interconnection of related projects. Such failures may not be totally the fault of the project owner or project manager. Thus, it can be said that Charles Babbage's Analytical Engine designed in the 19th century was in some ways a scheduling error. His project would have resulted in the world's first computer capable of solving fairly complex mathematical equations, far more advanced than his earlier Difference Engine. His Analytical Engine was stymied by budgetary problems, and also by the technical failure of Victorian engineering to produce parts with the required accuracy. The NASA space shuttle (see case study, p. 38) was a classic scheduling problem; a programme that was already running over schedule and being forced to cut corners (compromising safety) in the vain hope of getting back on track. It can be said that God is the only true master project scheduler.

Technical

This is usually a reason for failure or under-performance in high-tech industries, e.g. pharmaceutical or computer hardware/software. Companies involved in state-of-the-art research and development (R&D) are termed as the leading edge of technology – and also as the bleeding edge (see NASA case study). Project initiation usually gets the go-ahead to meet a set of desired or mandatory performance levels. When these levels are not reached, it is often enough to kill off the project mid-way. Biotechnology is an example of such a graveyard of once-aspiring projects. British Biotech, for example, was fined $50 000 by the US Securities & Exchange Commission over its press releases for its cancer drug, Marimastat.[24] Even the most eagerly-awaited drugs, such as Viagra pills for treating impotence, will have *some* side-effects. Companies have to be particularly careful over getting pharmaceutical product approval: a drug's healing properties, the validity of its testing, consumers safety and the verdicts of regulatory authorities are areas which could experience delay and pose schedule risk for the project. The delayed introduction of the Iridium satellite telephone system is another example. Technology is a potenti[al] minefield for projects that may seem promising initially.

Legal/regulatory

Supervisory authority within an industrial sector wields varying degrees of power that is occasionally brought to bear on companies and organizations. A project may be put under pressure to amend its course of action, perhaps by an industrial directive or fine. This may be intended to increase the period of testing, as in the pharmaceuticals industry, to enforce a design change in cars or buildings, or even to remove the operating licence from the project owner. It might, for example, be a Federal Aviation Authority ruling on flight safety and operating procedures. The options are usually to fight the regulatory ruling in a law court, pay any fine, change the jurisdiction of operation, or shut up shop. We explore this further in the chapter on legal issues.

Thus, operational risk influences, or even dominates, the other factors. An incompetent or corrupt project manager or project owner will put serious risk on the project. Once again, the model may have been a good idea, but a poor one to put into practice. Our DSL experience shows us that using a contract is best, certainly for large-volume projects. Smaller projects have to be judged on cost-benefit, where you decide if the costs of drafting a contract (possibly hiring a legal expert) are too great in relation to the total sum at stake. A surprising number of companies undertake projects without a full contract; in many cases, a letter of intent suffices to secure the production and order for the start of a large project. More often than not, small or medium-sized firms or one-man operations are constrained by money, time, manpower and lack of legal expertise to draft contracts. Therefore, the risk of non-payment for their services remains.

Risk analysis is knowing where the hazards are, and the likelihood of encountering them. It is like drawing a map showing dangerous mountains and deep seas. Risk management is knowing where not to fly and how to sail safely around icebergs. An accumulation of experience over industrial best practice provides us with a base for skilled project navigation. Project risk management is not pseudo science, it is putting knowledge into action.

Notes and references

1 *The Economist*, 19 August 1995.
2 The *Independent*, 16 January 1999, p. 6.
3 Bernstein, P. (1998) *Against the Gods*, p. 21, Wiley.
4 Foreign and Commonwealth Office and Control Risks Group UK, 1998.
5 Personal interview, Moscow, December 1998.
6 *Wall Street Journal*, 19 October 1998, p. 17.
7 *Wall Street Journal*, 19 October 1998, p. 17.
8 *Financial Times*, 2 October 1998, p. 8.
9 *Financial Times*, 23 October 1998, p. 6.
10 *Financial Times*, 11 January 1999, p. 22.
11 Adapted from *The Economist*, 'Tale of Two cities', 5 September 1998; and The *Observer*, 11 October 1998.
12 *Financial Times*, 24 November 1998, p. 27.
13 Soros, G. (1998) *The Crisis of Global Capitalism*, Little, Brown & Co.
14 *Financial Times*, 5 December 1998, p. xxvi.
15 ITAR-TASS, 25 November 1998.
16 *Wall Street Journal*, 1 December 1998, p. 1.
17 *Financial Times*, 5 December 1998, p. 3.
18 *Izvestia*, 1 December 1998, p. 5 (in Newsbase, UK).
19 *International Herald Tribune*, 14 December 1998, p. 1.
20 Fay, S. (1996) *The Collapse of Barings*, Richard Cohen, London.
21 Soros, G. (1998) *The Crisis of Global Capitalism*, Little, Brown & Co.
22 *Financial Times*, 2 December 1998.
23 Leeson, N. with Whitley, E. (1997) *Rogue Trader*, Little, Brown & Co.
24 *The Times* business section, 18 January 1999, p. 45.

4

Risk Management

" Protection is not a principle, but an expedient. "

Benjamin Disraeli

What is risk management? Risk analysis is like drawing a map of potential hazards and outlining the damage they could cause. Risk management is taking the map and deciding how to avoid the hazards.

The concern about risk in recent years has given rise to concerted attempts to define risk and risk management methodologies. One such example is the RAMP (Risk Analysis and Management of Projects) method launched by the Institute of Civil Engineers and the Institute of Chartered Actuaries in the UK. They have sought explicitly to provide a project framework to identify and reduce risks. The clear aim is to identify and act against risk factors that could lead to significant delays or overspending in projects; to combine risk analysis with risk management within the project operations arena. The system creates a comprehensive and logical framework for risk identification and project control. RAMP works by concentrating on detailing and quantifying risks in the life cycle of a project.

Some people may choose to view RAMP, and similar methodologies, as an assembly of common sense. Nevertheless, RAMP is better, in many senses, because it puts a structure or strait-jacket over some of the potentially wilder elements in a project. The aim is not to make paperwork and controls stop the progress of the project; RAMP tries to force the project parties into a rational series of procedures and enable them to continue to have scheduled risk analyses during the project life cycle. The price of proper project risk management must be cost-effective, i.e. the cost of getting there must be less than the value of having risk management. Risk management in itself is not the objective, it is a means to an end, to maintain the project on schedule and on budget. A case study of RAMP in action can be seen in a construction project for a tolled road bridge.[1]

Risk to the business plan brings in the uncertainty over an outcome where total investment cost will be greater than the final project benefit or result. Risk also bears on the likelihood that the project schedule will be longer than planned or not delivered at all. This opens the door to consideration of risk mechanisms – these can be exceedingly complex and form a major element of the risk analysis.

Risk is not constant over time within the project cycle. Work done at feasibility stage can reduce risk to a point where we can be reasonably confident that the outcome (likely profit) will be worth more than the investment. We still have to keep in mind what has been committed to – and what can still be changed.[2] The customer or project owner can try to come in forcefully mid-project and say: *'This is not what I wanted!'*

Placing a lump sum or fixed-price sub-contract reduces time and cost risk for the customer, but it may increase functional risk – what if a change is then required? We have to vary the contract and either the contractor or customer may pay dearly for the change. Alternatively, a cost-reimbursable contract does not fix cost or time but does give the project owner the ability to change the objective. There can be flexibility, but the project cannot be so fluid that it is in danger of falling apart. Project contracts, in this respect, are a compromise between structure and change.

Project risk management in a nutshell

Therefore, in the project environment we must keep track of time horizons. We can act on those which are prioritized, i.e. scheduled by urgency. Otherwise, we will be spread too thinly for effective action.

Risks in the future

Ahead of us, and possibly too far away to influence today's operations, are tomorrow's risks (Risk Management I). Nevertheless, there are various risk management procedures that can be established in order to handle future risks more effectively.

CASE STUDY

UK ambulance services

Many regional health authorities have decided to implement active deployment of their ambulance services. It is a progression from the earlier project view of an ambulance service: start – implement ambulance service – maintain service. Detailed historical data of accidents, plus records of emergency call-outs, give a picture of likely areas of need. The data can be linked with a GIS (Geographic Information System) that provides drive times and specific postcodes, plus centres of medical aid with clinical specialities to give a better pro-active picture ▶

▶ of health risk before the emergencies occur. The London Ambulance Service computer despatch management is an example of such a system. It is also a prime example of what can go wrong in a project – over-budget, late delivery, unfulfilled user expectations and lower performance than that of specifications.[3]

Thus, ambulances can be stationed outside their centres beside busy road intersections or in towns where there is a great likelihood of medical need. The appropriate medical staff can be placed on duty or stand-by where established patterns of emergencies needing medical attention have emerged. Less effective risk management is to pay no attention to past data and to wait for the need or accident to occur in the future.

Risks of the present

Risks of the present have an immediate effect; sometimes the project dangers are staring you in the face. Let us look at the case of individual finances. You could take a pension as your personal project to provide an income when you retire. In the mid-1980s Britain's Conservative government moved to shift the pensions burden away from the state and transfer it to the private sector – an attractive goal for government given the rise in the proportion of elderly and non-working population. The State Earnings-Related Pension Scheme (SERPS) was particularly targeted. Employees were given the right to leave their employer's pension scheme and transfer their money into private pensions. Immediate questions (risks of the present) spring up for the individual:

● am I handing over my money to the wrong pension company (counter-party risk)? It is not a simple case of them going bankrupt or absconding with the cash; the risk is that they will under-perform when they invest the funds in assets that do not appreciate adequately to pay off future obligations. The potential hazard is not just that I give my money to them improperly, but I also contract to pay them a cut of my future income.

● am I choosing an unsuitable pension scheme for my needs (market risk)? There are various options depending on the individual's age, savings, family circumstances, whether they are self-employed or not, the amount they can pay into the scheme each month, etc.

These are questions that reflect the risks in decisions that must be made. Let's look at the case of personal pensions in the UK.

> **CASE STUDY**
>
> # UK pensions
>
> Planning for a pension is a project calculus of the risks of the present and risks of the future. It also involves cash flow forecasting, plus an (implicit) calculation of the real net value of the future incoming pension. The investment costs, balancing out the risks, should be outweighed by the net profits.
>
> In 1986 the Conservative government instituted changes in SERPS to bring public sector savings. These changes meant that from 6 April 2000 only half of the SERPS payment would go to the surviving spouse. The Department of Social Security admitted it had not informed the public of the danger that widows' benefits would be halved. The use of a methodology such as RAMP or PRINCE 2 is an explicit attempt to ensure that the appropriate documentation is raised, and the relevant parties are informed. Otherwise, the real danger is people are not notified – those contributing into the SERPS pensions were not told for ten years.

Risks of the past

These are previous risks or hazards to which we were once exposed. We have now conducted comprehensive risk analysis to determine that these risks pose no major danger. We can release funds and resources so that we are not working against a risk that no longer exists but channelling much-needed resources into other productive purposes – it is a case of risk management making you money.

NB: we should make adequate effort to monitor the situation to ensure that our previous risk analysis was correct in diagnosing a dead risk. Volcanic eruptions and earthquakes are examples of risks that crop up even though they may no longer have been considered a threat. Earthquakes in Los Angeles and Kobe make us aware of the possible resurgent threat. We should track our performance on risk to allow us to add up …

Total risk

Sum of the above. This total risk changes over time and it must be understood each time we measure progress on the project. The project risk depends on:

- time – i.e., 1998, 1999 or 2000; summer or winter; before or after a market boom
- context – i.e., construction or retail industry; non-governmental organization, private or government body

- culture – i.e., old family manufacturing firm, new start-up, US-based or east Europe.

Sometimes, one or all three act in the wrong way for you. At other times, there are options that are not immediately recognized or obvious. Time can be on your side too.

CASE STUDY

Home income plans

Changing demographics lead to an increasing proportion of older people in the population. Governments and companies are becoming less willing to fund the rising costs of pensions. Older people are often faced with low pensions and little to fall back on to meet their healthcare and everyday needs. Home Income Plans (HIPs) are one way of providing a form of annuity to unlock capital. Let's look at the risks.

Risks of the present: Facing elderly people is the scenario of low pensions and little cash to spare. The pain of increasing healthcare bills leaves them with today's worries. A mortgage/annuity arrangement could give them the little bit of extra income they want. There were cases in the 1980s of HIPs being oversold, especially if the housing market fell.[4] The real danger is that elderly people fall for the smooth talk of an unscrupulous salesman.

Risks in the future: For the householder, there is the possibility that housing prices fall, so that if the annuities are fixed to the prevailing house price, what ends up in their hand is less than expected. Little or nothing of the house value may be left for heirs, although this is not a problem for single people without descendants. These people are in a cash-flow situation, just like the Reichmann brothers (see Canary Wharf case study, p. 159). There is a way out – but is the price acceptable?

> **CASE STUDY**
>
> ## A bank training course in Russia, 1997
>
> DSL came across an executive trainer in a German bank in Moscow. Stefan was very confident as he was gearing himself up for presenting a training course in marketing to Russian bankers. From other sources, we learned that his seminars were successful in Germany. On closer examination, we found some areas of potential difficulty, notably that this was his first time in Russia, he had no previous experience of handling the Russian market, he knew no Russians well, and he did not speak or understand Russian. The local trainees were, understandably, less than receptive to the project.
>
> Why did Stefan fail? Was the bank project manager at fault (using the wrong resource) or was it down to poor Stefan? Realistically, it was clearly not possible for him to do a good job; in many ways, he had been 'set up'. Another reading of the situation was that the bank really did not care who they sent out, or what kind of quality they achieved on the job – the money for it had already been earmarked. It is ironic that if they had sent Stefan out there a few years earlier, he would have been greeted with great enthusiasm. During the early days of glasnost and the opening of the USSR, it was unusual to be given much access to the locals; Stefan would have been a welcome rarity. After the fall of communism, and the influx of western aid and consultants, Russians became a bit tired of western people there to help them. Russian business people wanted real investment and real value-added services; they did not need or want western textbook solutions for an economic upheaval and a novel event in world history. Projects should provide real value for money.

Project management is the process of combining myriad available resources; it involves planning to reach a goal or to build an end-product. It is fraught with everyday risks. The readings of the foreign market must be up to date to come up with an accurate assessment of it. Prior research is always needed. In some ways, risk management is a risk-neutral attitude; it does not try to take an extreme view at any stage. Risk management is the process of noting the risks and taking active measures to operate better under existing business conditions. Risk management is not an optional bolt-on package, or something that is merely nice to have; it should always be there from the outset. It is a structural and iterative process that continues throughout the life of the project.

Risk management has elements of:

- risk precaution/planning
- risk action/implementation.

These use a combination of constituent parts to keep the project on track and to handle potential hazards.

Risk log

One of the key inputs to the project is a risk log or risk assessment at critical points in the project life cycle. It can take various forms; we use a construction industry example.

Table 4.1 ● Construction risk log

Beavis risk log for Avignon Housing Corp, France				Date: 7 July 2001
Overall status at: 1 July 2001				
Risk issues	**Checked**	**Sure**	**Remarks**	**Next action**
Contract	Signed	100%		
Planning permission	Signed	100%		
Suppliers	Pending	90%	Reinforced concrete to be confirmed	Get contract and confirm deliveries
Sub-contractors	Pending	75%	Carpenters, electricians and glaziers to sign	Sign contract, confirm number of workers and wage rates
Location	Hilly			Check drainage channels are free of obstruction
Ground	Chalk, firm	99%	Little history of subsidence in this area. Drainage is good	
Weather	Sunny	90% (now)	Rains a lot in September (average 7cm), frost possible in late-October, minimum winter temperature –14°C	Ensure tarpaulins and coverage during rain. Check warm clothing issued. Anti-freeze in stock
Project team		85%	Check competence of mechanical engineer; review CV and take references	Look for replacement M&E officer
Compiled by	*Pierre Newton*		Site engineer	
Checked by	*Thomas Pearson*		Project manager	

This log is only a cut-down part of a larger document; it has to be tailored to the needs of the company and the requirements of the project. It is simply a record of affairs, and is useless without appropriate preparation, planning and follow-up actions. Risk management is not an ad hoc, off-the-cuff affair. Similarly, risk management is rather worthless when we do not put plans into action and get real benefits.

CASE STUDY

The fall of Singapore, 1942

Risk management is an iterative process because our situation changes, and our knowledge of the risks also changes. British heavy artillery emplacements in Singapore during 1942 were the result of assessing the risk of attack; they were set in concrete casements for use against the Japanese assault but were facing in precisely the wrong direction. The British battleships *Prince of Wales* and *Repulse* were lost in a mismanaged attempt to thwart the risk of Japanese invasion. The ships were sent to an area off north-east Malaya where the Japanese were not present; they were later caught without any air cover by Japanese bombers and sunk.

Some post-war commentaries indicate that the project of defending Singapore was a fiasco in both risk analysis and risk management, with extremely high-profile political meddling by Churchill in one of his poorer judgements. The tally of mistakes continued to mount as panic began to set in. The causeway to Malaya was blown up to prevent Japanese troops from invading, but this also destroyed the only source of drinking water for Singapore. Morale dropped and rioting broke out among both civilian and military personnel. Defeat was only a matter of time. A business situation compares insignificantly against the terrible scenario of war. Nevertheless, both military and civil planning have to incorporate proper handling of risk analysis and risk management to obtain successful results. Risk management helps us to lower the likelihood of defeat in our handling of projects.

Let us look at a civil engineering example.

The Royal Opera House, London

This project had a £214 million renovation budget, funded by British taxpayers. The number of people involved in the project was large; it was steered by a committee of 22 people. The leadership was unable to deal with must of the conflict. We look at what happened to some of those involved:

1986 Jeremy Isaacs joined as general director
1987 Bernard Haitink appointed musical director

1996 Jeremy Isaacs left
1997 Lord Chadlington appointed chairman
1997 Genista McIntosh came in as chief executive
1997 Genista McIntosh left after 4 months
1997 Mary Allen joined as replacement chief executive
1998 Mary Allen left
1998 Judy Grahame, director of corporate affairs, left
1999 ROH closed for one year

The Commons Heritage Committee critical report in 1998 led to the resignation of the ROH board and Mary Allen as chief executive. Sir Colin Southgate, Chairman of the Royal Opera House, was fully aware of the negative publicity and pushed for new trade union working agreements, which also resulted in the Royal Ballet corps staff being cut from 900 to 700. Michael Kaiser, formerly Head of the American Ballet Theatre, arrived from New York as new chief executive. The new brooms have to be seen to clean up former working practices. Nevertheless, the accumulated deficit of £20 million showed there was considerable progress to be made.

The arguments among the ROH management came about partly from the clash of objectives – political versus business versus personal. Senior personnel had mixed responsibilities and different roles; the government had appointed a committee but then liaised with other project owners or interested parties. The rebuilt ROH was late and overrunning its budget, which led to strains on the company finances, schedule and staff – all opera performances were cancelled for 1999. Fewer performances meant lower revenue, less favourable publicity and lower staff morale. Haitink's international acclaim as a conductor was lost in an opera house without opera. It capped a management disaster that had involved the loss of three chief executives, two chairmen, other administrative staff plus the resignation of the entire board.[5] The loss of key management personnel on such a wide scale is symptomatic of a general malaise.

Extensive consultancy work was carried out but it was hard to see much concrete benefit for the ROH (see Consultants, p. 121). Furthermore, these external contracts involved significant sums that were not openly contested, and they were seen to have been awarded on a less than competitive or meritocratic basis. Financial controls were slack. The result was a project that was over budget, over schedule, and upsetting to many. Sadler's Wells threatened to sue when their 1999 productions, due to take place at the ROH, were cancelled. Sadler's Wells was paid £1.25 million compensation by the ROH.[6]

We look later on at the case study of a DSL client bank and its decision-making process for a major project (see Fig. 5.1, Chapter 6). We discuss more effective leadership when examining personnel, and look at the Project co-ordination committee, also in Chapter 6. One evaluation of the ROH committee was that it was so stricken by internal politics that it diverted a lot of time and resources away from music and the arts. This resulted in less time for creativity, lower staff morale, a low number of productions and a vicious downward quality spiral.

It should be noted that the ultimate goal of a project is not to please everyone all the time; a lot of potential project players will want to jump on the bandwagon. A large and unwieldy steering committee is not an appropriate vehicle to manage a project. The key is to include people who have deep interest in seeing the project succeed, and those who can complete the required tasks. There is also the political element; those who need to be consulted regularly and who can provide input to the needs and operations of the project should also be included, plus those who are able to exercise the political clout to finish the project when it meets opposition or hindrance.

Project steering

DSL experience tends to indicate that there is a compromise between involvement and anarchy. We should try to involve everyone who can contribute effectively to a project; but taken to extremes, this would mean that all the committee members would not be able to speak and discussions would be easily hindered by disagreement. The need for practicality has fashioned a trend for a 10, maximum 15, person steering committee; any more and it becomes potentially disruptive. See Fig. 6.1 in Chapter 6 for a possible structure for the steering committee.

The daily running of a project should be under the auspices of one person who reports to an appointed group. He/she should have the character and power to break a deadlock. It is imperative that the project manager has the clout to enforce decisions, which may be deemed unpopular by some, but ultimately necessary for the success of the project. Contracts to outsiders should be open to tender where possible, except for small sums or for very important work that has to be done quickly. This is part of the ITT (invitation to tender) process, which is discussed in detail in Chapter 8. The art of project management is not just creating the project, but trying to tread on as few toes as possible and to be seen to be professional and fair. This counts doubly when the project is a high-profile business affair.

There are few large-scale projects without any political problems or infighting. A project manager is assigned and paid to do a quality job; this automatically requires the diplomatic skill and political clout to get the job done. Project management means avoiding or handling the problems and risks when they materialize. Project managers are hired and paid to plan, then to fix things when they go wrong. And go wrong they do! There is no such thing as a problem-free large project.

The risk planning cycle

Risk management has benefits for the modern project manager. It has various uses as a defence (to avoid loss), or to go into attack (to seek profit). Thus, where the yield (or profit) curve is over-estimated, those players with better risk management can move in quickly to take on more profits. The risk-return ratio should be accurately assessed during the earlier risk analysis stage; some form of loss generally comes about when profit, costs or risk are over or under-estimated. We look at some aspects of planning.

Budgeting

One of the biggest risks facing most projects is that they run substantially over their allocated budgets. A set of accounts or a stock list gives us a snap-shot picture of where we are and how we are doing. This helps us to plot a course of where we should be going next. Potential budgeting errors can come from:

● under-estimating the fixed costs
● under-estimating the variable costs
● under-estimating the project schedule
● over-estimating the income stream.

Cost estimation

Project metrics are very difficult to master, even for the experienced. The estimation process is very complex for probabilities, for time schedules for tasks, and for revenue and cost streams. The assessment of future events can be scientific under project risk management, but it can also border on the artistic or gifted. Some project risk management experts are better at risk metrics and estimating schedules/costs. They do not always give full reasons for their thoughts, but sometimes elucidate their project prognostications on a 'hunch' or heuristics. Thus, there are experts who can sum up their forecasts cogently and accurately, sometimes without advanced mathematics or formulae. For example: *'I think we can make a decent 15 per cent net profit after three years.'* Or: *'Maybe it's not so good. I get a bad feeling about this project.'*

On a global scale, even the experts can get it very wrong. They may do so on the basis of unsuitable assumptions to justify their investment advice. George Soros has, ironically, been one of the most vociferous critics of the mainstream experts. He particularly criticizes those who trade freely but make the assumption that they will be rescued if they get their prognostications wrong. As he says:

> *'Financial markets are rather peculiar. They resent any kind of government interference but they hold a belief deep down that if conditions get really rough the authorities will step in. This belief has now been shaken.'*[7]

Sampling experts is an essential part of pre-feasibility, especially when we are dealing with longer time-span projects. Similarly, businesses operating under more unpredictable conditions, such as the emerging markets, have to be more accurate in their budget forecasts.

Project budget

This is one of the traditional structures, alongside the schedule, for exercising control over the project. It governs resource allocation and task prioritization. There are various ways to estimate a project budget, which are usually defined in three time periods:

1 long-term/strategic: roughly three years or longer

2 medium-term/tactical: one to three years

3 short-term/operational: 12 months or less.

Top-down

You can take a panel of experts (see Delphi group, p. 40) or a comparable past project to benchmark your next project. You can then subtract savings from this example if the project is smaller, simpler and more straightforward, or add contingency costs for unknown factors in the project to derive a revised estimate. This will give you an idea in terms of the big picture. This will be the same process for scheduling. The idea is not to predict all future events, or to try to foresee most of the outcome; the goal is to be more prepared to deal with events when they happen. Being stretched without contingency resources across the lifespan of a project makes us targets for nasty surprises. Nevertheless, it is the client/project owners who set the budget initially, if only because they hold the purse-strings. The project owner or directors set the strategic long-term budgets which have to be translated into action at the lower project operational levels. These are regarded as top-down budgets.

These budgets have to be implemented by the project manager downstream. The project risk is that there is a severe communication problem between top managers who do not understand the project nature or technical issues at the operational level. Then there are the project managers who cannot understand the resources available, or the general business objectives, on the wider scale of the whole company.

> *'This sub-optimality is a result of top management's limited knowledge of the specific of each project, task, activity, knowledge that is unavailable when preparing the long-range budget using the top-down approach.'*[8]

Bottom-up

This gives the project manager the opportunity to put a project proposal together, detailing the current project requirements. This will total the components, labour, and scheduling of tasks and deliveries, with a margin for project management services added. This budget can be passed up to top management for approval (or rejection). However, it is more usual to enter into a process of iterative budgeting, where the proposed budget is amended by top managers and the project manager until it is acceptable to both parties. Your project team or departmental experts can give you their estimates of what they think each of their sub-tasks will cost. You total these costs, add managerial and integration costs, plus a buffer or contingency fund for the unknown factors in this particular project, to come up with the final estimate.

Cost control

One of the ways in which people can rationalize a complex world is to use heuristics, or rules of thumb, extensively in business. These rules are based on previous experience, and may well have proven themselves to be very useful in the past. Some heuristics are based on sound mathematical proof and good business sense. Thus, for example, the 80:20 rule has many manifestations. *'Only 20 per cent of your components give you 80 per cent of all your maintenance problems.' 'Twenty per cent of your customers will give you 80 per cent of your revenue.'*

The problems come when we try to over-use heuristics in project management, or to use these rules in an inappropriate situation. Thus, people can easily assume that circumstances have not changed significantly; this will have a harmful effect on the budget, e.g: *'Our raw materials always cost us only 3–4 per cent more each year'*; *'I came from IT, the machinery there fell 35 per cent in costs each year. It must be the same in manufacturing'*; *'The directors will make up the short-fall in the budget. They did last year.'*

Project budgets tend to be either:

- fixed-cost
- cost-plus.

Fixed-cost takes most of the uncertainty and much of the risk out of the contract. The downside risk is that the actual costs for the contractor may rise during the time of the project and leave the contractor with low profits, or worse, a loss. Fixed-cost is preferable when contractors tend to be hit by strikes or materials shortages; the cost of employing staff and capital equipment rises alarmingly, but the client is committed to a fixed price. There is usually a force majeure clause where such incidents can be ruled outside the control of the contractor, so the fixed price becomes increased accordingly. The client or project owner may make a mistake in accepting a high price, when the real costs of materials and labour are lower than originally believed. This is a common feature in the case of corporate employees who are paid a fixed rate for expenses, e.g. $200 per night for hotel accommodation, and $80 per day for food allowance for project work away from home – whatever their eventual costs. There is no guarantee that hotels and meals are not cheaper, which would save the client money.

Nevertheless, DSL would recommend the fixed-cost method as the preferred way to commence a project, certainly from the client's view-point. There are a number of reasons for this:

1 knowing the budget at the outset makes it easier to sell the project
2 setting the budget enables the project manager to set mile-stones at each stage
3 cost control for the accountant becomes stronger.

Cost-plus: The downside of this is that there is little incentive for contractors to minimize the cost of their raw materials and time if they are billing for labour in man-days. This method falls out of favour when contractors are found to have inflated their costs, thus overbilling the client. It is still commonly used, however, when the price of raw materials is well-known and fairly constant. Another name for this way of billing is the time and materials system. Carpenters and other tradesmen working in small businesses often quote prices on this basis. NASA used it during its early days of space exploration.

CASE STUDY

NASA cost-plus pricing in the 1960s[9]

This example involves a space research and development multi-phase project, started in the 1960s by NASA. It demonstrates the choice by NASA of a fixed-price contract for the initial phase, followed by a cost-plus (CPFF) contract for the next phase.

> 'Phase 1 was a $25,000 fixed-price competitively awarded study contract with a major aerospace firm. The second phase contract (resulting in several hundred thousand dollars of funding) was won by CPFF without competition, which involved continuing study tasks and an aircraft flight test programme.'

The say the first one will always be the toughest. The risk/reward ratio for the first contract was decidedly high-risk, but it was sweetened by the opportunity to win a follow-on contract. The project manager (Mike Kolker) was able to win more support beyond the initial $25,000 funding. The first contract carried additional significance because it was the first NASA prime contract won by the newly formed space division. The project manager had to establish his bona fides in order to build bigger success upon a smaller project success. Some companies will do just about anything to prove themselves to the client even if it means not covering costs, that is, a loss-leader. This was the old sales tactic of getting your foot in the customer's door.

The flight test equipment was supplied by NASA, and the flights were piloted by NASA personnel. Ground truth ocean surface characteristics were also partly monitored by NASA staff. The flight tests were a collaboration between contractor staff and NASA resources funded by the NASA programme office.

> 'Therefore, it would not be feasible for NASA to fund the contractor with a fixed-price contract. From our company view this meant there was no downside financial cost risk in this programme phase. However, with a fixed fee there was no upside incentive for increased profit. The CPFF contract inefficiencies were the use of funds without pressure on the NASA flight centre and us to achieve a fixed dollar target with a profit incentive. However, the risky nature of any flight test effort (e.g. the weather) and the lack of direct management control by the NASA programme office over the NASA centre obviated (the possibility of) a fixed price contract. While the contract was CPFF, obviously there was a limit to the NASA programme office funds for this phase. We were aware of the approximate funds anticipated for the contractor portion. Thus, the programme had mainly schedule risk; the longer the aircraft test burned up funding, less was available for data analysis and study tasks. Since there was no clearly defined flight test objectives, it was really defined by funding availability.'

Success was a matter of getting the contract, and ensuring that it was awarded on a suitable contract basis (i.e. fixed-price or cost-plus). The funding, and the whole project situation, can so easily change in the market. See Budgeting p. 78. Let's look at a tough case.

See Budgeting p. 78.

CASE STUDY

The Channel Tunnel project

The saga of the Channel Tunnel is well known, and it provides lessons to be learned. The initial players were asked to fund the tunnel's construction, which ended up as one of the world's biggest projects, costing £12 billion. They were unable to obtain a return on their capital because of cost overruns and the project falling behind schedule. Over-optimistic rail freight and passenger forecasts further reduced the eventual revenue stream. First to be hit were the banks and shareholders. Even with some operating profits in 1998, the time it would take to provide them with a return on their investment grew longer.

'Eurotunnel spent £12 billion building the tunnel and now it's celebrating that it's collecting £129 million operating profit. It's like building a house, and boasting that you are getting some rent.'[10]

The financial risks in this project are well known. The initial construction budget of £5 billion in 1990 has been overshot by almost 150 per cent. In 1998 it was estimated that it was unlikely to make a profit before 2005. Passenger and freight loads were lower than projected by Eurotunnel, the tunnel operator. This made achieving real profits and meeting the original pay-back period for investors very difficult, if not impossible.

'When they built this thing in 1987, they said the dividend was seven years away. Today, the dividend is eight years away – it's slipping away faster than time itself.'[11]

If the project manager or owners and backers of the scheme had been armed with better revenue forecasts, they would have used project risk management skills to raise profits/reduce costs. Potential investors with good risk-return evaluation could have budgeted the revenue stream better and may have avoided the project completely at the start of the share offer. The Eurotunnel share price hit 600p in 1994, but then fell dramatically to a low of 53p in September 1998. Interest payments were so large compared to the revenue stream that a debt-for-equity swap was inevitable in May 1997. This exchanged £1 billion of debt for shares, which cut the interest payments by half from £15 million to £8 million per month. This may have saved the company, but shareholder relations were damaged.

There were visible personality clashes between the British and the French, and disputes between the building contractor Trans-Manche Link (TML), the builders of the rolling stock, and the rail service operator, Eurostar. The ill manner in which

▶ disputes were settled highlights some of the hazards that can bedevil a project. The project manager has to have the diplomacy to defuse arguments, and antennae for sensing future disputes, especially when project owners are strong personalities. The conflict between the bankers and Sir Alistair Morton of Eurotunnel was legendary, and it culminated in his departure from TML in 1997.

The threat of fire became a reality in 1997 when a cargo wagon entered the tunnel alight. The resulting blaze put one side of the tunnel out of use for months, further curtailing any chance of revenue growth that year. The incident exposed deficiencies in fire detection and design of car transporters. There were significant doubts, even at the end of 1998, over the ability of Eurotunnel to ensure that safety standards were adequate. A later check (see project auditing/review, p. 146) showed room for improvement. This audit revealed that safety patrols were not able to cover every emergency within 15 minutes as recommended. Patrols operated for only 15 per cent of train running times and not round the clock as advised.[12]

The Channel Tunnel is a successful feat of engineering, but it does not fill with confidence those who expected a higher rate of profit when they first bought shares on the back of the Eurotunnel prospectus. The dividend for shareholders is like Waiting for Godot. Godot never arrives.

Project overruns such as these illustrate the need for contingency funds to bail out project tasks that have gone over earlier estimates. This may be due to unavoidable factors or because of optimistic budgeting. A knee-jerk response can be to allocate a large fund to cover most events – saving up for a rainy day. We will show that this can be wasteful when the project no longer needs that particular contingency funding. Therefore, the tied-up resources should be released for more productive purposes.

Resourcing

It is important that the project manager ensures the project is given the resources it needs for completion. If not, the PAR or project is not being prioritized properly by top management. This can be the case when the project does not have enough, or key, project champions in management to support it, or when the project overlaps with someone else's patch and creates conflict in management ranks. It is up to the project manager to attempt to win the resources needed for the project's successful completion. It can be a tough political fight. Fighting skills are a must for success. Yet on the other hand, there are many times when projects should be killed off before they waste resources or cause damage.

Project termination

There are various reasons for terminating or canning a project. We list them in order of frequency.

Reason	Technical	Economic	Market	Other
1. Low probability of achieving technical objectives or commercializing results	X			
2. Low return on investment		X		
3. Too costly to develop individual product		X		
4. Low market potential			X	
5. Technical or manufacturing problems not solved with available R&D skills	X			
6. Higher priority of other projects	X			
7. Change in market needs			X	
8. Too much time required to develop				X
9. Negative effect on other projects				X

Shtub, A. et al. (1994) Project Management Engineering, Technology and Innovation, Prentice Hall NJ, USA.

Critical success factors for an IT project

> *'Executive support – it is essential to have the sponsorship of senior executives where enterprise-wide information systems are being implemented. These systems impact almost all areas of the organization, and they are fundamental to the future operation of the organization. They also impact a broad range of end-users and so the ability of executives to take the arbitration of sensitive issues is extremely important. In addition, where additional funding is required due to cost overruns, then it is typically an executive decision to release further funding.'*[13]

DSL has found that a project that does not have top management support is set for trouble, and will hit hurdles in the path of its successful completion. Directors may think up project ideas, then pass them on to project managers, saying: *'I can't help you any more. You're on your own.'* Or, just as bad: *'This is outside my job description.'* A project manager may be left in the lurch. Achieving success can involve getting big guns on your side when the project comes under fire.

Notes and references

1 RAMP, 1998, pp. 81–7, Institute of Civil Engineers & Institute of Chartered Actuaries.
2 Refer to *ACE Client Guide* (1998) The Association of Consulting Engineers, Thomas Telford.
3 Flowers, S. (1996) *Software Failure: Management Failure*, John Wiley.
4 *The Times*, 17 October 1998, p. 55.
5 *The Times* 12 October 1998, p. 1 and p. 3.
6 *The Times*, 13 October 1998, p. 1.
7 Soros, G. (1998) *The Crisis of Global Capitalism*, Little, Brown & Co.
8 Shtub, A. et al. (1994) Project Management Engineering, Technology and Innovation, Prentice Hall NJ, USA, p. 379.
9 Kolker, M. (December 1998) personal interview and correspondence.
10 *The Times*, 22 September 1998, p. 29.
11 *The Times*, 22 September 1998, p. 29.
12 *Daily Telegraph*, 21 November 1998, p. 29.
13 Bishop, H., ibid. December 1998.

5

The legal process and risk

ff If you desire peace, prepare for war.99

Sun Tzu, *The Art of War*

Contracts form a fundamental part of risk management in projects, both in a positive way (the carrot) to define roles and rewards, and in a negative way (the stick) to state potential punishment or penalties.

The value of a contract or law suit

It must be said that the value of a contract or law suit should be called into question sometimes. The practicality and worth of contesting a legal action may be less than it first appears; depending on the circumstances and country, it may even be pointless. Emerging markets highlight many of the risks involved in dealing with the validity and enforceability of legal contracts (see DSL's work in emerging markets[1]). The value of a contract in the former USSR is less than clear-cut. There are a number of reasons:

1 the legal system changes from day to day; laws are brought out or amended
2 views and interpretations vary according to which agency you deal with
3 your ability to enforce the law (if known) may be limited
4 the cost and time in seeking legal redress may drain you, and your project, of resources
5 the plaintiff may not exist any longer, e.g. it may be a bankrupt company, or the party may have disappeared.

It helps to know where the lines of responsibility and direct control lie, and if there is a contractual relationship. This line of responsibility will be academic if the sub-contractor goes bankrupt. The aspect of control is also open to question in instances where the sub-contractor is registered abroad, or resides under a different jurisdiction. Position yourself on the same footing as others on the project.[2] The following example is of a construction project in Moscow in which DSL was one of the sub-contractors.

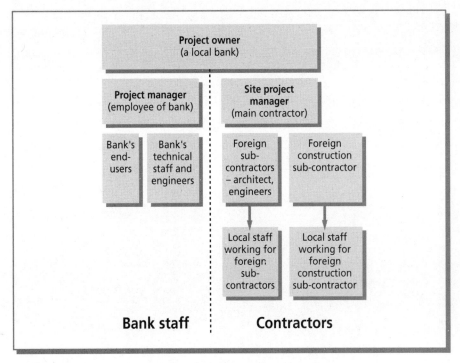

Fig 5.1 ● **Project responsibilities in a Russian construction project**

Accounts and assets of foreign investors can be frozen or sequestrated, or their outstanding debts can be left unpaid despite repeated calls. The choice is often to use lawyers to try to have debts settled. The ultimate action is to go to an international court of arbitration for settlement (see Project penalties, p. 93). Canadian authorities impounded an Aeroflot aircraft when the airline was judged to have defaulted on debts. Foreign companies can also appeal to the court of arbitration for redress.[3]

The use of contracts and hedged investments in Russia proved to be of little value in the economic crisis of the summer of 1998. The Russian government put a 90-day moratorium on foreign currency hedged forward contracts; thus, investments were unprotected as the rouble slid from Rbl 6.1 to $1 to Rbl 17 and lower. Currency hedging contracts were therefore ruled out by force majeure; you couldn't get your money out in hard cash (US dollars usually).

The contract

It is occasionally necessary to point out that a signed contract offers only part protection in a project's lifespan. The practicality of securing adequate compensation, or encouraging other project parties to collaborate in full as stated in the contract, has to be examined. The cost of obtaining legal counsel, and the time needed to secure compensation, must also be factored into any decision to pursue a potentially protracted trial. There are various forms of contracts and many ways of detailing the costs and returns for the parties involved. You should also be aware on whom the contract is binding, when it is binding, and what activities it covers. The lines of contractual obligation can be quite complex and they are illustrated in Fig. 5.2 for project teams collaborating on a hydroelectric project.

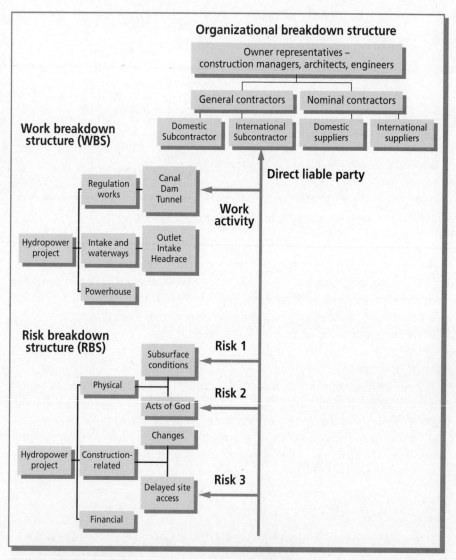

Fig 5.2 ● **Risk and liability identification of work activities**[4]

CASE STUDY

BCCI (Banque de Credit et Commerce International)

This case began in 1991 when Deloitte Touche acted as liquidators for creditors in a suit seeking $11 billion in damages over the failed BCCI. Allegations involved collusion and fraud by individuals in the bank and some of their customers over depositors' funds and shareholders' interests. Many of the depositors and shareholders were members of the Pakistani business community in the UK and abroad, and other depositors were local councils in the UK. This legal battle pitted Deloitte and its clients against Price Waterhouse as main auditor of BCCI, and Ernst and Young (then Ernst & Whinney) as group auditor. Deloitte finally settled for $200 million seven years later.[5]

Three apparent lessons come to mind:

1 You might have to wait a long time to receive damages

2 Your damages may be less than you requested

3 The costs of legal counsel may be substantial compared with money received.

There is no such thing as a certain victory in legal battles; even if you think there is, you will have to factor in cost and time to see whether the victory is worthwhile or Pyrrhic.

Strikes and industrial action

Here lies some of the greatest potential for causing project damage. A good project can be derailed, sometimes permanently. Standard university textbook theories on project management can be made almost redundant overnight because of personal or political disputes in a project.

CASE STUDY

The London Jubilee Line strike

This £2.8 billion project nearly came off the rails in 1998. Apart from being 18 months behind schedule, political flak and adverse media coverage gave it a pretty rough ride. The crunch came when it appeared the rail link would not be ready for the opening of the Millennium Dome, the centrepiece of the UK's millennium celebrations. Bechtel, which has its headquarters in the USA, took control of the project away from London Transport when it appeared the project was in trouble. Bechtel was also managing the construction of the first stage of ▶

91

▶ the £5.8 billion Channel high-speed rail link to London. The company is seen by some as a trouble-shooter for difficult problems. The new term, possibly, is crisis manager.

Analyzing the problems that arose depends on which version of events you wish to hear: the electricians' trade unions said delays were due to Bechtel trying to steamroll the project into a tight schedule and thus to compromise safety measures. The project managers felt the electricians were delaying the project on purpose. The pay rate is quite high in many technical projects – £1150 (c. $1900) per week for electricians on average.

When many projects finish, contract workers are left to seek jobs elsewhere; striking or delaying a project can lengthen employment and increase pay-cheques. It was reported that electricians wanted £5000 ($8000) as a bonus to open the line in time for the Millennium.[6] This tendency is not specific to any particular type of project. The Jubilee Line was particularly affected when vital signalling cables were found to have been cut. It was not known who had cut the cables because of a lack of surveillance.

Despite all the major delays and project disputes, the Jubilee line extension of 5.5km to the Greenwich Dome was opened in May 1999 in good time for the Millennium celebrations. This Jubilee line was opened in sections bit by bit in a *'phased implementation'* project. This meant that a public transport route to the Millennium Dome is rolled out as tried and tested parts of the route to be used immediately by passengers. Thus, a travel route can always be offered in part, if not in full, under all circumstances.

Project momentum can easily die towards the end of a project; it is up to the manager to get it back on track.[7] There is no single recipe that guarantees to avoid industrial disputes. The methodologies given do not present a one-size-fits-all solution. The key steps are:

● use a methodology or toolkit that structures the project with key controls
● monitor the situation to spot troublesome areas of conflict
● assign skilled negotiators to handle the situation
● be prepared to give and take; use the carrot and the stick occasionally
● implement solutions and learn from the situation.

The key to conflict resolution is to take the right stance:[8]

● study
● understand
● listen to all points
● defuse the situation
● counter-offer
● conclude negotiations.

It helps to understand that few projects are intentionally killed off by their project team during infighting. Rather, by agreeing to participate in the first place and to sign contracts, the project team has already decided that the project will be completed. The sources of conflict arise over the lesser, but still fundamental, issues. Questions that have to be addressed are:

- how should the project be done?
- who does a specific task?
- when has it to be done by?
- what will be the cost for this task?
- what are the performance criteria of this task or product?

Project penalties

A performance bond is a contractual assurance that the project will be done on time, on schedule and to the desired quality for the client or project owner. It is an insurance against under-performance. A good-performance bond or payment can be secured from the contractor beforehand to exert more pressure for a high standard of work. In order that the project's progress is maintained, the project manager may be asked to submit a good performance guarantee, which can be issued by a bank or credit institution operating legally in the host country where the project is based. This is in order that the contractor cannot exert pressure on the bank or credit body not to honour the bond in the event of a dispute. The guarantee will cover a percentage of the project's total value, or a sum, such as 20 per cent of the project manager's fees, including or excluding tax.

Writing bond contracts may be relatively easy; getting remuneration from bonds drawn from a bank can be fairly easy; getting remuneration from insurance bonds can be relatively difficult because they have to be vetted by insurance company investigators. The fact that a bond may be pulled from a project manager or contractor does not signify that the project manager is at fault; there may be valid force majeure conditions why he could not fulfill the terms of the contract.[9] If so, there is likely to be legal wrangling as to what these mitigating circumstances are, and whether force majeure clauses can be exercised legally. Furthermore, there are instances where the client tried to withhold the bond from the contractor. It could be that the client never made any attempt to pay the project manager or contractor. The performance bond serves only as an excuse to withhold payment. Some customers appear very reasonable at first sight – but look before you leap!

There are various forms of phrasing, of which the following is only one example indicative of contracts with penalty clauses:

1 *'In case any clause of the contract to be signed is violated, not executed or not properly executed according to the standards set out in the technical appendix, the client is entitled, without any other formality or prior notification, to rescind the contract. The client will collect the good performance and the advance payment guarantees, due to penalty clause and claim damages from the contractor for any loss incurred, arising from the violation of the contract's clauses.*

2 *In case of dispute over the standard of performance, either party may take the case to arbitration, the court in question being the ICAO in Stockholm, Sweden. The decision of the ICAO court in Sweden shall be final and binding upon both sides.'*

Delays and underperformance

Delay penalties are often placed on contractors to ensure that the project is delivered on time, on budget and to an acceptable quality. The project manager is obliged to pay a penalty depending on the tariffs set out in the legal clauses. The following percentages of the project's net value are only representative:

● *for a delay of up to ten days, 0.1 per cent per day*
● *for a delay exceeding ten and up to 20 days, 0.15 per cent per day*
● *for a delay exceeding 20 days, 0.4 per cent per day*
● *the delay penalties rise to a maximum 15 per cent of the project's total net value*
● *the total penalties for delay cannot be more than a maximum of £150 000.*

If the deadline (e.g. 30 days) lapses and inadequate action has been taken by the project manager to rectify unsatisfactory work, the customer may be entitled to take further action. This may be cancellation of the contract, plus any other damages stipulated in it. Cancellation may not necessarily prejudice the client's future course of action in claiming further damages for any loss incurred in the project. This type of contract cuts both ways; the client may act unreasonably to delay a project. The contractor has to be able to hit back.

CASE STUDY

Architecture and the art of feng shui

Tom Tow and Melanie Francis of Singapore run a firm of architects and design consultants involved in building projects around SE Asia and China. They take on all types of building work, from creating design drawings for the whole project to its interior design. It tends to be the interior design that causes the most headaches. (See Prototyping, p. 22.) Because of the prominent presence of a Chinese business community in Asia, clients sometimes call in a Chinese diviner of spirits to find the ideal placement of architectural features to allow for best working conditions. Feng shui is the Chinese practice of arranging household and office space, and objects in it, through interior design. Certain architectural features may be changed, objects repositioned, or even the building relocated on the advice of the feng shui practitioner. It is an ancient belief that is part spiritual and part ergonomics, and involves an appreciation of negative and positive energy. It does not have a 100 per cent scientific base by any means.

Feng shui can create a real headache for Tom Tow and Melanie Francis as the lead architects on the project. A previous client called in a feng shui practitioner to devise the best lay-out for his building. Work stopped for the inspection, building plans were redrawn to conform to the feng shui recommendations, and the interior design was adjusted. The arrangement was deemed to be the best for the client. However, the client was not completely satisfied with the feng shui, so he called in another practitioner. This happened three times. Each time building work was halted because the feng shui recommendations involved something slightly different. There is no standard for feng shui operations, nor is there a guild of feng shui practitioners; it is an open field and anyone can recommend the best feng shui arrangement. This means that a building might never be completed.

Delay and unreasonable conduct by the client can be curtailed by clauses in the under-performance or delay section of the contract. It is also less damaging to the architect, sub-contractor or project manager when the budget has been drawn up to take these risks into account. There are various forms of ground rules that could lessen potential damage:

- penalties placed on the client for delaying the project unnecessarily
- unacceptable behaviour and interference
- cost-plus budgeting
- time and materials budgeting.

The project manager can be obliged to pay the bulk of costs in such a case.

Contracts are fine for the large company with a legal department and a team of lawyers free to draft contracts, but they can be of little use to small and medium-sized enterprises and sole proprietor operations. Let's look at one of the myriad City of London SME firms, such as DSL, that are commissioned to write management reports for clients on various subjects, e.g. risk management, IT and emerging markets.

Formating and sending an invoice is the easy part; chasing up payments is more difficult. Reminder telephone calls and faxes can be the order of the day for the more difficult or forgetful client. One way to avoid credit or default risk is to work with screened or well-known clients. Another is to operate in a small community, such as the City of London. This village atmosphere means bad debtors find it harder to operate, as their reputation goes before them. If they step out of line, you can put the word out and it gets around rapidly. Another method is to develop the skills to write, first a formal reminder, and then a pro forma letter threatening legal action. It helps to have good relations with a reputable law firm or barrister if you have to go the whole hog.

You can also establish good relations with a larger company – if the debtor withholds payment, you can bring in the full resources of the big brother to threaten legal action. An agent in a larger company has the personnel and clout to get payment in most cases. Sometimes a factoring agent is used. Such a company will guarantee a fixed percentage of your fee, e.g. you will receive 80–85 per cent of the full fee, it takes the rest. This is certainly an option, and depends on your circumstances. Smaller companies might not resort to such measures for cost reasons.

CASE STUDY

Project payment for Tom Tow

'Negotiating fees often requires a face-saving gesture. It is customary to quote for services with a future discount, to be offered during negotiation, in mind. But certainly some reduction, even token, is de rigueur in the east. Everyone knows one does not do business without a contract. We seldom do, but even so, they do not ensure payment. One learns to bill promptly and to follow up with a telephone call or reminder notice when that payment is delayed. When these simple measures are not effective, we have been known to sit in a client's reception area for that cheque.'[10]

This shows that business reputation is an asset that even the most unruly client is unwilling to lose in a hurry. Yet, the client may still be prepared to face off the project manager to get the tiniest discount or trivial concession. Consultants such as Tom Tow and Melanie Francis might have to sit through protracted negotiations and still make concessions. It is interesting to see that face or honour is so important in business. We can shame difficult clients at times, and on occasions it is the most viable way to deal with a non-payer.

Change management

This covers the enormous and varied transition processes during the project's life. The fundamental changes that affect people and their work environment are often under-stated in the engineering view of a project. Yet one of the main stresses on a project that can potentially cause it to fail is the element of change management with its strong social factor. If top echelons of the company are unwilling to embrace the project, the life of the project is surely limited. Change management is detailed in other major publications and remains one of the hot business subjects both in and out of university.[11] Projects create change, and they are likely to face opposition from all quarters. Managers who cannot handle the introduction of change are facing a risk that their work will run straight into a brick wall.

Documentation

Documentation exists to give us an accurate picture of:

1 where we were on the project
2 what our project status is now
3 where we want to get to next on the project.

This has serious implications for those who manage to lose themselves in the maze of project paperwork. Sometimes you or your project manager may forget or lose track of tasks to be done. At other times, external players who are not necessarily in the project team can exert disproportionate influence over the project. When the project encounters severe opposition, there may be enough unsympathetic voices that can win enough votes, or exert enough power, to kill the project. At the very least, documentation serves as an *aide-mémoire* to remind the project leader and project team of what to do and where to go. It is also part of the arsenal to defend yourself and the project – it is a risk management weapon.

Those who wish to hurt the project, intentionally or otherwise, have to fall into the change management documentation process. This has the effect of:

- slowing them down
- forcing them to spend valuable resources filling in the necessary forms
- giving them adverse publicity they may not want
- involving them in paperwork they may have no experience of.

PRINCE 2 plays a significant role at every stage. For example, at the start of the project there are standards for processes and documentation. They will involve:

- project start-up
- authorizing project initiation
- project initiation
- stage selection.

Next, there is control over the running of the project. It covers:

● product description
● tolerance
● work package authorization
● project issues
● change control
● risk log
● checkpoint
● highlight report
● exceptions report
● end stage assessment
● end stage report.

PRINCE 2

PRINCE 2 is one of the methodologies that require documentation to be an essential part of the project process. It serves as an inherent series of checks and controls, and ensures that things are not forgotten that could crop up later with a vengeance. Tasks that have not met quality requirements or other specifications have to be attended to again; paperwork checks ensure that such requirements have been met, and that nothing can be incorporated into the design of the final project unless it has cleared quality checking. PRINCE 2 serves to keep project tasks in a more or less straight progression. It is not intended as a quick solution for a fast job; in fact, it is precisely the opposite. The job will be done on the right quality and performance stipulations or it will not be done at all. Most PRINCE 2 project managers are cautious enough to devote adequate resources to documentation and implementing stipulated amendments. The job can be delivered with quality. (Note: PRINCE is a registered trademark. It is the property of CCTA, UK.)

| CASE STUDY

The European Space Agency's Ariane project

The launch programme of the European Space Agency using Ariane rockets to put telecommunications satellites into orbit is one of the most complex of pan-European projects. It is an example of the double-edged sword effect of working in advanced research and development – you are either at the leading edge of technology or the bleeding edge. It also demonstrates some of the potential perils of the space industry, both political and technological.[12] It is a high-risk and high-gain industry, a market worth some $60 billion over ten years and faced with increasing competition. The NASA space shuttle disaster showed some of the downside risk at its worst. The Ariane-5 was involved in a spectacular explosion after a 36-second test flight in 1996, which was televised internationally, and there was a failed second attempt in 1997 before a successful flight in October 1998. The French said they had $3.4 billion worth of orders for 39 satellite launches.[13] Ariane was vital, and without it Europe was out of the satellite launching business. Space technology is about success; failures are bad for business.

The Ariane-5 has been developed by ESA, a French-led consortium that launches its rockets from Kourou, French Guyana, and which puts change management into the inherent structure of the company. Many other organizations are set in concrete, and do not want to change or find it difficult; ESA had no choice, because of challenges from Russia and China after the end of the cold war. It also has a fall-back option (contingency) in the tried-and-tested predecessor, the Ariane-4, in case things go wrong again.

Contingency management

The management of a project is a dynamically changing series of decisions and re-allocation of resources to get the job done. A project that does not see change in allocation of funds and manpower is either running smoothly, or is stagnant. Having a back-up rocket for launching a satellite is one contingency option. Other contingencies take a more pessimistic view of human ability; uninterrupted power supplies (UPS) or stand-by generators are used if an electricity supply company is not able to provide adequate power for various reasons. They can kick in when an electrical power loss is detected, and are a way of buying time if a total loss of power is feared. Project management is also the art of coping with the unexpected, or with detrimental effects of unforeseen events. Contingency management is a necessary part of combating operational risk, such as fraud.[14]

Laxity is common in many business areas. Looking at the problems of introducing economic and monetary union in Europe, or those of the millennium bug, we can show that business leaders or politicians sometimes ignore or procrastinate dangerously over major IT projects.

> CASE STUDY
>
> ## The IT millennium bug
>
> This risk of computer chaos arose because dates were not programmed, for example, '97, 98 and 99', meaning the millennium could easily read as 1900 instead of 2000. The risk of disruption or complete shutdown is significantly greater in mission-critical IT-based system such as air traffic control, hospital life-support systems, and bank systems trading billions of dollars. It is necessary to define risk impact first, then prioritize action. The slow response to the problem by many private companies and the public sector means that time to deal with it has been running out fast.[15] Given such tight schedules, analysis is trimmed down to:
>
> likely case – the most probable outcomes
> worst case – the highest damage caused.
>
> Contingency work for a possible millennium bug disaster entails forward planning that pays dividends in the long-term. Hospitals have arranged to put important staff on 48-hour shifts over the critical 31 December–1 January 2000 period. Prior analysis and planning in the best-run hospitals has included the designation of many spare beds in case of emergencies. Police forces in England and Wales have decided to cancel staff leave for the millennium in case of civil disturbances.[16] Backup telecommunications and electricity facilities have been installed in various companies.
>
> Many organizations have produced operations manuals with details of what staff should do if computer problems arise. The names of essential staff, with their addresses and telephone numbers, are given. Emergency procedures need to have been practised, to help expose potential glitches. If a company wants to have effective use of its resources should things go wrong, then practice makes near-perfect.

Obviously, some companies and organizations come out of such crises much better than others. They had recognized the nature of the risks and problems early on, so they were well organized. This took the luck element out of project management. They may later ask with justification: 'What crisis?' However, some companies even go bust because their systems cannot cope with the demands of technology and the market.

The way in which we handle market dynamics demonstrates that management change is evolving. We are seeing changes in the market away from the *ad hoc* seat-of-the-pants attitude that permeates slack project management which has little recognition of risk. Such an attitude only causes the panicky fire-fighting syndrome where one fire is nearly put out and another one starts in a different location. Risk management involves a lot of preparation and prior analysis to ensure that impromptu fire-fighting is kept to a minimum. We cannot assume that the business problems we face will always be small ones or be easy to solve. It is so easy to believe that there will be someone out there who can fix the company's problems quickly, and at little cost. If only this were true.

CASE STUDY

Airline reservation systems

These have been operating since the 1970s in the USA; Apollo is the one used by United Airlines, and the American Airlines system is called Sabre. The main European computerized reservation systems were started in 1987: Amadeus for Air France, Iberia, Lufthansa and SAS; Galileo for British Airways and other airlines. Amadeus and Galileo now each handle over 300 million customer bookings per year.

Most major airlines overbook their flights in the expectation or contingency that some passengers will change their flights or miss their connections. This provides the airlines with added revenue and spare seating capacity. But in case the number of passengers who turn up for the flight is greater than the seats available, airlines can always change the flight allocation or bump passengers to a later flight. In case of customer complaint, they are prepared to pay compensation, arrange hotel accommodation or give an upgrade to business or first class. It is a case of planning contingencies upon contingencies. This is the practice of keeping something in reserve, specifically aimed at coping with an event that could otherwise disrupt your plan.

CASE STUDY

DSL in office design

DSL experience with integrated office environment design highlights the need for such a reserve. We use the same principle for all our customers, whether they are the Sports Council in the UK, Pepsi Cola, Moscow-Narodny or Natwest Bank, and recommend that computers have more memory and processing power than is usually needed. That way any increased system loads and demands can be handled. Sensible installation of cabling allows for increased electric, voice and data needs to be easily met at a later date, and means the office does not have to be dug up to lay more cables. Our sub-contractors dealing with specialized furniture arrange for delivery of desk panels and tops with specific measurements or complex shapes which are cut onsite to allow an exact fit. There is a spare supply of desk in-fills, tops and fastenings to replace defective parts, or furniture that has not been delivered or is sub-standard. The care taken is doubled when the project is abroad and delivery, with customs clearance, is more difficult to arrange at short notice. The aim is to be prepared for project surprises.

In 1989, a Chinook helicopter crashed on the Mull of Kintyre in Scotland, killing senior police, army and intelligence officers working against terrorism in Northern Ireland. Britain's counter-terrorism capability was badly affected. The tragedy has some similarity to the plane crash in Munich in 1958 that killed most of the Manchester United football team. The difference is that a football team cannot easily fly on separate aircraft. Counter-terrorist personnel, with military air support, can more easily be split up. Key staff should travel on separate vehicles if possible. Have a contingency plan if one vehicle is late, or fails to arrive. You never know when problems might arise.

It should be remembered that in many countries, medical services are below standard. Those in Russia and some ex-Soviet countries, for example, are extremely under-funded and highlight some of the difficulties faced by state-run enterprises in the transition economies. Doctors and nurses are among unfortunate state employees who are victims of the backlog in unpaid salaries. Under-investment in state hospitals around the world is more of a rule than an exception. Your staff would not really want to have to undergo intensive treatment in these facilities, so you may have to think about insurance, adequate first aid, or even stand-by emergency evacuation services in extreme cases.

Succession

It happens in all areas of work, whether business, sport or the arts – a top manager may leave an organization at short notice. Disagreement over work conditions, low performance, conflict with colleagues, or the lure of higher pay elsewhere – there is a multitude of reasons. Succession is one of the main worries for a company, but it is not often addressed properly. The departure of a top manager creates stresses and strains for the whole organization; these may be enough to endanger projects and the survival of the company itself. Often, top management may be too occupied with other matters to notice the warning signs that key staff may be about to leave. Or they could choose to fire them without the slightest idea of a replacement. A project run without crucial staff runs the significant risk of severe under-performance. All projects, particularly longer term ones, need to withstand the stress of staff turnover or attrition.

One example was the sudden departure of Richard Brown of Cable & Wireless of the UK to America's EDS.

> *'He was the single architect of the group's transformation from an unloved and disparate telecoms holding company into a much more focused shareholder-friendly group. ... It is undoubtedly a very big blow for Cable & Wireless.'*[17]

'But Mr Brown may be leaving at a time when Cable & Wireless needs him most. For starters, his particular legacy, a can-do operational style with little patience for poor results, has increasingly become part of Cable & Wireless's culture, and a replacement may not be easy to find.'[18]

DSL experience with Cable & Wireless's arch-rival (British Telecom) shows that it is the relationship with particular individuals, not just with the whole corporation, that creates value. Knowing key individuals gets the job done, or helps to get it done faster.

Contingency funds come to mind, the squirrelling of finances to meet the damaging effects of some event. Some funds are salted away for a rainy day; these may be used to pay for damage caused by flooding, thunder or subsidence. Insurance is usually involved.

Insurance

Some incidents will happen through no fault of your own. For instance, thunder may hit all major overhead electricity pylons that supply your company. Or negligence on the part of a supplier may be involved, such as the power cut which plunged parts of New Zealand into darkness for a lengthy period during the winter of 1998.

Insurance kicks in to offer some protection against damage involving:

- loss of assets during the project
- loss of revenue
- liability to third parties
- liability to injured employees
- liability to regulatory agencies, e.g. those covering health and safety, the environment, and pollution.

Keeping contingency funds in a proper state of readiness, and their sensible deployment, is the key to contingency planning.

Running a hospital is becoming increasingly fraught. Medical negligence suits can be a big drain on a hospital's budget, not to mention bad publicity through the media. One way to protect against such lawsuits is to obtain insurance cover. Personal indemnity insurance is becoming big business. It is an example of risk-sharing in practice. What would you do if you were a hospital manager? Wait for a law suit to hit your hospital? Sometimes there is little choice.

Effective risk management is the process of meeting or coping with future risks, not just current fire-fighting in one crisis after another. SMEs have to get away from purely day-to-day operational thinking, and start to think of

> **CASE STUDY**
>
> ## Medical negligence in UK law suits
>
> (a) A woman doctor pricks herself accidentally with a discarded syringe in a hospital. She develops a fear of contracting Aids from the needle. She becomes phobic about all needles used in her work, and becomes too stressed to work. She sues the hospital and is awarded £500,000.[19]
>
> (b) A boy is permanently brain-damaged through an operation. His parents sue the hospital for a life destroyed. They are awarded £3 million in damages.[20]

strategic risk management. However, there is a need for basic cost-benefit analysis here. 'Are the risk management services and charges that I pay really needed?', you have to ask yourself. Careful consideration is particularly crucial for the SME when funds and manpower are tight, as they usually are. With shipping insurance there is a need for market research before each shipping charter or project. For example:

● what do you want to do or carry in your project?

● where do you want to operate or ship to?

● what do you want to cover?

● how much do you want to pay?

● where will you obtain this cover from?

● is this the best source of insurance?

CASE STUDY

Alex K. & Associates, a small shipping company based in Athens

Alex picked Malta as the preferred place to register his cargo ship. The place of registration is based on cost-benefit analysis – costs are a very significant factor for small companies. Risk factoring comes in automatically because his ship sails with insurance from Lloyd's of London. This means that the ship is covered, even though it can sail without any cargo insurance if so wished. The chosen country of registration for a ship is usually the one with the cheapest costs that satisfy certain minimum criteria. For this reason, Panama and Liberia are the largest 'flags of convenience'. There are cheaper flags, but if they do not have a good record in adhering to international codes of safety and pollution, ship-owners using them tend to be penalized or even rejected by:

- banks (which give finance to buy ships)
- underwriters (which insure ships and/or cargoes)
- and charterers (whose primary concern is that the cargo carried will arrive safely and quickly at its destination).

Then there is the question of what is the preferred material to ship? Liquid products are easier to ship, because they are more homogeneous and easier to load/unload (you need only a pump and pipeline). You have to examine risk-return ratios for each shipping project, plus the costs. For example, the flag of registration can be a minor risk and cost factor. In our case, with a very small ship, flag costs amount to about 2 per cent of turnover. For a larger ship, the costs will fall to a fraction of 1 per cent. This is a classic risk analysis/risk management operation in comparing the costs of different flags of convenience. There are cheaper registrations than Malta available, e.g. Liberia, Guatemala, Russia or even land-locked Bolivia. Perceived corruption and violence in the country of registration is of minimal importance (hence the success of Panama and Liberia in the number of flags of convenience). Malta is seen as a low or acceptable risk by Lloyd's.

> 'In our case, we originally chose the Maltese registry, which is a little more costly than Liberia or Panama, because Maltese ships were given preferential treatment in the port taxes that were payable in Black Sea ports. This was a benefit that we estimated far exceeded the additional costs of the Maltese flag. The higher port fees and other costs have to be weighed against registration fees, insurance, charterers' costs and other considerations.'[21]

This is a prime example of a cost-benefit analysis with risk factors examined for a small or medium-sized enterprise.

Alex says of present conditions in shipping insurance: ▶

▶ *'This need not be purchased from Lloyd's – in fact, over the last few years, other underwriters are gradually taking an increasingly important share of the marine market. Also, you should not confuse cargo with hull insurance – in the event of a casualty, the insurers will pay only what is insured (ship, cargo, both or neither).'*

Think of the what, where, how much questions in your project.

Risk analysis is becoming standard in projects both before and after completion, not just when there is a disaster. It is better and cheaper to correct a design error in a project at an early stage than to wait for disaster to strike. Prevention is better than cure.

CASE STUDY

Piper Alpha oil drilling platform

This was an oil drilling platform destroyed by an explosion in the North Sea in July 1988 with major loss of life. The $3 billion platform had a design error that was not corrected at the computer design stage. Piper Alpha was essentially a vertical structure, with workers' accommodation housed above the equipment storage compartment. Cracks in the gas riser, corroded steel platform legs and other design faults were a recipe for disaster. When the explosion occurred, its shock waves were transmitted into the sea as had been forecast during the design stage on safety matters, but not completely as should have happened.

The use of comparative benchmarking through risk analysis would have revealed structural errors. For example, builders of Norwegian oil platforms are obliged by government rules to conduct risk analysis before and during project design. Their design allows for and has a longer structure that separates accommodation quarters horizontally from the oil-gas production process. In addition, steel doors are put in place to shield workers from explosions. In the case of Piper Alpha, stress from the explosion destroyed much of the superstructure and crew quarters, leaving 167 dead.

> CASE STUDY
>
> # Russia's bond market
>
> There were warnings in 1997 about impending fall-out from the Russian economic crisis. The problems revolved around the insatiable desire of foreign investors for fast and high profits, and a lack of willingness to learn from previous mistakes in dealing with emerging markets.[22] Investors were slow to implement risk management strategies, and they were none too keen to monitor the situation thoroughly. There was little or sometimes no contingency procedure; this would have included a get-out or exit strategy. In the bond market, $11 billion of foreign holdings in Russian bonds were frozen when Moscow called a debt repayment moratorium.[23] Even investors' hedging strategies proved to be less than effective because the Russian government essentially defaulted on its debt and put on exchange controls. This was construed as a force majeure situation, but it did not stop some western creditors from seeking redress in court.
>
> The effect (see Risk impact, p. 36) on industry varied from company to company and also depended on the type of industry involved and what risk management tactics were being used. Many Russian companies went bankrupt, the end of a capitalist dream. Western companies also suffered, although to a lesser extent. It really depended on how exposed they were to the Russian market.

Market exposure

London Forfaiting, which buys exporters' trade debt and re-sells it to banks, was badly hit. It was heavily exposed to the Russian debt market, and in 1998 its share price tumbled from 475p to 83p.[24] It was reckoned that if London Forfaiting was exposed by £50 million in Russia then it would survive; if the exposure was £150 million, the company would go bankrupt.

Investors have various choices in countless similar situations, depending on their initial position:

- if they are already share-holders – sell up or reduce their holding, or stay put and wait for the economy to recover;
- if they are not already involved – rush in on a speculative play, or stay away and wait for a clear signal about market conditions.

A mad rush is clearly out for most long-term players. Nevertheless, some investors may be willing to take a chance on daunting odds. Venture capitalists, for example, are often willing to get involved in high-risk projects. Figures show that many start-up firms in the UK are likely to go bust within their first

three years. Venture capitalists are prepared to invest and protect these investments by a policy of diversification and risk absorption. They will pick a
portfolio of promising companies and expect that some of them will go bust
within one or two years. But the venture capitalist also expects losses from
these firms to be more than covered when a start-up firm thrives so well that
it can be floated on the stock market after three years, and the venture capitalist can sell his stake and pocket a vast profit.

In the world of portfolio investment it has been proven that a well-managed,
balanced amount of risky investment can increase potential returns while
actually reducing overall risk. For a well-balanced fund, a modest proportion
should be invested in riskier markets to increase the potential return while
cutting by a relatively small amount the overall risk on the portfolio. The same
principle applies to most corporate activity, where exposure to high-risk, high-
reward markets can cut the risk of missing out on a trend – the so-called rule
of 'tipping points'. Here, a new product or service will have gained critical
momentum before more than a handful of people have spotted it.[25]

Nevertheless, it is crucial that the investor or manager chooses his/her
project team with care and due skill before 'cherry-picking' projects and
potential investments.

Notes and references

1 DSL Consultants (1997) *Risk Management in Russia and the Baltic States,* FT Publications.
2 Refer to, for example, 'ICE Conditions of Contract' and 'ICE Conditions of
   Contract: Guidance Notes', 1991, 6th edition.
3 *Wall Street Journal*, 1 December 1998, p. 11.
4 Charoenngam, C. and Yeh, C. Y. (February 1999) IPMA (International Project Management Association), *International Journal of Project Management*, p. 31, vol. 17,
   no. 1, Elsevier, UK.
5 *The Times*, 22 September 1998, p. 27.
6 *Financial Times*, 8 January 1999, p. 6.
7 Refer to, for example, RAMP, Institute of Civil Engineers and Institute of Actuaries
   (1998) *ICE Conciliation Procedure*, Thomas Telford Publications, London.
8 Meredith, J. R. and Mantel, S. J. (1995) *Project Management*, ch. 6, John Wiley.
9 Refer to, for example, RAMP, Institute of Civil Engineers and Institute of Actuaries
   (1998) *ICE Arbitration Procedure*, Thomas Telford Publications, London.
10 Tow, T., personal interview, December 1998.
11 Refer to, for example, Kanter, R. (1985) *The Change Masters*, Allen & Unwin, London.
12 *International Herald Tribune*, 22 October 1998, p. 1.
13 *Financial Times*, 22 October 1998, p. 5.

14 Refer to 'Fraudstop' (1996) FBI, City of London police with Coopers & Lybrand.
15 *Computer Weekly*, 6 August 1998, p. 1.
16 *The Times*, 18 January 1999, p. 1.
17 Bloomberg & Reuters, 11 December 1998.
18 *Wall Street Journal*, 11 December 1998, p. 3.
19 *The Times*, 12 October 1998, p. 1.
20 *The Times*, 14 October 1998, p. 1.
21 Alex K., personal interview and correspondence, Athens, December 1998–January 1999.
22 DSL Consultants (1997) *Risk Management in Russia and the Baltic States*, FT Publications.
23 *Financial Times*, 15 October 1998, p. 24.
24 *Daily Telegraph*, Business, 31 October 1998.
25 Interview with George Littlejohn, Emerging Markets Forum and Citybridge Research, London, January 1999.

Business roles in the project

> **❝** All the world's a stage, and all the men and women merely players. **❞**

Shakespeare, *As You Like It*

Business involves a lot of interaction with many players. These people have different roles and responsibilities, and differing views of risk. Some people, such as accountants, those with large families and salaried jobs avoid risk if possible. Others live for risk and adventure, whether they are explorers, soldiers of fortune, gamblers or speculators on the stock market. Such people all have different roles to play in their projects, and different risk attitudes.

Project team members

The project sponsor/client

This is the customer, a project role with the highest or most traditional profile. The old adage that the customer is always right still applies, even today. Traditionally, the customer outlines his requirements and signs the pay cheques. That has not changed much. What has changed is that the project is usually of such a complex nature that the project owner – the customer – is unable to say exactly how she/he wants the end result to look. The customer, however, must look at the project's goal in broad terms, and should not let small matters stand in the way of this. It is the project manager who has the eye for detail to make this strategic goal a reality. You have to keep your eyes on the prize.

CASE STUDY

The Royal Infirmary, Edinburgh

It is rare to find a project with a greater mix of parties involved than the UK health service: it includes government, regional NHS areas, hospital committees, trade unions, private finance initiatives backed by banks, vendors and other project owners. A multi-million pound healthcare budget has to be monitored and kept on track by the management. The prevalent practice of changing customer requirements before, during and after a project is likely to create a loss in schedule or budget.

> *'Historically, IT projects that started two to three years previously, when delivered have no longer met the needs of the business because the business has changed much more rapidly than the initial technology implementation. It is inevitable with such long-term projects that the initial requirements will not in fact reflect the final requirements for the system. Certain (hospitals), such as the Royal Infirmary, Edinburgh, now understand that it is a worthwhile exercise to carry out a review of IT alignment with key business objectives at critical phases of the project.'*[1]

Project progress checkpoints or milestones are an essential part of spotting deviations from the business plan. Top management should not only informed but involved and supportive of projects, particularly longer term ones. Otherwise the supervisors can take their eyes off the goals and let the project slip. Keep your finger on the pulse, and keep your project on track.

The project manager

The project manager has sometimes been compared to a government civil servant. Ministers have the visionary zeal, while the bureaucrats work to transform this message into reality. The project manager needs to combine funds, skills and raw materials, and co-ordinate departmental requirements and the work of external contractors. The art of reconciliation and compromise figures greatly here, and a good project manager also has to be a great diplomat or politician at times. He or she has to tie up all the loose ends that invariably occur; which will include conflicting interests and statements between the project participants.

Examples of project arguments or conflicting needs are:

● sales manager has promised a building will be completed in three years; construction and engineering department says at least four years;

- plans are finalized and staff are set to commence work, but lawyers have said that planning permission cannot be secured for about six months;
- the client wants an electrical generator of 135kW for a building, but the dimensions of the generator room seem too small to fit it in;
- the local council now wants a school built for 1800 pupils, but the contract stipulated 1500 children plus staff;
- the local health and safety executive office says emergency exits are insufficient for the number of staff working on a site;
- telecoms officials say you must meet a different certification standard to the approval you have already got;
- the computer centre in your office now has to connect all the new staff from the recent merger – this was not in the original specifications.

Cases of conflict are different in nature and scale. You must:

1 assess the significance or likely delay/extra cost/damage
2 find parties to assign to it and get them to confirm the impact on the project
3 see whether you are already covered, or have the funds to meet this new task
4 if covered, bring responsible party to complete task
5 if not covered, allocate staff and resources
6 monitor progress, and check if done satisfactorily to set standards.

The manager has to keep control over any project infighting. A good team culture and identity is crucial.

The sales and marketing executive

Normally, a sales and marketing executive is an extroverted adventurer who is open to new markets and therefore to more risk. They will go into regions where they have little local knowledge, or knowing that the areas are not as developed and protected as their domestic markets. These regions are often termed emerging markets, or those that have not reached anything near market saturation. There is also a temptation, or risk, that sales staff will be pressured into securing a sale through offering either:

1 lowest price or substantially discounted price from normal
2 higher quality service or performance product than usual
3 faster delivery/installation time than average.

There is no doubt that this is a high-pressure job that can determine the health or survival of a company. We have come across many examples where it is a job done well, and others where it is done badly. The actions of the sales and marketing staff can have significant ramifications for a project, particularly when these sales staff have not consulted other colleagues in the company or the supply chain as to whether quoted price and delivery conditions are feasible. There may be a significant risk of non-performance through eagerness to close a deal. Make sure that what you can deliver for a reasonable profit ties in with what your sales people are promising the clients.

We have also seen the old ploy of delaying signing contract papers in order to put pressure on the salesman, who is already under pressure to secure the contract if he is to be awarded sales commission. Sometimes the contract arrives at the last minute, and it is often impossible to scrutinize all the wording before signing it. Sometimes this can be a tactic used against the client or project manager, and is one of the oldest tricks in the book. It is a project risk to avoid if possible. Something invariably slips through.

The accountant

A chief accountant is traditionally an introverted and risk-averse character who is unwilling to commit the whole company's health to one move or gambit. Extensive use of budgeting, cash-flow forecasts and expense sheets signed by the authorized gate-keepers tend to ensure that the lid is kept on profligate spending.

The accounts department acts in two important capacities:

1 paymaster
2 policeman.

A good company needs the department to carry out both roles well. It is the heart of risk management operations in smaller to medium-size firms because of the traditional role of accountants in overseeing cash-flow.

A market incorporates the actions and roles of both types of business player, the extrovert and the introvert. Most companies cannot survive without the roles played by each of these types. The crucial thing is to know how to achieve the best mix of the risk-averse and risk-seeking character, and when to take risk and when to avoid it. A gambler on a winning wager is sometimes considered a genius, or a mindless fool when he loses.

The banker or financier

These are the people who determine the flow of funds to the project. They regard themselves as the facilitators in that a cleverly-crafted deal can create a clear view of the project finance, with risk-managed positions for both the banker and project owner. The terms of finance can be attractive, or they can be so constricting that they strangle the project early on. Where backers are not flexible enough to provide attractive financing, project owners may go to the type of financier sometimes dubbed 'vulture capitalist'.

Bank provision for bad debts, loans to firms which cannot or fail to repay them, can vary between 1 and 3 per cent of total lending. Venture capitalists often operate on the basis of 20–30 per cent of their investment projects failing. This is why they retain a basket or portfolio of investments – a classic example of diversification to take on risk but spreading it over a range of investments. Venture capitalists recognize the inadequacy of the traditional tools of discounted cash flow, internal rate of return, or net present value on their own to deal with risk. So their targeted net returns are at least 40–50 per cent in order to justify the risk.

The engineer or designer

They have the task of doing the productive work, creating the finished product. Proper design and testing are particularly crucial in mission-critical applications (see NASA space shuttle case study, p. 38) where life or major loss is possible. They have the most input in terms of finished product design, but they have to work in tandem with the demands or advice of the accounts department and sales and marketing. Research and development for a new product or service is the stage where the project is most vulnerable: a lot of money going out with no visible sales or cash inflow. A good project manager and research team who can distinguish a fine pheasant from a turkey are essential before much time and money is spent on a worthless project.[2]

The lawyer

It is the lawyer's duty to see that the terms of a contract are crafted in the best possible way for the company. Risk management dictates that threats of damages or some redress be specified in the contract to wave the stick. Redress specified should be practical, realistic, clearly understood and believable to all involved. The benefits or carrot waved under the noses of project members serve as the incentives for keeping people focussed on the project. See Chapter 5.

The health and safety manager

A risk management view of a project invariably takes a look at human causes of accidents and damage. DSL staff were passing a road project near our construction site in Moscow, where temperatures were –10°C. It was a chastening sight seeing a worker sprawled on the ground after he had dug his power hammer into a live electric cable. Had the road been scanned for underground electricity and gas pipes? Highly unlikely.

You as the project manager have the task of ensuring the project follows the correct health and safety procedures. These involve the possibility of large negligence claims if ignored, and you also have to deal with the introduction of new employer liability regulations. Indemnifying yourself and your operations covers only part of the whole project environment. The need is paramount to review professional ethics and risk management. Health and safety hazards affect you through your involvement with external sub-contractors, even if your direct employees are fully trained and risk-aware.[3] Safety equipment and safety clothing should be issued to all staff who require it. Proper standards are not always exercised by any means. Health and safety remains a sensitive issue because of the emotional factor. Yet it is often necessary to push to get health and safety on the project map, and have the necessary resources allocated. Unfortunately, the perceived risk of injury is often taken to be low, and the escalation of health and safety concerns as a high priority may come only after a bad accident. Health and safety is, sadly, sometimes seen as a luxury, a cost that projects can do without.[4] Regulatory authorities have to ensure that health and safety is an intrinsic part of training in projects, and that standards are enforced.

| CASE STUDY |

The Heathrow tunnel collapse

The Health and Safety Executive (HSE) initiated a civil action in which the court fined Balfour Beatty engineering £1.2 million for the October 1994 Heathrow tunnel collapse.[5] The judge also fined Geoconsult, the Austrian tunnelling consultant.[6] The tunnel collapse would have been potentially devastating if the debris had fallen on the Piccadilly line trains. The HSE has to send the message that slack running of projects that endanger lives must be punished. Your project should have someone with projest risk experience who is devoted to handling HSE factors.

A London hotel visited by DSL & Associates

This is a restaurant and hotel in London. It is popular and the staff are busy. There was a lot of clutter – papers and books on the shelves, for instance. A fan heater was hanging by its cable from a coat-hook, and it was switched on. Water had come in through the roof and was dripping through the ceiling. There were no visible fire escapes. Residents could have been trapped. Our visit, six months ago, coincided with the fire brigade being called out to deal with a kitchen fire. There had been a build-up of paper and litter outside the building. Our questioning of staff revealed that there had been a fire the previous week because of a large fat accumulation in the kitchen ventilation cowling. This was the same reason for the fire at London Heathrow airport in 1997 that caused millions of pounds of damage and shut down a whole terminal.

The question is: where is the risk awareness? Answer: accidents happen because people let them happen.

Government and regulatory agencies

Taxation laws are set out at central and local government levels. These are not limited to personal and corporate income taxes, but also include land taxes, operating taxes, capital depreciation, tax-breaks and subsidies. The successful project manager or project owner can see through the maze of regulations to equate downside tax risk against benefits from the tax structure.

Look at Asea-Brown Boveri (ABB), an engineering group which was headed by Percy Barnevik. He not only determined that ABB needed to be more global ('think global, act local'), he could also see there were benefits (i.e. positive risks) from re-locating the headquarters to Switzerland from Sweden. The taxation structure in Switzerland was very attractive compared to Sweden. Another similar example is CALTEX, the oil and engineering multinational of the US. Shifting the headquarters to Singapore meant lower personal taxation bands, plus tax incentives for the corporation.

> **CASE STUDY**

Formula 1 Grand Prix racing

The $2 billion bond offering by Bernie Ecclestone, who heads Formula 1 racing, was a good example of regulatory authorities in action. The bond offering was initially troubled because of relevant questions that investors should ask before they accept an invitation to take part in a project.

- who ultimately controls the company?
- what do they own?
- how much do they owe?
- who do they owe it to?
- what is my likely profit?
- who are the regulatory authorities?
- what can they do?

The formula One bond offering was an example of risk versus return in a complex situation. For example, the regulatory authorities such as the European Union's agencies were known to be conducting a review of broadcasting rights and tobacco advertising. The EU was known to be adopting an anti-smoking stance, and had instituted bans against cigarette advertising and sponsorship. Formula One racing is partly dependent upon this sponsorship. Hence, the likelihood of external intervention from regulatory agencies alone would have added to the perceived risk, hence potential investors would have liked a higher return.

Agents and intermediaries

A company or organization interested in entering a market or a new country has various choices, and may use an agent or intermediary. DSL has come across many such agents in emerging markets. Penetrating a market in a new country will probably take a large number of agents or intermediaries. Some of them may be efficient Mr Fixits or trouble-shooters, others may be only trouble, producing no results for the client. There are two main options:

- go in on your own. This will involve more work and resources. Your company will have to handle the company registration and operating licence application, find suitable premises (offices or production site), recruit staff and find the best sources of raw materials. It is therefore a capital-intensive and time-intensive process to establish your market presence. The advantage is that you can try to keep a lot under your own control. It is often the option chosen by a company wishing to keep its operations or products secret, or not trusting outsiders to market or produce its products/services to required standards;

● use an agent, or existing firm in a joint venture. This is often the most time/cost-effective method. Your company has to choose a suitable partner for an agent or intermediary. There are usually lots to choose from, and agents are forms of risk management experts. Take a country like Russia, and this description of agents there:

'They are experienced in overcoming bureaucracy, corruption, a legal system still evolving to meet the needs of foreign investment, and a rapidly changing security system.'[7]

They should help you formulate your marketing and distribution plans, and give advice and assistance on forming influential links and setting up your security arrangements. Vet your agent or you run the risk of less control with an unsuitable partner (see Counter-party risk, p. 54).

CASE STUDY

Volvo in Russia and the Baltic states

Volvo transports cars and spare parts directly from Sweden to Russia and the Baltic states. The vehicles are put in bonded warehouses for secure storage and customs clearance, then moved out to the company's local dealers. Volvo's first foothold in Russia was in small premises in Moscow in 1984. Sales took off when it established a joint venture with a local company, MTDS, in 1989. Volvo then wanted to exert more control, and all distribution in Russia is now done by a wholly-owned Volvo office. Similarly, Volvo entered the Baltic states in 1991 via a local importer. This kept its initial risk exposure low, in case there were any major problems. Doing business like this allows companies to learn about local conditions and then increase investment when they are more confident. Volvo is happy to test the waters initially with a joint venture, then expand and upgrade if this enterprise is successful.[8]

Project risk management services on the market

The size and complexity of projects, and increasing changes in regulations and regulatory agencies, mean that even large companies are hard-pressed to find internally all the up-to-date skills they need. These often come in the form of risk-takers or risk-sharers, external parties who are happy to take the risk, or some of it, for a negotiated fee. Outsourcing, the hiring of skilled staff or consultants is now commonplace.

It is estimated that outsourcing will grow by two-thirds in the UK public sector in the five years from 1999.[9] But the hiring of specific project management skills on the market can open a can of worms. It is generally a trade-off between:

- project objectives
- availability
- price
- performance
- reliability.

Assessing bids from outsourced contractors

You, as project manager or client, have to follow your procedures on how to choose between various project bids. The best private-sector bid is usually the one judged to be the most financially desirable; for instance, the lowest bid wins the contract. But you should review your appraisal technique. Look at risk probabilities and downside scenarios. Consider, for example:

- the extent to which the contractor can manage the various kinds of project risk
- the contractor's strength and management experience
- their financial backing and how they can withstand the impact of an unwelcome event or accident.

There needs to be risk analysis before valuable functions are given to the marketplace.[10] IT and accounts are two key services that are often outsourced, but these are valued functions that tell a lot about a company. Banks and other companies naturally have some misgivings if their IT databases are to be held in the same data centre (perhaps a disaster recovery centre) as those of rival banks. What if their data got mixed up? Who really controls the data centre? Confidentiality is just one issue.

> *'By entrusting its IT function to others, a company risks outsourcing part of its brain.'*[11]

Consultants

The management consultancy services of the Big 5 accountancy firms are widely used. Potential investors, banks and credit agencies often prefer large accountancy firms when auditing company accounts and valuing assets, particularly when calling for work done according to International Accounting Standards (IAS). The larger and prestigious firms also carry higher bills, but you would still be advised to go searching for the best value-for-money services on the market. Management consultancy can be a high-margin business where fee revenue is currently rising at double-digit percentage growth each year.

Training is one of the biggest cost burdens for all management consultancy companies because often the trainee is kept away from doing billed work. It is essentially 'dead time'. However, there is a great temptation to send out inexperienced staff to learn on projects. This means that you might get inexperienced consultants or 'green beans' sent to work on your project. You end up paying for their training on the job and get charged at the standard daily rate. This is a 'win-win' situation for the firm and not necessarily for your project.

DSL direct experience working alongside many consultants leads us to recommend that you should conduct prior checks to ensure that the final project staff you are sent are experienced in the business field.

A German project manager has valuable experience on the cost-effectiveness of using consultants from bigger companies. His opinion is:

> *'If you choose the right people, then they help you. If you just go for the name of the bigger (well-known management) consultancies you might get stuck with low-quality people for a high price. But if you get the right people, they can help by using their international network of information.'*[12]

Thus, should they fail to deliver the project, you will suffer project schedule slippage or have to employ other consultants or deploy your own in-house staff. Giles Pallister, IT Manager of the UK Royal Academy, is of the opinion that using the large established consultancy firms is not cost-effective.

> *'We are very price-sensitive and, in addition, we do not feel that we will get a favourable price-quality ratio by using people from the prestige consultancy firms. We have enough to do selecting outsourced services and products. We currently have to do a lot of vetting to separate claimed levels of service quality from reality.'*[13]

You should set consultants to work where there are concrete, measurable benefits. The idea is not to get them to provide you with endless analyses and feasibility reports on the project. Paperwork will cost you money, and possibly delay your project. The objective is to get the job done, and to get value for money from outsourced services.

There are quality control procedures that you can use. Otherwise, you may be billed for time at a high rate for junior lawyers, accountants or engineers. Ensure that the project team promised on CVs or other documents is the same as the one which eventually does the work. You may run the risk of falls in project work quality by using less experienced staff. You should find out what the penalty is for employee substitution. Just say that those you require are off ill, on holiday or working elsewhere. What do you do? You also need to look at team skills. The USA's men's Davis Cup tennis team had the best individual seeds in 1998. They were whitewashed by the Swedish team that won the final against the Italians. Doubles tennis saw the reign of the Woodies (Woodforde and Woodbridge) as the world number one doubles team during the 1990s, yet neither was a top thirties singles player. You should get a team player who performs well on your project.

The key is to select the best mix of personalities and skills. See Risk management as a cultural issue, p. 136. People who do not get on with each other can harm the team. An advance scout, such as a sales executive who is abrasive, can easily kill a project's chances of success.

Project co-ordination committee

Typically, a project such as the construction of a sales call centre, or a computer networked office, has a complex mix of roles and tasks. The large number of staff and associated contractors involved, plus the large number and variety of tasks, means there has to be close project co-ordination. A sample co-ordination or steering committee can vary in size and composition, but it can involve:

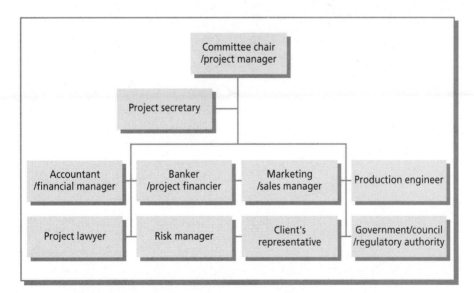

Fig 6.1 ● **A sample co-ordination committee**

Notes and references

1 Bishop, H. and Casterton, P., personal correspondence, London, 1998.
2 See RAMP, Institute of Civil Engineers and Institute of Actuaries (1998), Thomas Telford Publications, London, for project selection.
3 Refer to 'Health and Safety for Engineers' (1998) ed. Martin Barnard, ICE.
4 Refer to Chicken, J. C. and Posner, T. (1998) *The Philosophy of Risk*, Thomas Telford Publications, London.
5 *Financial Times*, 16 February 1999.
6 *The Times*, 12 February 1999.
7 Overseas Trade: Russia (April 1998), Overseas Trade Services, DTI, UK.
8 Interviews with Volvo, by Tomas Gilsa, Stockholm, 1997.
9 *Financial Times*, 2 December 1998, IT, p. 2.
10 Refer to RAMP, Institute of Civil Engineers and Institute of Actuaries (1998), Thomas Telford Publications, London.
11 *Financial Times*, 22 October 1998, p. 9.
12 Winkler, K., interview and personal correspondence, December 1998–January 1999, Telepassport, Germany.
13 Pallister, G., personal correspondence, January 1999.

7

Operational risk management

> **" Life is a joke that's just begun. "**
>
> W. S. Gilbert and A. Sullivan, *The Mikado*

This covers some of the greatest potential hazards in the project and includes the most unpredictable factor: human beings. Apart from errors in IT and information systems, we can attribute various deviations in planned performance to a variety of phenomena: lack of training, inexperience, incompetence, corruption, criminality, kidnapping, etc. The joke could be on you.

CASE STUDY

Volvo

This is a world-famous corporation with strong backing. It has a large profile and is active in many of the world's emerging markets where western cars are prestigious. Its executives have a reputation for being well-trained and, certainly by many foreign standards, well-paid. Top executives have the use of a chauffeur-driven car as is normal in many corporations. But these local transport arrangements are geared to save time and 'hassle' rather than to maximize security – local drivers know the best way to drive around town. Also, if they get caught for traffic violations, it is the local driver who gets jailed or fined rather than the Volvo executive. There is little evidence of intimidation or 'attacks' on the company's western or local staff. It seems to have a policy for staff to keep a low public profile. Volvo security measures seem to vary from place to place around the world. The company has encountered relatively few major problems of a violent nature. Volvo prefers not to comment on its security arrangements which they wish to remain secret.[1]

Volvo has had better luck than other organizations and companies, such as the Red Cross, or Granger Telecommunications of the UK, which have seen staff killed in Chechnya.

> **CASE STUDY**
>
> ## Granger Telecommunications
>
> Granger lost four staff killed in Chechnya after they were taken hostage in October 1998. The Granger case was tragic: the severed heads of the four men were found in December 1998 after failed negotiations with their kidnappers and a botched attempt to rescue them. The four cellular telecoms engineers had a protection squad assigned to them, but this proved ineffective when they were abducted. The UK Foreign Office had already issued warnings to British citizens about travelling to Chechnya, and the warnings proved apposite. A company and project management team should evaluate all potential risks before going ahead with a local project. Projects do not always live up to expectations. In this case, it went tragically wrong.

MIG (Merchant International Group, UK) estimated that risks in emerging markets cost businesses £15 billion in 1998. These risks range from the misunderstanding or underestimating risk of different corporate and country cultures, to real dangers posed by bribery, nepotism, fraud, unfair rival's tactics, or poor legal and operational safeguards. Poor risk analysis and risk management lead to poor project results; a MIG estimate is a loss of 8–10 per cent in expected returns. A realistic risk attitude and an effective risk management strategy are needed for project success.[2]

Insiders and corruption

One of the most under-emphasized aspects of running a project is the need to take on staff of integrity and honesty. Most major damage in companies nowadays is done by insiders, those who have intimate knowledge of company operations. Perhaps the most worrying aspect of operational risk is that the threat comes from 'one of our own' within the company. It is often assumed that we are safe with the people we know – better the devil you know than the devil you don't! This attitude leads companies into a false sense of security; as the German proverb goes: 'An old falsehood is always more popular than a new truth.' It is even more ironic when the fault lies in top management. See Barings Bank case study, p. 60. Beware the enemy within.

> CASE STUDY

The 'Mars bar thief'

Martin Keys, a warehouse manager, was sentenced at Gloucester Crown Court in the UK to five years' jail. He had been a shift supervisor at a warehouse and was instrumental in a conspiracy to steal confectionery from the stock, managing to steal eight lorry loads of Mars bars and other chocolate. The stock taken weighed around 300 tonnes and was worth more than £500 000. Keys was estimated to have pocketed about £156 000 from the crime.[3]

All companies and projects, big or small, run the risk of not knowing what their current stock, cash or net balance situation is at vulnerable times. DSL has found that with some companies this is due to poor position-keeping and inadequate controls at senior accountancy levels. Unfortunately, they may not want to know about it or admit it. For example, banks are resigned to the need to counteract the risk of fraud in their operations, though not all devote adequate resources to combating operational risk. The way in which banks and other companies use resources to achieve adequate security raises questions. DSL experience with some banks in the UK, Russia, the Baltic states and North Africa shows that there is some cause for concern.

Security guards at the entrance to premises, time-locks on deposit boxes, sophisticated accounting software systems, and closed-circuit cameras to monitor teller personnel, amount to a daunting security arsenal. The rigorous checking and re-checking of money banked is commendable, but it limits the view of the company's overall security level. We should search wider:

> *'If you wish to spend thousands of dollars checking the till-girls who might walk away with a couple of hundred dollars, then why don't you do the same with traders who might lose a few million dollars?'*[4]

There is an inconsistency in the risk analysis of banking operations if it does not cover the full range of risk. Risk management personnel often try to cover the visible risks while leaving other sources of risk neglected. One British consultant said of local banks before the Baltic banking crisis: *'Any one of their dealers could rip the arse out of the bank!'*[5]

The 1995 Baltic banking crisis hit Latvia initially, where the biggest bank, Baltija, went bust. Public confidence was badly dented because of the large proportion of private savings which were lost. Baltija bank was duly investigated and deemed to have been mis-managed, under-capitalized and laxly monitored by the banking regulators. A related banking crisis affected Lithuania in the same year, which saw the closing or freezing of Innovation and Litimpex banks plus other smaller operations.[6]

A similar scenario struck Russia in August 1998, badly affecting foreign investor confidence in the economy. The Russian crisis continues and there have been various explanations for it. Blaming it on the South-East Asian economic slump is flawed because this ignores the interplay of structural banking inadequacies and the existence of systemic risk more akin to the mis-management of the Baltic banks in 1995. History re-visits us every so often.

Staff may be damaging your company for a variety of reasons, including:

- greed (wanting more money)
- revenge (settling old scores, or perhaps for not being given promotion).

Such risk is much more difficult to deal with when you are running a project away from home soil and you do not have many, if any, local established contacts. Bribery may be endemic in the country where you are operating. Ratings agencies such as Moodys, Standard & Poor's or Fitch-IBCA provide classifications of countries to reflect where bribery operates. It is a practice that cannot be ignored; some view it as a form of tax or levy and factor it into their operating costs. It may involve some of the biggest household names such as Lockheed, or NEC whose chairman (Tadahiro Sekimoto) left in October 1998[7] after the over-billing and bribery scandal. This is especially the case for anyone going into a new market. There are some basic steps to follow when recruiting staff, such as:

1 selection
2 training
3 monitoring and detection
4 punitive action or counter-measures.

CASE STUDY

A department store in Russia

An interview in Russia with Wackenhut, a security services company, with head-quarters in the USA and branches in Russia demonstrated some good reasons for screening your own staff. Wackenhut was brought in as an independent external security company after a major incident in a large Russian department store. A store manager, who had worked there for 18 months, had embezzled a large sum of money and fled. A shop assistant was killed in the process. Checks on the backgrounds of store staff revealed organized criminal links and police files on 30 per cent of staff members. Staff were found to have committed a variety of misdemeanours in the past, including civil disobedience and drunken and disorderly behaviour. Wackenhut was brought in to act as a 'clean broom', to screen staff and help the store to start afresh.[8]

This sort of thing demonstrates the need to tread carefully, doing initial staff screening, then setting up your core team. After all check-points or gateways are cleared, you can then think of expanding. Even top western firms make the mistake of offering large salaries and remunerative packages to prospective staff without even the most basic security checks.

We should examine the value-added chain of risk management to see where it would have the best effects. It is tempting these days to buy and install a risk management system that operates by means of a nice computer, but this alone is inadequate. Companies need to assess the value and suitability of any risk management system proposed, then implement it correctly to suit their requirements. There is a tendency to go solely by the looks of a system, then not to use it properly. One bank was asked, after it had fallen for a salesman's talk, why it had bought a particular computer dealing system. It replied: 'Because this good salesman came to see us and sell us his system.'[9]

Research tends to confirm the risky downside of being taken in too much by a salesman's promises.

'It seems that the sales hype which took place ... early in the project, raised expectations well beyond what the project was subsequently able to deliver.'[10]

Technology alone never solved a fundamental risk management problem.

Table 7.1 ● An operational risk health-check

Number	Question
1	Does your management board understand operational risk?
2	Has it set up a risk management committee?
3	Has the committee established op risk procedures?
4	Has it done a company-wide op risk audit?
5	Has it written op risk resourcing procedures?
6	Does it have adequate staffing?
7	Are the staff of the right skills mix?
8	Does it have an adequate budget?
9	Does it have adequate power/authority?
10	Has it ever exercised punitive measures?

One quick way of looking at operational risk is to examine what is right, and what is possibly wrong, at top management level.

A committee of directors that rubber-stamps an executive's decision can cover up anything embarrassing, but only for a short time. The emperor cannot go on wearing no clothes. Risk analysis exists to pose rational and occasionally very awkward questions to determine investment soundness. These questions are useless when business investment projects are run on the star system – when the previous excellent performance or reputation of an individual or a company overrides all else. The LTCM hedge fund fiasco typified the way in which intelligent people were blinded by the supposed intellectual brilliance behind one fund management outfit and the high profits it seemed to be making (see LTCM case study, p. 165).

'*Hedge fund's star power blinded savvy investors to enormous risks,*' ran one headline.[11]

The project manager or the project owner should ask probing questions, no matter if they are embarrassing, and deploy resources to get maximum value in coping with risk.

Buying investment funds or shares

Before handing over anything to anyone who wants your money, or signing a contract with them, possible questions to ask are:

- 'who are you?'
- 'what is your background?'
- 'what is your company's background?'
- 'what is the track record of your company's investments?'
- 'what is the background of your company's chairman?'
- 'why did he leave his last job?'
- 'was he dismissed, and if so, why?'
- 'what are you selling us?'
- 'how long have you been working on what you are selling?'
- 'do you understand what are you selling?'
- 'where is the bulk of the investment to be located?'
- 'what is the total cost now?'
- 'what is your company's total exposure or value-at-risk?'
- 'what is my maximum total exposure from my investment?'
- 'what is the likely return over a year?'

- 'what are the assumptions for projecting these returns?'
- 'what are the effects of an adverse 1 per cent change in UK or US interest rates?'
- 'how sensitive is your company to a 10 per cent drop in demand next year?'
- 'what risk management functions are there to guard against these potential losses?'

Unfortunately, as we have seen, such questions and a company's entire risk analysis can be sidelined when a senior executive is taken in by a salesman's personality and is keen on his product, or overrides the warnings of the risk manager. Risk specialists are not necessarily blameless here because project managers are fallible creatures who will opt for the most sellable option. It is in the interests of the project manager and the project itself that the whole project picture is kept in view. Risk analysts have to be able to communicate their cases convincingly without the use of too much technical jargon. Furthermore, they should be able to provide solutions to problems; the last thing any project manager needs is to be told that nothing can be done because of the likely risk involved. There has to be a viable option.

Leadership, team, task and the individual

The project can often be thought of as a human project – how to get the best performance out of a combination of staff. This applies whether it is an investment bank, a construction company or a football team. Project members can be complete strangers to the project manager. There are potentially rewarding and productive relationships here, but there are also numerous possible pitfalls – a project manager can, for instance, put too much trust in the supposed ability of a member of staff. The process of management is somewhat akin to tending a garden; look after it carefully and it grows, mistreat it or neglect it and it may fail. A garden in bloom enables the gardener to take the credit, and it is this desire to earn or share the plaudits that can lead to a project being given the go-ahead prematurely and the entire risk analysis procedure being bypassed. LTCM serves to show the banks can lose control by delegating the investment of large corporate funds to one or two directors on the basis of a sales pitch. Adequate risk management dictates that investments must be justified, and not made because of appealing personalities or business stars who can do no wrong. Worshipping stars is fine for rock 'n' roll; let's keep it out of business.

One of the biggest names in the investment world is George Soros. But even he has admitted that mistakes are made when commencing or continuing a project. As he says:

'I would consider it a greater accomplishment to have the courage to wind up a failed foundation than to have the vanity to set up a new one.'[12]

It is essential sometimes to consider terminating a project. This has to override any moves to keep the project running merely because of what it has cost or the publicity it has attracted.

The method of staff selection that suits your project is determined by your business and your current situation. Unfortunately, some businesses do not make enough effort to get the right personnel for the right job. This may be due to circumstance, such as staff being inherited from a take-over, or staff being connected to the owner as is often the case in smaller family-controlled enterprises. Questions have to be asked about staff vacancies:

- what you need the person for?
- how fast do you need the position filled?
- how much do you wish to spend on selection?
- how much are you willing to pay?
- who do you have to carry out the selection?
- who do you have who might fit the job requirements?

Sadly, these questions are sometimes ignored; the staff selection process for a project may be carried out on a more immediate basis; for instance, who stands out as a possibility when a decision has to be made.

Screening project staff

Sometimes, uncertainty over whether you have hired the right person can affect the success of the entire project. This problem can be cleared up through a questioning process at the interview stage. Most project leaders try to conduct face-to-face interviews because they trust this method the most – they can see the goods first before they buy. There is a risk, however, that the interviewee may have been involved in fraud or malpractice, and be prepared to be involved again.

The use of conditional or Bayesian probability enters into our calculations. This means we have to examine the likelihood of an event given a previous outcome, i.e.

$P(A|B)$ = probability of B occurring given A

For independent events, there is no change, e.g.: A coin has 0.5 chance of heads [H] or tails [T] turning up.

$P(H|T) = 0.5$

133

Therefore, there is no change on the basis of a previous coin toss.

For modern risk management, a project leader or analyst must examine the conditions and the probabilities as strands of evidence, much in the same way as a criminal case. Evidence should be unearthed, and the reasoning explained to all those on the project. Thus, in a murder case with a gunshot victim, we can say when viewing a suspect:

Probability (guilty) = 0.5, i.e. Guilty [G] or Innocent [I]
In reality, we are forced by the law to assume that a man is innocent unless proven guilty, so officially, P(G) is zero or negligible at first.

Evidence: the bullet has come from a Magnum .357 pistol.
P(G) = 0.65. Reason: suspect is known to possess a Magnum .357.

Evidence: the suspect's gun barrel tracks match those on the bullet.
P(G) = 0.85. Reason: suspect's gun was used in the killing.

Evidence: the suspect's fingerprints match those found at the murder site.
P(G) = 0.95. Reason: suspect has been at the site of the killing at some stage.

Evidence: suspect seen approaching site of killing shortly before murder.
P(G) = 0.99. Reason: suspect's whereabouts ascertained.

Picking staff through questioning

A project leader is often unaware of the real capabilities and integrity of the individual being interviewed. Thus, the screening process looks for evidence which will help avoid the risk of taking on bad staff – P(B) – as opposed to a good worker – P(G). Initially, P(G) = 0.5, that is to say either equally bad or good.

Example: a job interview

Question: 'which large projects have you worked on previously?'
Answer: 'I worked on the Trans-Sahara road project.'
Evidence: this is a large well-known project.
P(G) = 0.57. Reason: applicant has some relevant experience.

Question: 'How would you rate the Trans-Sahara road project in terms of schedule?'
Answer: 'I think it was very successful. We finished it on time.'
Evidence: the road was 18 months late opening.
P(G) = 0.35. Reason: applicant known to be imprecise.

Question: 'what responsibility did you have on this project?'
Answer: 'I was assistant project manager.'

Evidence: this was high up in the project staff hierarchy.

$P(G) = 0.30$. Reason: applicant is associated with a failed project.

Question: 'how would you run the Trans-Sahara project if you did it again?'
Answer: 'we would run it more or less the same way. We're very proud of it.'
Evidence: the road was late and over budget.

$P(G) = 0.15$. Reason: applicant known to be unwilling to learn.

Evidence from someone who worked under him: 'this man is difficult to work with and is unsystematic.'

$P(G) = 0.05$. Reason: applicant's skills severely criticized by former staff.

Decision: we are 95 per cent confident he is a poor project manager. Reject this candidate.

CASE STUDY

An interview with DSL

We were given an opportunity to interview an applicant for a banking job. Later, we had to sift through the claims he made, the truths and the half-truths. The applicant's CV included senior jobs with good companies, but there was a lot of chopping and changing. When asked about this, he had said: 'They were consultancy assignments. Contracts were finished at the end of their term.' Then again, how could he have been so senior for such a short time? Surely these were permanent positions – wouldn't companies want continuity rather than using short-term contractors? He could give no satisfactory answer.

He said he had written and designed a banking system. Where was it? We asked for evidence of his work. He couldn't show it. Did he have a laptop PC? Yes, he did. Then why couldn't he show his work? Client confidentiality, he said. We asked about his client's policy on confidentiality, and he gave a garbled answer. Was this the same in all firms he had worked with? What about his own designs done to his own specification? Nothing.

Conclusion: his story was full of holes.

There are two ways to handle a job interview:[13]

Structured interview – go through a check-list and search for all the relevant questions on it. Sometimes you can go for the jugular by skipping some questions and going to those which really matter. 'So why did you leave your job as financial controller at Acme Real Estate in 1999?'

Unstructured interviews are those that have little pre-set agenda. It is often a preferred way of getting more fluid answers from the respondent, and allows the interviewee to ramble – a little discipline and reversion to the core questions is often needed. There is a great opportunity here to find out about someone's creativity and what makes them tick.

For instance, in one unstructured interview carried out by a DSL manager, the candidate was asked a question which was both a way of finding out about his analytical skills, and checking on his claim about his competence in chess.

What do you think of this sequence of moves, he was asked.

e4	e5
Nf3	Nc6
Bb5	

It's the famous Ruy Lopez opening![14]

The initial questioning could be as wide-ranging as you want, but once you have a target – hit it! 'You mentioned bridge; what do you think of the Blackwood system?' 'A classical music collection? Which Elgar "Enigma variations", do you have?' You may be happy to let the interviewee skirt around the question and answer it in his or her own way. Or you may witness the interviewee falling into a trap. As the saying goes: Give them enough rope to hang themselves.

On the positive side, the answer may be cogent and truthful, enough to justify your view that the candidate is fit for the job you have offered. We feel that on balance, most interviews should usually combine elements of both the structured and unstructured technique, with most emphasis on the structured type to maintain standards for comparison between candidates.

Risk management as a cultural issue

The sales effort

This is one early phase of a project where risk management is often omitted. The growth of international trade means that more sales staff are travelling further, often to strange lands and cultures. We can use project leaders as the best-qualified and most culturally-aware scouts. They may have to beat a path to the project owner's door and find a way in. They must not smash the door down and trample over the prospective customer's feelings. The customer is king (certainly in his own home country). The list of objectives in a sales campaign runs something like this:

● get the introduction or lead
● get your foot in the door
● explain the project or product
● close the sale, and sign the contract.

> **CASE STUDY**
>
> ## British sales manager for airport construction
>
> A large British company was going into Malaysia on a major sales campaign. There was a raft of contracts up for grabs with the large Sepang airport complex due to replace the ageing Subang terminal. The lead sales manager, or project manager, of the sales campaign was visited by the deputy prime minister. The sales executive put his feet up on his desk (exposing his shoe soles, which is very rude in Muslim communities) and pompously asked his visitor without realizing who he was: 'Who are you?' Needless to say, British hopes of winning some contracts went straight out of the window.

The need for key project team skills means that we are moving away from ad hoc recruitment or staff selection to the more structured approach. Whichever project methodology we choose will have a section on job description. This should have an outline of what job titles are for the project, the responsibilities and duties, and the skills required. There are various formats, but they serve to put a structure on what has often been a hit-or-miss affair. It may once have made sense for companies to give the sales job to the biggest talker, for instance, but the need for a structured project means that staff selection has to be a well thought-out affair. See the following simplified example:

Table 7.2 ● Job descriptions

Job description for:	Telecoms engineering services marketing executive
Vacancy opened:	12 January 2000

Essential skills

1	Telecoms engineering, more than ten years
2	Marketing and sales, more than three years
3	Team player
4	Mobile

Desired skills

1	PABX telecoms experience, more than ten years
2	Financial institutions experience: banks and insurance companies
3	Languages: French or German to IOL 3 conversational level
4	IT/telecoms degree to BA level

Description Executive for developing European telecoms market to work in team, leading five to eight team members. Executive will progress sales leads and liaise with clients' management and IT departments. Has to support and brief legal and design teams. Main targets are medium to large banks and insurance companies. Contracts size typically € 3–5 million.

Reports to: Vice-president (sales)

Remuneration Depending upon experience, €45,000 base + commission

Step	Staff	Date	Status
1 CV/resumé	Received: J. R. Adams	8 Feb 2000	Proceed
2 Telephone	Done: R. S. Stephens	21 Feb 2000	Proceed
3 Interview No. 1	Done: RSS, CJD, ARW	14 Mar 2000	Proceed
4 Interview No. 2	Done: CJD, REW, WDE	4 Apr 2000	Accept
5 Offer	Sent: J. R. Adams	8 Apr 2000	Proceed
6 Accept. letter	Done: RSS, CJD, ARW	14 Apr 2000	Proceed
7 Check refs	Pending: RSS		Waiting
8 Check qualifs	Pending: RSS		Waiting
9 Contract	Drafted: CJD		Waiting
10 Induction		16 May 2000	Scheduled

Introducing team risk awareness

Team members may not all have worked with each other before. The aim is to focus their resources and abilities towards successful completion of their project. We examine this in depth in the section Building consensus and project focus, p. 141.

The first thing many companies do is try to create a corporate identity or communal working spirit. Workshops, brainstorming and project team events are examples of this. American companies, in particular, are keen to promote these types of events, ranging from meals, barbecues, dressing-down days, concerts or opera visits, bar evenings, and playing frisbee and softball. It has become something of an established *modus operandi* in western Europe and North America, although it is not common in all cultures. Nevertheless, it is clear that team-building is a constructive way to help reduce the risk of internal project team conflict. As John Neerhout, chairman of London & Continental Railways, said of building the high-speed rail link between London and the English Channel:

> *'A works picnic is cheaper than a walk-out.'*[15]

This binding process is doubly important following a take-over or merger. However, in some countries it is actually preferred for managers to be distanced from line workers in a project. Getting too close and intimate with junior staff may lead to senior personnel losing the respect of others. Britain seems to be trying to go down less formulaic avenues.

> *'The acceleration of change within the business world means people are having to adapt, be more flexible and have a higher level of communications ... New teams have been formed and people know those in their teams but haven't got to know each other cross-functionally.'*[16]

Projects create change in people's working conditions, and this may be against their wishes. One of the keys to project success is introducing and maintaining proper change management. This is a crucial note when there are some social habits or working practices that are deemed to be vitally important. Some things are almost sacrosanct in certain countries.

> *'The answer lies in an ingrained business culture that, while not exactly resistant to change, is certainly wary of it. German managers on the whole adopt as a matter of course a 'show me' attitude for new methods of working. German companies, for example, were slow to adopt PC technology.'*[17]

Telephoning people, or forcing them to work, during lunchtime is regarded as unreasonable in some cultures, as is giving people less summer and winter holiday time, despite offers of greater remuneration. Parents in a project team may need extra time off to look after their children, and project managers should be sensitive to these needs within reasonable limits. Insensitive managers rarely succeed because they cause feelings of resentment and alienation in the project team in the long-run.

> *'CEOs still think that they can simply throw people of different cultures together and they'll get on. Yet that rarely happens in one's own country without skill and effort, let alone in multicultural groupings.'*[18]

Ironically, it seems that some multinational projects have fewer problems over different languages than with overcoming quirks of the local culture.

> 'There always seem to be communication problems, not so much with the language, but with things that people take for granted in one country but not so much in another country (for example, German punctuality dictates that things have to be delivered on time). So my understanding of an international project team is to get the same level of understanding (rules of the game) first, and then start working as a team.'[19]

Language is important, but good business in Russia can still be done in English or German. Language can blind you to what is more important for the project – understanding the local market, the country and its people.[20] For instance, the process of negotiating fees often involves an initial ploy that borders on outright effrontery. We have come across this in Russia and South-East Asia, where often an outrageous price is demanded, then a face-saving compromise is later reached. It is common for price quotes to have an in-built buffer to allow for a future discount. Negotiations can be long, and they may seem over-heated at times, compared to those in the west.

Other research on international project teams shows which nationalities team members prefer to work with.[21]

Nationality	First preference	Reason
American	British	Professional approach
British	American	Positive attitude
Danish	British	Positive attitude
Dutch	German/American	Professional approach
French	French	Know where you stand
German	German	Market access
Swedish	American	Professional approach

Building a project team rests upon trust. This depends on a feeling of respect that transcends international and cultural lines.

> 'Yet at least one in four US managers and one in seven UK managers are estimated to fail on international assignments. Learning how to handle culture shock is essential.'[22]

Inevitably, significant cultural differences will arise when you try to build a mixed-nationality project team. For example, the French like long lunches but like to discuss business only afterwards. The Chinese are very flexible but are difficult to pin down on schedule and delivery times. The Americans have much less experience of European cultures and tend to believe that the US business culture is the right one. Managers who are regarded as individual high-achievers can excel in the west, but they can be seen as too impatient and intolerant in a more consensus-led decision-making process in international projects. You should pick the right person with the most suitable technical and cultural skills.[23] We have seen how foreign arrogance and failure to look at things carefully in Russia can easily destroy a project team. Many western companies have tended to send product specialists to Russia who know little about the country. But it is preferable to use Russian specialists who know about your product.[24] We need to understand the country we are operating in, in order to do good business and achieve project success abroad.

David Platt, ex-manager of Sampdoria football club is a good example. Not only did he learn Italian, he learnt the local Genovese dialect.[25] He also went so far as learning the most important language for the job – the language of the club. David Platt was sacked as manager of Sampdoria after six league losses.

Note: There is no magic recipe on how to form a great project team whose members are guaranteed to get on with each other.

Building consensus and project focus

A project manager has to build a cohesive team around project objectives. If he neglects this task he will bring about ill-defined use of resources and a fall in staff morale. The project manager bears the burden of having to pull the team together, and keep it that way. This requires a set of soft skills that are not easily picked up in a university course or a college textbook. A lot of companies and project owners place a high value on traditional intellectual and academic achievement, a reflection of a possible obsession with IQ. There has been some backlash against this emphasis on traditional hard skills and measurements of intelligence. There is a growing realization that the success of a project can depend on these practical skills, or emotional intelligence, which do not readily manifest themselves in a curriculum vitae or degree certificate.[26] They comprise social and business elements:

1 Self-awareness – recognizing your strengths and weaknesses
2 Self-regulation – the need to keep emotions under control and be mentally open
3 Motivation – equipping yourself with the drive to attain success
4 Empathy – awareness and understanding of others' dispositions

5 Social skill – an ability to form and maintain creative socio-business relationships.

Such talents are essential contributions to the success of a project. Treat your counter-party or partner with respect. Learn their characteristics; people in some countries, for instance Russia, like to do business only if they understand the social persona of whoever they are dealing with, not just the business persona. Business trust is earned and not given.[27]

Sport is a prime example of a pastime that has been developing into a business. Yet, project goals are essential and the process of team-building critical if you are to achieve your objectives. A team's foundations are trust and respect, of which money is only one motivator. Channelling your resources effectively is essential for success.

CASE STUDY

Professional football

Winning the English league championship or the UEFA cup is a major project for any football team. The large English clubs have faced a massive change of culture from merely sport to business as well – including the value of their land and buildings, merchandising operations, and the value of the players themselves. Furthermore, a club's intangible asset is its goodwill. A football manager has to be an adept player, businessman, diplomat, politician, change management guru and, finally, a leader.

Newcastle United under Kevin Keegan epitomized an attacking style of play, popular with TV, the media and the public. The choice of Kenny Dalglish as manager marked an emphasis on a defensive style of football, partly due to his inability to buy in more skilled players because of the relatively limited budget. Ruud Gullit, as the new manager since 1998, had gone for a return to the Keegan-type attacking style. But Gullit had only £7 million to spend on buying players in contrast to Keegan's £60 million and Dalglish's £38 million.

Football is a business that needs to please the fans, TV, the club, the players, directors, merchandisers, shareholders, and the stock-market.

There are many other examples of managers who left their clubs; for instance Bertie Vogts, Germany's 1998 World Cup manager, Russia's head coach Anatoly Byshovets, Barcelona's Johann Cruyff, Brazil's Mario Zagallo, Christian Gross at London club Tottenham, and Luigi Simoni at Inter Milan. They have disagreements with their clubs, particularly after a series of losses which is possibly no fault of theirs, and they leave. Sometimes the fault can rest with the club or the players, or in the case of a company, with the client.

You need to build a team that can handle the project. Obviously, Sir Alex Ferguson found the right formula for building a winning project team on Manchester United's way to the League, FA Cup and European Cup victories in 1999.

The Fat Man restaurant, Malaysia

There are restaurants in South-East Asia that provide low-priced breakfasts and lunches for the local workforce. The proprietor may set up the restaurant with an infrastructure of awning, tables, plates and cutlery, while the catering is subcontracted to freelance people who pay a cut for the use of the premises and for the washing-up to be done. One famous example is that of an entrepreneur in Kuala Lumpur, known as the Fat Man. He built up a successful restaurant with good cooks and a loyal clientele. Then, for whatever reason, he lost the team of cooks and his customers. As the saying goes, people chose to vote with their feet. Either he lost sight of the goal or he lost the power to keep his team together.

There is a lot written about the art of management that completely ignores the risk to a project from anti-social behaviour, mental illness, drug-taking, alcoholism or other things. They can cause serious damage to your project.

Empowerment of the project team

Having an enthusiastic and capable project team is of little value when they have neither the resources nor the political mandate to succeed in their job. DSL has found that a project assigned to a team with neither funds nor authority is liable to fail, either inadvertently or deliberately. A project without influential friends, and a project team that has inadequate status or reputation, is likely to run straight into the ground. There sometimes is a need to win friends and influence people. Let's go back to NASA for an example on winning friends.

CASE STUDY

NASA satellite research

Extensive contacts were made with oceanographers and the scientific community at UCLA and Ohio State University. In essence, the contacts were both technical and political to ensure that the scientific community would accept the study results as credible and conclusive and would support NASA's plans to implement a satellite programme.

It is imperative to project success that we get the best people for the job, and that the recruitment process be done professionally and independently. The European Union (EU) is a good example of some of the problems that occur when running multicultural projects in what may develop into a politically charged environment. Things can get out of hand.

CASE STUDY

European Union fraud team

The EU independent report by five independent experts revealed modern hazards in project management. The Report examined mismanagement and fraud in the EU Commission and showed how Commissioners had created a 'state within a state'. It detailed the lack of control in project management and the scrutiny led to all 20 European Commissioners resigning.[28]

The Report's relevance to our study of risk and project management is in terms of:

Corruption and the Invitation to Tender (ITT): corruption and favouritism was exposed when contracts were awarded in competition tenders. Projects were open to bribery, which posed a serious risk to the efficiency of operations and the chances of success. EU contracts for handling security were awarded to the companies IMS Group4/Securitas. These were not won on a fair and openly competitive basis, nor were the staff regarded as professional in their quality of service – see Chapter 8, p. 153 (Invitation to Tender). Similar doubts were expressed in the report over the tender for various contracts in the Leonardo da Vinci programme.

Recruitment and consultants: the Leonardo da Vinci youth training programme was awarded to Agenor, the French company, on a non-competitive basis instead of according to a value-for-money rationale – see Chapter 6, p. 121 (Consultants).

A Leonardo daily rate of 2677 euros was paid to a UK academic who 'apparently did not produce any scientific services which could justify the considerable fee'.[29] Two Commissioners were implicated for hiring acquaintances: Mrs Edith Cresson for employing her dentist friend as a 'visiting scientist', and Mrs Monika Wulf-Mathies for awarding a temporary contract to a legal expert married to an old friend.[30]

Top management responsibility: top management must bear responsibility where the project failures are systematic. Little or no firm action was taken by the commission for years to eliminate corruption and fraud. It took four years until the EU fraud-busting group investigated the awarded security contract. By the beginning of 1999, 76 bodies or individuals were the focus for criminal investigation in the Commission's Tourism Unit. But the Commission chose to ignore or discredit the allegations.[31] Like the LTCM failures in managerial control discussed earlier in Chapter 7 (see p. 131), accountability must go to the top of the project management hierarchy if controls are to be successfully applied. Otherwise, your project carries significant downside risk.

According to one senior London policeman, business can face similar bureaucratic obstacles when calling for international police co-operation over fraud.

'The only two things that the criminal really fears are the custodial sentence and the loss of profit from crime. The results have been disappointing, with very few convictions in any participating country. Many hardened professional criminals now regard fraud as the safest method of committing crime.'[32]

As if that is not bad enough, many companies are so embarrassed by financial mismanagement or fraud that they do not report it to the police.

'... many organizations do not report fraud because there is a belief that we do not regard the recovery of stolen funds as a priority.'[33]

Those involved in fraud are adept at setting up front companies abroad, including offshore companies. Connections may be clouded or deliberately hidden.

'Money launderers can set up hundreds of companies as a conduit for their funds and the trail is almost impossible to unravel. The use of separate jurisdictions greatly complicates the investigators' task.'[34]

If you are in any doubt about your counter-party or partner, and think they might be involved in fraud, the risk strategy should be to stay clear. Where fraud is undetected in companies or organizations, this may be due to a basic empowerment failure through:

- no fraud prevention policy
- no planning for fraud analysis
- inadequate staffing in numbers and skills
- no support from top management
- poor or non-existent implementation
- little fraud or project review
- too much political obstruction.

Review of the project team's results

This is the crucial stage to see how well we have performed, and whether we have really reached our goals. It is for such reasons that a project auditing/review (PAR) is conducted. We have to learn where we are, the effectiveness of the process that lets us get there, and how we can do better.

Project auditing/review

A check of the project's status is necessary to ensure that it is meeting expectations. If we are to meet our objectives and be less vulnerable to nasty surprises, then checks and controls become a fundamental part of risk analysis and risk management. The project auditing/review process becomes a necessity, rather than a luxury.

There are several PAR objectives:

- identify potential problems earlier – fewer surprises
- improve project performance – total quality management (TQM)
- reduce the number of mistakes and their impact
- reduce costs
- reduce schedule overruns.

PAR involves fairly in-depth questioning of not only the direction but also the manner in which the project is running.

1 does the current progress meet with our planned expectations?
2 are budgetary and scheduling changes likely?
3 what is the status of critical tasks that can affect/delay the project?
4 what is the likelihood and impact of these hazards identified?
5 what data from this PAR affects other projects, or the whole organization?
6 what were the limits or remarks of this PAR operation?

Notes and references

1 Interviews through Tomas Gilsa, journalist, Stockholm, April 1997.

2 Merchant International Group (MIG), 'The intelligence gap', March 1999.

3 *Daily Telegraph*, 21 November 1998, p. 3.

4 Personal interviews with British banking consultant, Latvia, December 1994–July 1997.

5 Personal conversation with western banking consultants, Baltic states, 1995.

6 See DSL Consultants (1997) *Risk Management in Russia and the Baltic States*, FT Publications.

7 *International Herald Tribune*, 24 October 1998, p. 13.

8 Interviews with Anatoly Ilyin, deputy general director, Wackenhut, Moscow, July 1997.

9 Personal interview, bank manager, Moscow, May 1997.

10 Fowler, A. and Walsh, M. (1 February 1999) 'Conflicting perceptions of success in an information systems project', IPMA, vol. 17, no. 1, pp. 1–10.

11 *International Herald Tribune*, 24 October 1998, p. 13.

12 Soros, G. (1998) *The Crisis of Global Capitalism*, Little, Brown & Co.

13 See, for example, 'Employment of key personnel' in *Profit from Loss* (1998), Maxima Plc, UK.

14 Lopez, R., sixteenth century Spanish priest and chess player, who is renowned for the famous Lopez chess opening move. The modern international chess notation is preferred these days.

15 *Financial Times*, 24 November 1998, p. 18.

16 *Financial Times*, 16 October 1998, Mergers and Acquisitions, p. 6.

17 *Project Manager Today*, July 1998.

18 Andersen Consulting Change Management, in *Business Life*, November 1998.

19 Winkler, K., project manager, Telepassport Service, Germany. Personal correspondence, December 1998.

20 Trusswell, S., British Embassy, Moscow. Personal interview, 4 January 1999.

21 Cooper, Prof C., the UK's Manchester School of Management, in *Business Life*, November 1998.

22 *Financial Times*, 21 January 1999, p. 14.

23 Marx, E. (1999) *Breaking Through Culture Shock*, Nicholas Brealey.

24 Trusswell, S., ibid.

25 *Guardian*, Sport, 3 February 1999.

26 *Financial Times*, 24 November 1998, p. 16.

27 Trusswell, S., ibid.

28 'Report on allegations regarding fraud, mismanagement and nepotism in the European Community', 15 March 1999.

29 *Financial Times*, 17 March 1999, p. 3.

30 *Financial Times*, 17 March 1999, pp. 2–3.
31 *Financial Times*, 17 March 1999, pp. 2–3.
32 *Financial Times*, 15 October 1998, p. 9.
33 Correspondence with senior officer, City of London Police Fraud Squad, January 1998.
34 *Financial Times*, 2 October 1998, World Economy supplement, p. 8.

8

Quality assurance

❝ But yet, I'll make assurance double sure,
And take a bond of fate. **❞**

William Shakespeare, *Macbeth*

Introduction

We use the term quality assurance or QA to describe project control over the production process to ensure that performance goals are being met. Internal operating standards will define levels of quality and performance, and acceptable tolerance limits.[1] We have manufacturing standards to produce 12mm metric nuts and bolts to, say, plus or minus 0.05mm. Banks can stipulate that customers should queue for no more than 120 seconds. And, we can be certain of getting our dry cleaning back by ten o'clock the following morning.

Many of the ideas for quality assurance were advanced with the concept of total quality management (TQM). TQM was essentially born in the engineering environment, but it has applications in service industries too.[2] TQM seeks to promote a strategic drive towards satisfying the customers' needs faster and better without detriment to company employees. It covers a methodology that is geared towards a more efficient and less wasteful production system.

There are international and national operating standards for product compliance. The driving forces behind these are the national and international standards bodies, the British Standards Institute (BSI) with its BS5750 quality standard, and the International Standards Organization (ISO) and its ISO9000 series of quality standards. Companies that have been quality-certified by the BSI or ISO are deemed to have successfully passed the certification processes, but this does not necessarily mean that everything these companies do or manufacture is of quality. One of the main questions is over the competence of our business associates and suppliers. Thorough investigation is required here to ensure that they can provide quality.

Tom Tow, an architect with 20 years' experience in the USA, UK and Singapore, has had various dealings with ISO9002 contractors, both good and bad. What we can say from our DSL experience is that ISO9002 is only partially useful – it is a pre-qualifying hurdle that favours the larger companies,

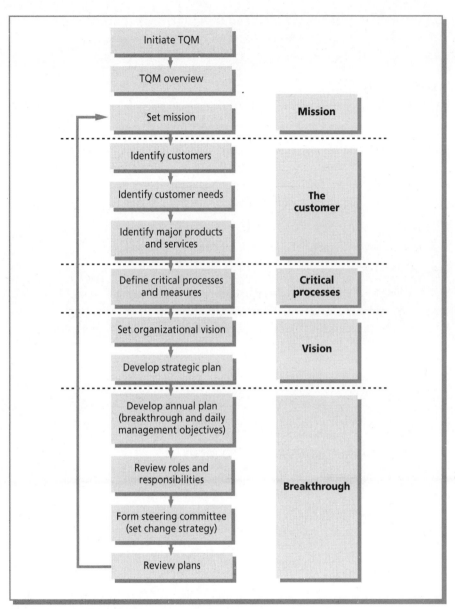

Fig. 8.1 ● TQM in projects[3]

especially when a government awards contracts to those with ISO9002 accreditation. Tom Tow has come across companies who have done the paperwork but cannot deliver the goods. We have to say that DSL has encountered similar companies. What the regulatory authorities have done, in our view, is to put too high a value on paper qualification. After all, would you hire an ISO9002 accredited decorator to renovate your house? Reality tells us there might be other things more important than paperwork. Experience and ability count more than an international symbol on a business letterhead.

QA checking

Quality assurance occurs in all industries. One example is the QA check to see that the product or service meets the specified targets. This process is methodical and time-consuming; it is not rocket science, but it is an essential part of a project. This process can be illustrated in the 'snagging report' that DSL compiles when it is involved in designing and implementing an office environment. The sequence of actions is simple:

1 analyze (spot)
2 document and distribute to relevant project team members
3 act (follow up).

It also helps to have some threat or incentive to encourage the other party to act on your requirements, such as withholding or releasing payment. Otherwise, there is the risk of not getting what you want. We might imagine a simple purchase of office furniture.

CASE STUDY

A simple purchase of office furniture

SNAGGING REPORT: DESKS ref: DD/2001/0301a

1 March 2001

Project Leader
Ruritanian Bank Project
Hi-tech Furniture Inc.
New York

System delivered: 25 February 2001
System installed: 25–28 February 2001

1 Total number of desks ordered was one hundred (100). Two (2) had to be rejected. These two desks came in a size 1590mm wide by 1190mm deep – 1cm different from the others. These must be delivered in the correct dimensions of 1600 x 1200mm. Please provide delivery for us, latest by 12 March 2001 onsite.
2 Wood finish (mahogany) was of inconsistent colour in five (5) desks numbered D056–D060. Please arrange for dyes and colours to be corrected. The linoleum in-fills in desks D031–D033 have to be re-glued.
3 There were scratches, varying in length from 15–65mm, on desks D031–D037, please correct with filler and re-colour. We advise you to bubble-wrap all the

desks to 15mm thikcness to protect them thoroughly from potential damage.

4 Desks D045–D046 are missing one drawer cabinet each. Please deliver.

5 The pull-out/slider for PC computer trays on D029–D030 are stiff. Please correct.

6 Back panels (mahogany finish) of desks D031–D032 need to be connected. A 3mm gap has appeared.

7 One desk top 2-gang electric isolation switch is missing on desk D014. Please send one.

8 The desks D076–D077 are mounted 756mm high. Please drop to 750mm work surface height.

I will issue instructions to release the second part of the payment to you when I have seen these defects put right. We need this done urgently by 12 March. Please confirm to me in writing by 5pm 5 March 2001.

D. Marchmont
Assistant Project Manager

The invitation to tender process (ITT)

This phase of a project can be very costly and fraught, and may involve more political infighting and manoeuvring than almost all the other phases combined. There is also a chance of bribes and other incentives, official and unofficial, occurring here. These go beyond the wining and dining that forms part of standard public relations. Bribes are likely to be part of a business transaction in some form, and are very difficult to detect and prove in an increasingly global world.

At DSL we start the ITT phase by obtaining the external party's literature. This usually comprises:

● company background

● services overview

● product overview

● technical documentation.

The next thing is to assess the prospective contractor; his body language can give you an idea of what he is like. For example, a contractor's discomfort can betray his inexperience with working on a project such as yours. Unfamiliarity with the literature about his company's services or product may indicate that the contractor does not really believe in the literature, which may be misleading. A search on the company and its key personnel usually involves getting previous client testimonials and references. An independent third-party recommendation should be sought, someone who can testify to quality of work.

A deeper look at a company's operations

If you are thinking of contracting a company to act as your project manager, take a close look. It could be worthwhile.

● scheduling – are its projects usually delivered on time? What percentage of deviations are there?

● budgeting – are its projects usually delivered within budget? What is the percentage of deviations?

● employee count – does it have enough staff?

● employee quality – are staff trained and experienced? Are there significant staff changes on the horizon, lay-offs, for instance?

● what is the composition of the project staff and what are their CVs like?

A tactic often used by contractors is to put forward their best or most qualified staff for the interview or ITT to win the contract. Once the contract has been won, you may well find the bulk of the project work is to be done by a less experienced employee. This person may not have the direct project experience that you came to expect from the initial contact. You can get around this tactic by specifying the staff to be used, or requiring all curriculum vitae to be submitted before the start of the project.

Forensic accounting

Further detective work is usually advised, and a search on the integrity of a company and its finances is essential. Public databases cover Fortune 500 or FTSE-100 corporations, and the individual proprietor. There is a wealth of information available on these databases on a company's record, compiled from publications like *Business Week*, The *Wall Street Journal*, The *Financial Times*, The *Economist*, and other newspaper articles. Check with S&P, IBCA and Moody's credit ratings for previous annual performance and likely patterns. Follow up with a search of analysts' and agency projections of your target company's future performance.[4]

● balance sheet – how are its assets and liabilities structured?

● capitalization – is it secure, and can it handle your project size?

● profitability – does it make any money in this industry?

● is the company trying to hide information or cook its books?

A lot of the detailed information from then on will be gathered through interviews and face-to-face discussions. It may become apparent quite early on that the company does not possess the skills, manpower or equipment to handle the job you need done.

Matrix evaluation in response to ITT

We can use an evaluation matrix on a company's past performance to indicate how we think it is going to perform. In an open market, it is often worth shopping around for the best price and quality on the most favourable terms. This is an extract from an ITT for one of our clients who was buying advanced telecoms equipment.

CASE STUDY

An extract from a DSL system evaluation

Selection criteria	Supplier A	Supplier B	Supplier C
Price	£250 000	$410 000	DM950 000
Delivery	£15 000	$30 000	Included
Tax included	No	No	Yes
Maintenance p.a.	11 per cent of price	$25 000	DM95 000
Extras needed	None	$15 000	None
Guarantee	12 months	2 years	1 year
Customs clearance	Extra	Extra	Included
Functionality	Excellent	Excellent	Good
Ease of use	Excellent	Excellent	Excellent
Training included	Yes	Yes	Yes
Quality of presentation	Good	Average	Excellent
Quality of client list	Excellent	Good	Average
Experience in this country	Yes	Yes	No
Maintenance track record	Good	Good	Average
Selection overall: weighted points awarded	99	94	84
Overall rating	**First**	**Second**	**Third**

Benchmarking

The job of comparing, or 'benchmarking', during an ITT will become much easier with widespread use of the euro currency. Even trade partners outside the EU could be persuaded to give price quotations in euros rather than US dollars in order to win Europe-based business. The main goal is to get an idea of where you are, and often where you want to go. It is also a way of letting the customer judge value for money.

155

There are various forms of benchmarking:

1   Comparing with the lowest performer. This is sometimes useful if you need the lowest common denominator to make your evaluations. It is not particularly useful if the benchmark is in a significantly different market sector, for instance, contrasting the handling characteristics of a Mercedes with a three-wheeler Reliant Robin.

2   Comparing with a specific rival. This is often the favoured method, and might involve Texaco being compared with Exxon, Safeway with K-Mart. The ITT selection matrix above is a classic example of lining up all invited suppliers to be judged in the beauty contest. Marks awarded to each category have to be weighted for importance according to your project needs.

3   Comparing with the best industrial performer. A company seeking a contract might use this method to see how things are done by others in order to try to catch up. Or it might concentrate on its value for money and win in the comparison process. Thus, although a Volkswagen VR6 is slower than a Ferrari F40, the Volkswagen is faster around corners and narrow urban roads, at a much lower price.

4   Comparing with best practice. This is often the technique used for a company to get a health check or evaluation such as an operational risk audit. The company can run through a list of checkpoints to see how it fares, and how it matches up to best levels. Most companies do not score 100 per cent, because such a score would reflect the sort of company that does not exist in the real world. It is important for a company to note where it falls short. It is not a matter of getting the most ticks on the score sheet, it is imperative to get the ticks where they matter most. Furthermore, a yes or a no answer does not always mean what it says in the analysis of comparisons.

Further study would be required and then the resources invested to correct operating inadequacies in the project.[5] The type of benchmarking a company needs is determined by the type of business and situation – what it needs it for, how fast it needs the results, how much it wishes to spend, and who it has got to research it.

Notes and references

1   Refer to standards of, for example, FIDIC (Federation Internationale des Ingenieurs Conseils), Switzerland, or IEEE (Institute of Electrical and Electronic Engineers), USA.

2   Deming, W. E. (1986) *Out of the Crisis*, MIT, Cambridge, USA.

3   Shtub, A. et al. (1994) *Project Management Engineering, Technology and Innovation*, Prentice Hall NJ, USA.

4   Refer to, for example, Walsh, C. (1998) *Key Management Ratios*, Financial Times Management.

5   Refer to, for example, Institute of Civil Engineers, Institute of Actuaries, London.

9

Finance in project risk management

> **❝** You pays your money and your takes your choice. **❞**

Punch, 1846

Cash flow

Cash is like ammunition for troops in a war; no matter how much you have, you will end up needing more. You can never get enough. Cash flow under conditions of uncertainty is one of the greatest hazards for a business. Limited cash flow or problems in properly managing it, are the main reasons why businesses fail. Whether Brunelleschi's dome in Il Duomo, Florence, or a modern suspension bridge over San Francisco Bay or the River Tay in Scotland, project finance is a real *sine qua non*. A list of major project risks provides reasons for and sources of risk in project funding. These can arise from the client running low on funds, the discovery that there is more work to be done than foreseen, the need to satisfy planning regulations, and having to pay more because a subcontractor has gone bankrupt.[1]

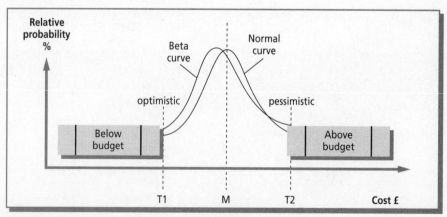

Fig 9.1 ● Relative probability curves for a project

There is a desperate need to model how the relative probability curves of your project look, even if only laid out on a simple graph. The most likely project cost lies between the optimistic T1 and pessimistic T2 values. Most projects go for T1, or the middle average value M; they should also be aware of the pessimistic value T2. Being aware of the downside risk, or pessimistic value, further helps to reduce nasty surprises. These are not restricted to the small business that is a few pounds or dollars short of the rent. Let's look at a big project that had huge assets but no available cash reserves.

CASE STUDY

Canary Wharf, London, and the Reichmann brothers

This was the biggest construction project in the UK, if not Europe, at the time. The Reichmann brothers faced 1991–92 with enormous capital tied up in land and buildings in London's docklands. There was a major economic recession, and the banks were breathing down their necks. Less than 50 per cent of Canary Wharf's office space was rented and revenue was not coming in fast enough.

This is a classic case of a cash flow problem, and an illiquidity phenomenon; it is not a case of being poor, but of being in a bad situation – resource-rich but cash-poor. The Reichmann brothers had to face their financial backers and play a game of chicken on the lines of: 'Give us your best financial terms or we go bankrupt.'

The 71-acre (29 Ha) site now makes more than a fair profit based on its near-full occupancy and guaranteed income from rents. It provides a prime example of cash flow problems that can drive even large companies into near or actual bankruptcy. It went into administration in 1992, and passed to a group of banks in 1993. It was then sold in 1995 to the Saudi Prince Abdula Aziz who was given two bits of advice by Paul Reichmann:

'Two things you should never do – never over-leverage, and never put everything under one umbrella because they implode or explode together.'

The lessons from the Canary Wharf project are still valid:

- avoid over-borrowing where possible, or get the best terms for loans and try not to be over-extended. Use risk management tactics; for instance, take a stronger partner with good financial backing, pick fixed-interest loans (these reduce uncertainty, even if you might pay a little more interest eventually) or create a contingency fund;
- diversify your assets among a portfolio of balanced investments to avoid having all your eggs in one basket, with the risk of big losses that can ensue.[2]

Canary Wharf shows us that project de-scoping, or slimming down of earlier project ambitions, may be useful in running a successful project.

We are not saying that good projects using risk management are never late and never experience cost overruns. We are saying they are likely to suffer less damage, and be more beneficial to the project owner. It may even be that all projects we are examining here have gone over budget. Thus, comparing median cost overruns, risk-managed projects have average overrun-1, less than average overrun-2 where there is little or no risk management. See Fig. 9.2.

Look at two Project Managers (or Contractors); each one's projects run over budget but by different average overruns. Yet the average cost overrun of Manager 1 (with risk management) is less than the average cost overrun for Manager 2. Calculate the project cost savings against the additional cost of implementing the risk management procedures. If you save more, then you're in the money.

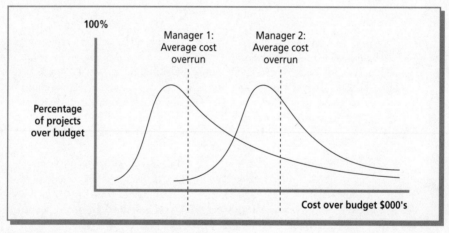

Fig 9.2 ● A comparison of cost overruns

Revenue protection using trade financing

Risk management is the process of gathering resources together, or protecting them, to accomplish the project. Trade financing can be seen as saving the project from a cash flow crisis and possible bankruptcy. It is a means of preventing a project becoming a non-project. Here is one such case.

CASE STUDY

A Siberian paper mill

Tony Carter is a manager in the project finance department of Halliburton, Brown & Root. He has considerable experience of structuring financing deals for projects in various parts of the world, including emerging markets in Africa and the former USSR.

A successful structured transaction was the funding of the purchase of pulp and paper mill equipment in Siberia by a multinational group. The funding was provided by a western bank secured by a sales contract for pulp with a major Swedish pulp and paper trader, supported by political risk insurance. As sales were made a proportion of each sale was placed into an escrow account with the lending bank, the amount being sufficient to ensure that there were enough funds to meet the quarterly payments of principal and interest. In the event of a default … any outstanding sales were paid to the escrow account.[3]

As we have seen, the protection of project finance is highly desirable in risky projects. The case study outlined by Tony Carter mentions the use of escrow accounts where money is tied up or locked until all satisfactory conditions have been met. We have already read how such guaranteed sums can be held by the client in an escrow account, in the section on performance bonds. The money will be returned only on full and satisfactory completion of the project. This is a highly effective way of securing a hold over project finance where there is a credit or non-performance risk. It does, however, have more significance for larger projects than SME projects which may not be able to afford the resulting overhead. Many projects can be classified as being long-term, and therefore unacceptable to conventional project finance. This means that projects (e.g. Project A in Fig. 9.3) that break even early on in their cycle tend to get backing. Project B and other longer-term investments may be rejected because their break-even point is too far in the future, and they therefore carry unacceptable risk.

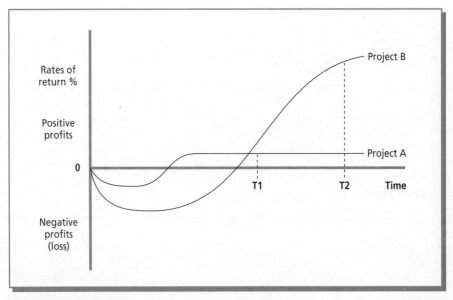

Fig 9.3 ● **Project returns**

Bechtel and London & Continental Railways

Some of the rail infrastructure projects associated with the Channel Tunnel, and handled by Bechtel, are key examples of the neeed for adequate financing to support the project. It is likely that even such a large, complex project like this – the construction of a high-speed rail link to London by Bechtel and London Continental Railways – can fail or stall because there is not a reservoir of sufficient resources to pay the bills. Having no cash in the kitty can be the kiss of death for a project. The essence of a successful project is to have a large surplus of cash to support it through both easy and hard times. Bechtel is unlikely to commit itself to a project and a fixed deadline unless it has sufficient funds to see the project through to its conclusion. Bechtel has raised more than $12 billion in project finance since 1990.[4] It needs this safety buffer or comfort factor to feel secure. Project managers are likely to feel the same; an unsure or rapidly dwindling cash reservoir causes anxieties and is a risk to the project being finished successfully. As John Carter of Bechtel says:

> 'We take positions in areas like finance and technology so we can understand the game.'[5]

The game goes as far as an equity stake in the project. Bechtel took an 18 per cent holding in LCR to be in a position to influence the development and direction of the project, as well as sharing in its profits. This was in direct contrast to the earlier Eurotunnel experience (see Channel tunnel case study, p. 83) where the banks and shareholders were essentially forced to accept a redistribution and dilution of the equity in a debt-for-equity swap – a position of weakness. Bechtel had made it its goal to gain control at the beginning – a position of strength. Bechtel also feels able in such a dominant position to get its own way.

The Channel Tunnel debacle involved conflicts and disputes that led to major delays and counter-claims. In its project, Bechtel attempted to avoid returning to the strife-filled labour relations of the 1960s and 1970s, and the earlier Euro-tunnel experience. The Bechtel message is to avoid conflicts and disputes that create cost and budget overruns.[6]

The use of future revenue as collateral to obtain finance of large initial capital outlays in projects is risky – the ground rules can change rapidly to work against you. For instance:

> *'Indonesian officials said that they would change mining royalties and ... local governments would be given more authority over permits – a concern to mining companies, which already complain of a double layer of bureaucracy.'*[7]

Changes in operating regulations and licensing can be swift. You have to watch out. Figure 9.4 has two scenarios for calculating the likely pay-back from the project at present value. The optimistic view is that the project breaks even at T1. The pessimistic view is that things do not go so well at first, so break-even is reached only at T2.

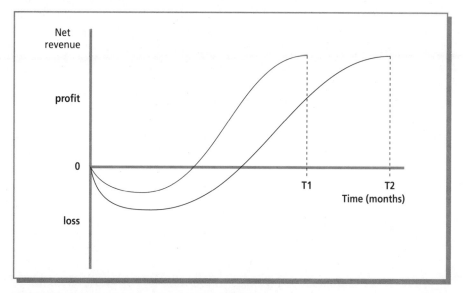

Fig 9.4 ● Financial risk management and derivatives

Derivatives

These investment trading vehicles were originally set up as risk management tools to counter adverse price movements in interest rates, currencies, commodities, shares or bonds. They could be used to protect the principal sum at risk by taking a position on an opposite price movement. Another way of operating would be for the trader to lock in to an exchange rate for a fixed time despite the world's foreign exchange markets experiencing volatile movements.

For example, if you were a project owner based in Germany and you took on a US contract payable in dollars in six months' time, you could protect the value of the contract, say $10 million should the dollar's value fall against the Deutschmark. You could pay a sum to insure against a devaluation of the dollar. You could buy futures contract on the $10 million for six months ahead, for let's say DM250,000, locked in at a fixed rate of DM1.6666:$1. So, in six months' time, you know for sure that you will receive the equivalent of DM16.66 million, less the transaction costs for the futures contract. Here, the reduction risk comes from minimizing the negative effects of fluctuations in $:DM exchange rates. You do not intend to make a profit on the whole hedging process; you seek to protect the value of your agreed payment when you get it in six months' time. (You may wish to study more detailed descriptions of derivatives and hedging tactics in *Financial Engineering*, or *The Financial Risk Manual*.[8])

The goal is to make high returns through investing in a variety of derivative instruments. Because the value of derivatives can rise in a falling stock market, it is tempting to buy derivatives to make profits under all market conditions. Another tactic is to sell short, take a negative view of the market and sell a share, bond or commodity that you do not currently have, with the aim of buying it later at a lower rate and making a profit. The downside is if the price rises and you are legally obliged to later buy it at a higher price than you had expected to pay. Japan, and the London Metal Exchange, have taken measures to stop short selling of shares and commodities to stabilize the market.[9]

Yet, potential profits are seductive. A stake or punt on the market, perhaps of $1 billion, could leave a company with a potential profit of $50 billion. Conversely, it could also have a $50 billion loss. Look what happened to Britain's Barings bank due to actions by rogue trader Nick Leeson in its Singapore office. In reality, a hedge fund, such as Quantum, Tiger or LTCM, engages in speculation on one-way movements in interest rates, currencies, shares or bonds. If you are interested in how billions can be made and lost in seconds, read on.

'*The increased liquidity in the market and the increased unconstrained capital flows make the chances of a catastrophic event more likely because the flow of funds is so large it can overwhelm any economic fundamentals. A lot of the big movements recently have been one-way, whether one-way down or one-way up. The FX market, for example, was originally a place for transactions based on the economic objectives of exporters and importers. There was usually some strong economic rationale for market movements, perhaps that one country's balance of trade was improving. However, all that has now been overshadowed by unconstrained capital flows in and out of markets.'[10]*

There is sometimes a divorce between theory and practice. We can look at an example that could have come out of the Hollywood film *Wall Street*.

CASE STUDY

Long-Term Capital Management (LTCM)

LTCM was one of the breed of prestige hedge funds that emerged in the late 1980s. They managed to parlay a stake of $4 billion into an exposure of about $200 billion, i.e. leveraged 50 times by 1998. Any extreme leverage is dangerous for a company; it means it will be unable to pay off obligations because of under-capitalization. LTCM said the Russian and Asian economic crisis had created gigantic losses for it. The US Federal Reserve felt compelled to step in with a consortium of 14 banks and inject $3.6 billion to avert LTCM's bankruptcy.

Just like Hollywood, we have to take the glitz away to find out what sort of project risk management existed. This saga exposed the inadequate way in which a few key personnel dealt with a situation where they thought they had the answers. The system of checks and controls that were meant to be in place were clearly overridden or subverted.

> 'LTCM ... may be exceptional ... but this is a sector full of exceptional ego-maniacs who believe that they can consistently beat the market ... But the hedge fund sector trades on its star culture, and greedy investors are easily seduced by the manager who promises to be up in a down year.'[11]

Risk management was not properly undertaken at LTCM, possibly because some clients may have been in awe of the hedge fund's founder, John Meriwether. A trader who claims investments will give a good return at low risk does not represent risk management. Risk management is an intrinsic, rational and iterative process in projects; it has often been confused or blurred by the cult of personality. The project manager or the client has to be able to question the expert to get a straight, down-to-earth answer.

Responsibility, risk and monitoring risk

High-risk, high-return projects should force you to analyze the likely risk present, implement risk management structures, assign responsibilities and to act decisively. Some individual experience or project brilliance accounts for accurate assessments of picking sure winners or setting up defensive project risk strategies. Other successful projects tend to have a good line of command that force people to weigh the scales of likely gain against probable loss. This management structure brings up checks and balances all the way to assess profit under risk various conditions. Methodologies such as RAMP or PRINCE 2 influence projects to consider the risk conditions at key stages – they do not necessarily change the management culture, especially where the project leaders are hell-bent on taking risks or adopting short-cuts. Thus, the chain of necessary events in project risk management can be easily broken, not only in emerging markets. Even the most 'respectable' company can fall victim to hubris and the smooth sales technique of a vendor selling a project. The project owner and project manager must always balance risk versus return. Ask yourself: *What is an acceptable project risk?*

Project risk management is not limited to the executive director of risk strategies. All your project members must have a hand in it if your project is to succeed. Many companies and projects are too small to have a hierarchy where a specific individual or group carries the sole responsibility for project risk management. Risk shoudl report all the way up, while responsibility should go up as well as down. Some projects, especially those running through a crisis or a failure, lead to recrimination – someone has to carry the can. *It is easy to pick scapegoats.* But, it is essential that those truly responsible for project failure are held to account for their actions. This is because:

● they learn not to repeat their mistakes in a hurry
● others are not led to believe that monitoring and accounting functions are weak
● we need to learn about risk and project failure just as much as about project success.

The Federal Reserve spearheaded the rescue bid to bail out the sinking LTCM. This occurred without an adequate investigation into how the disaster happened, who was responsible, and if those responsible should be punished. Critics were out in force. James Leach, chairman of the banking committee in the US Congress said that the US had lost 'moral authority' in banking.

> *'The Fed's intervention comes at a time when our government has been preaching to foreign governments … that the way to modernize is to let weak institutions fail and rely on market mechanisms rather than insider bail-outs.'*[12]

What LTCM really shows us is that greed can consume a project, with control and accountability going straight out the window. Clearly defined responsibility, and proper monitoring, are required but do not always happen. The lessons for handling risk that LTCM provides have yet to be fully taken in by banks, fund managers, and financial market regulators. Big money is sexy, but sometimes sexual attraction gets out of control.

Lessons of derivatives trading

It is ironic that derivative instruments were originally created from a desire to conduct risk management in foreign trade. But in the areas of foreign currency trading, futures and options, the derivatives markets themselves now pose a potential risk; they already account for a sum at least 50 times that of total annual world trade. Was any real wealth created by the growth in these markets? None. Yet, some hedge funds can and do report consistent profits. Should we worry? There is major cause for concern because many enterprises and organizations that are not considered to be hedge funds or investment banks have lost heavily in this type of activity. Let's have a look at some:

- Orange County, California
- London Borough of Hammersmith and Fulham
- Bank of England
- Bank of Italy
- Bank of South Korea.

The Bank of England lost some $20 billion during Black Wednesday in 1992 when it tried to support sterling at DM2.95. The central banks of Italy and South Korea were caught out in the LTCM fiasco. It seems there are a lot of taxpayers and shareholders around the world who are victims of losses incurred in the derivatives trading game. The gambler's winning streak has to end some time. Trading losses have been recurring through banking history, whether it is Barings, Sumitomo, Deutsche Morgan Grenfell or LTCM. There is certainly a lot of confusion about how investment funds and trading operations work. Let us clear up some used (and abused) definitions:

- arbitrage is a risk-free enterprise because it deals with price disparities which create certain profit when simultaneous deals are made. This means that a trader buys something in one country or market for a known price, X, and sells it in another market at a differential X+y per cent to reap instant profit;
- a hedge is a relatively risk-free capital venture; its explicit purpose is to preserve value or minimize risk of loss. There is no net profit or loss intended;

- speculation is a one-way bet on short-term price movements; it can be a high-risk venture, and can involve high loss or profit. Most hedge funds work on this basis, even if they are reluctant to be regarded as doing so. They would not want to attract the sort of unpleasant publicity that would come with calling themselves 'speculation funds'.

DSL looks forward to futures and derivatives trading being done at market-to-market prices within standard company reporting structures. Some of the proposals for reducing the risk of derivative losses are outlined in a publication by Chong (1999).[13] We wrote a management report for Financial Times Publications in 1997.[14]

> *'Banks and companies wishing to trade on the ... financial markets indulge in the zero-sum game where one trading loss is balanced by a trading gain – a form of mercantilism. This is almost certainly the case with derivatives trading, because no wealth is created, they are derived products of an underlying security that already exists ... what the player can put at stake (into the gambling pot) is partly governed by the regulatory authorities or banker.'*

It is likely that hedge funds and risky bets on derivatives will continue largely uncontrolled until central banks, stock exchanges and regulatory authorities really clamp down on them. We have to come up with sensible risk management in capital markets that explicitly attempts to examine project investments along the lines of: 'What is a reasonable risk and what is a reasonable expected return?'

How these banks can explain their large gambling stakes and huge losses in LTCM to their shareholders is another matter. The US push for market transparency allows shareholders to launch law suits against directors who seem to be underperforming or neglecting their duties. One group of shareholders sued, alleging that: 'The directors violated their fiduciary duty because they didn't comply with ... policies on protection against undue risks.'[15]

Then again, a few lines of small print under 'capital adjustment' might slip past without people noticing. This is not risk management. Risk management means occasionally using all methods, including law suits, against the offending party, which might even be your own side. The principle that trading in instruments that are higher risk but potentially high-profit can be conducted off the balance sheet is a dangerous one. The practice of investing large sums of the company's money without adequate monitoring or accountability is inadvisable. Futures and derivatives trading should be done within standard company reporting structures.

Project accountability

Without adequate reporting and controls, we are resigned to another LTCM-type fiasco happening again soon. Normally, investment banks use an operational process known as due diligence to evaluate the soundness of, and justification for, potential investments. When one person takes over the process as a personal fiefdom with disregard for all other opinion, then due diligence becomes a sham. Managers may go through the motions of checking and controlling risk, though they are not necessarily doing anything positive. Projects should be managed by responsible staff who work conscientiously and diligently in handling large sums of money on behalf of their clients and shareholders. But banks often trade in derivatives which do not show up in normal accounting procedures – these are referred to as off balance-sheet transactions. Careless project monitoring can make a mockery of the apparent health of an investment when it is judged solely on its current balance sheet or cash flow.

International accounting standards are not yet fully implemented to monitor and restrain wayward derivatives trading, although the International Accounting Standards Committee (IASC) and the US Federal Accounting Standards Board (FASB) further developed and advanced their interim standards in 1998. The FASB's version is Accounting for Derivative Instruments and for Hedging Activities. In the meantime, such trading continues as a sophisticated and potentially costly form of gambling. We have not seen the last of large capital losses on investment projects gone wrong. It is a case of *caveat emptor*. We really must hope that such committees do actually have the power to get results.

Chinese walls

Management can use so-called Chinese walls to create a barrier. Project staff are meant to be separated from other projects by these invisible Chinese walls, so as not to introduce conflicts of interest – for instance, people initiating company mergers do not talk to share traders. The intention is good but the practice may be poor. Can you really ban people from meeting friends and strangers in restaurants and bars? Can you stop them talking?

Practicalities of futures and options contracts for small firms

What relevance do multi-billion dollar deals have for SMEs and single-trade businesses? To be frank, little or next to nothing. Take the example of one small business.

CASE STUDY

Miss X, self-employed UK art and antiques dealer

This is a short study of a successful art and antiques dealer and how she handles derivatives and futures contracts. Basically, she doesn't. The art business involves a large number of international transactions. The problem is that if a foreign exchange rate changes significantly between the start of the contract and the time payment is made, Miss X may be faced with a loss. Small businesses cannot afford, nor do they understand in detail, financial derivatives and futures contracts. The time factor stipulated in a futures contract may not be enough for the SME proprietor because the client may delay payment, thus collecting more interest on the money. It is better and less costly to allow more time, rather than make calculations on the presumption of prompt payment. Thus, Miss X builds in a time comfort factor that copes with payments that are not settled in full for, perhaps, six months to a year. Then again, she incorporates profit margins of 30–40 per cent rather than 10 per cent. This is a risk strategy for an SME; it is risk-absorption in practice. If Miss X is prepared to accept a lower margin on the whole transaction, she can form a temporary partnership for the sale, risk-sharing and splitting the payment 50–50.

Businesses can use threats, such as imposing 0.1 per cent interest per day on outstanding payments, or demand payment in 60 days or the deal is off; or they can always start a law suit. There are inducements, too, such as a 2 per cent reduction if the bill is settled in 30 days.

The key points for an SME are:

1 practicality (what can you afford?)
2 familiarity (understanding how to hedge against risk or cope with it)
3 internalization of risk (including confidentiality).

The emphasis must be on what is practical for the SME.

In managing project risk, we are increasingly more willing to take a wider view. Traditional college textbooks or strict engineering tactics have their limitations.

> 'Several factors have influenced this shift. First it is clear that typical classroom teaching may not be the most effective way to learn many of the admired business skills.'[16]

Skills may be bought outside a company, or outsourced. See Consultants, Chapter 6.

The UK Private Finance Initiative

The changing demographics of the western world are having a huge effect on public budgets. Ageing populations mean that the increasing proportion of older people, and their pensions, will have to be supported by a smaller working population. This has had a massive effect on public services and construction projects. There is a greater demand for healthcare services, and places to base them, and a need to fund the expansion of both public and private sector pensions. Many of these areas are being outsourced to the private sector, and it is now more common to find staff saving up with a private pension. It is no longer politically acceptable, nor economically feasible, to place such financial burdens on the relatively shrinking working population.

The aim of the Private Finance Initiative (PFI) is to transfer major project risk from the public sector to the private sector, for an agreed price, and the UK government has been keen to transfer a wide range of projects and their accompanying risks into private hands. This is intended to help reduce public expenditure burdens and to encourage the initiation of projects that would not have gone ahead if based on traditional methods of public–private sector collaboration. The PFI involves a form of structured trade finance with access to private long-term institutional finance on the markets. In successful cases, it can bring desired risk capital and risk management skills to public-private projects, avoiding dependence solely on public skills and purse-strings.

Accurate risk analysis and negotiation with contractors will be needed to create an appropriate balance of risks between the project parties. The public body involved would have to ensure that:

- the project is politically feasible and acceptable
- the project parties have the skills needed to control the various kinds of project risk
- the major project risks have actually been transferred to the private contractor
- the expenditure of this transfer is cost-effective compared with keeping it in the public sector
- the financial reserves of the contractor are adequate
- the contractor's quality and reliability have been investigated and ascertained
- unexpected financial strains on the project can be withstood by both parties.

The PFI has shown the need for accurate assessment of transferred risks and capital burdens. Acceptable criteria for performance quality – Performance

Bonds (see Chapter 5, p. 93) or Service Level Agreements[17] – and financing limits have to be drawn up to serve as the basis for selecting private sector bids – see Chapter 8, p. 153 (Invitation to Tender). When obstacles in a PFI deal are identified, appropriate professional advice should be obtained, for example from PFI-experienced actuaries, engineers or project managers.

Hospital construction has come under severe financial pressure because of the fast-rising demand for care against a progressively smaller working population. Similarly, public projects ranging from bridges, roads, schools and universities are faced with lower revenues from the traditional tax base. The solution points to public–private, or wholly private, project. The time-scale may be long: several years, perhaps, for a bridge, highway or building. The PFI is, in many ways, a form of trade financing. (See Chapter 9: Trade Finance).[18]

The PFI can be a successful way of ensuring the finished product is handed over to the customer on time and on budget. In some cases, it fails in the same way as other project methods, but what the PFI does is to change the ground rules as to who bears the burden. Whereas before a contractor might have passed on higher construction costs to a client, the new equation makes things more complicated for him. One factor about the PFI is that, while total government funding has not changed, contractors are probably not going to be able to get so much out of public funds. A contractor may build a hospital for a National Health Service trust. The trust will provide the healthcare facilities and functions, though the building is operated and financed by the contractor. It therefore becomes a collaborative venture between the trust and the contractor after the building is completed.

There are a few caveats when it comes to the PFI, however. When a big contractor seeks to become involved, he can easily deter any competition in the invitation to tender field. The big contractor may do so by having greater international backing for an integrated operation that includes construction, engineering, IT, and finance capabilities, as well as that great bidding quality – proven relevant project experience. Ironically, this poses a potential risk for the project owner, usually a government agency or council, if the PFI auction therefore attracts only a single bid. (See case studies on London's transport system, p. 174 and the UK law courts, p. 175). The bid, as it is the only one, may not be as low as desired. The length of the project and its purpose are politically-sensitive issues, as is the cost to the taxpayer.

The public body involved will be anxious to lay as much of the risk on the private contractor as possible, and to get maximum value for money. The risks and final cost should not be excessive for the public body, whether central government or local council, compared to what the cost would be by doing the same project in-house (if it could). The private sector players are keen to ensure that these costs and risks are not an unacceptable drain on their balance sheet. They may be given a licence to collect revenue from the finished product, and they will need to ensure that the period and conditions of the contract allow them to recoup their costs and make an adequate profit. Negotiating skills and a clear head for risks and costs are crucial.

> 'PFI projects are usually complex, requiring the interaction and integration of a multiplicity of agents, functions and time horizons ... Each of these individual organizations and the public body itself will have different corporate objectives, management structures, time horizons and risk profiles. A vast array of technical, legal, financial and organizational functions will have to be integrated. Risk analysis and management is crucial to the success of PFI projects.'[19]

PFI usually means a long-term commitment, although it is possible for the client to pull the plug mid-project. The contractor tends to recoup money on his investment somewhere in the fifth to seventh year on average, so a project cancelled before the pay-back period will show up as a loss. The contractor has to submit a bid that take these possible risk factors into account.

CASE STUDY

Privatization and the UK railways

PFI tries to be more than just a straightforward industrial privatization exercise. Selling off Britain's railways epitomizes elements of what can go wrong.

> 'The performance of our privatized railways is a national disgrace, with service reductions, failing performance, increased fares – despite having twice the subsidy that British Rail [the nationalized system] did.'[20]

The 25 privatized train operating companies have had an increased public subsidy of £2,000 million, and a record number of customer complaints have been lodged with the Central Rail Users' Consultative Committee.[21] Privatization has the benefit of reducing the workload of the public sector and the burden on the Exchequer's purse, but it still carries the risk of budget overruns and lower service performance. The combination of poorly drafted legislation and a meek regulator demonstrates the pitfalls of controlling a private industry that also relies on public subsidy.

The spirit of the PFI lies in a reasonable share of the funding burden, plus the risks, between the private and public sector while maintaining standards of service and performance. The high-speed rail link from the Channel Tunnel to King's Cross station in London is a classic example of major political and financial pitfalls that have not been fully resolved by the PFI. The key is an acceptable project risk-reward distribution – that is the theory and goal.

CASE STUDY

The London Underground and bus transport system

Years of underfunding in the world's oldest urban rail and bus transport system left London Underground with a projected requirement of £6000 million to provide for staff costs, new rolling stock, refurbishment of stations, tunnels and all capital equipment. It was unlikely that the British government would be inclined to fund this. The plan was to involve public and private companies to bear the load of urban transport needs. The 18-month delay in completing London's Jubilee Line extension, plus the maintenance problems of the new trains, underline the room for errors in project management. An overhaul like this has to be taken in careful steps.

The bus system was hived off from London Transport, the core public organization, and operating licences were then awarded to private bus companies. This had the effect of reducing the number of public sector workers, and cutting down on the public capital needed to invest in a large fleet of buses and associated infrastructure. Once again, as with the privatization of the national rail networks, the plan sounds good but the devil is in the detail. The costs of the new ticketing system for the Underground, with the microchip-based Smartcard, alone came to £1400 million under the PFI. The contract was awarded to Transys, a consortium of EDS and Cubic of the US, with ICL and WS Atkins of the UK. The contract was for a 17-year operating period, with the £1400 million to be recouped over this period. Under PFI, the contractor gets a substantial cut of the revenue generated by London Transport rail customers. This is similar to trade financing where the financier gets a proportion of future operating revenues. Transys is forecast to invest £200 million in the new system.

Government-backed bodies trade the flow of revenue against the large capital costs of investment; they pass the risks of construction and operation of the system to the consortium of contractors. As in all projects, there are hiccups, one being that the bidding process for this PFI contract was somewhat marred by the absence of competition. Rival consortia led by BT, IBM and Andersen Consulting pulled out of the bidding, leaving Transys in a one-horse race. This is not the idea of an ITT, where competition should give the client the best price. PFI, like many good ideas, needs to be applied properly if it is to be more than just a good idea.

Running a large project is a compromise between functionality, budget, time and skills available. A higher functional specification is always favoured initially by the client, but reality usually forces us to seek a balance through functional de-scoping or slimming down of the project ambitions. Whey trying to keep everything else fixed (i.e. time and money spent) higher functionality becomes almost synonymous with high risk. Let's take a look at a large UK government project that met this fate.

PFI in UK law courts

The PFI project for new IT systems to link magistrates' courts showed that inadequate control over projects can create poor results. The PFI bidding system is based on competitive tenders to come up with the best service and product at the best price. The magistrates' new IT system showed that PFI principles do not always deliver.[22] ICL and EDS competed for the contract, and the result was:

- system requirements were not properly defined, and specifications were not agreed
- EDS pulled out of the bidding
- ICL won the bid in a one-horse race
- the IT systems were not ready in time
- the courts had to continue to use a manual system for a longer period.

The users called this auction, with just one company bidding, a farce.

PFI and similar ITT processes cannot be said to give unquestionable value for money if there is no competition involved. What PFI has done is to intensify the need for risk management in projects. This applies to both the public commissioning body and the private contractor – both sides stand to lose or gain.

Project ownership

Britain's Post Office is an example of the quandary facing the country's public sector industries. It is burdened by relatively high labour costs and the threat from rivals in an increasingly competitive industry. Difficulties in the privatization issue include how a public company is sold off or how it receives public subsidies, although Post Office Counters Limited has made a profit.

The idea of selling the Post Office is an attractive one for many parties. A way of doing this could be to attract private shareholders, keep government involvement low, ensure the activities of the company are kept under control, and appease the trade unions. However, this is a political minefield.[23]

One option in potentially difficult projects is to avoid political infighting where possible; we have seen examples of conflict in earlier chapters. Another option is to take the bull by the horns. The choice is yours. One way of trying to make a project succeed is to bring project team members and associated players together. It is better to head off potential conflict at the start.

CASE STUDY

DSL & associates in a construction project

This was a large overseas project to build a bank. The goal was to create a dealing system for the bank that was to be operational very soon. The only way to keep a project on schedule is for strong leadership, often backed by a steering committee that keeps people involved. This means that you, as the project manager, occasionally have to be tough with opposing forces. There is a limit to how much agreement can be achieved by use of consensus and soft negotiating skills. The compromise is a balance between command and control versus democracy. Too heavy a hand in a project can stifle creativity and destroy staff morale. Too much democracy lets just about everyone have a say in the project; it seems fair, but it means the project may be put at risk through anarchy and loss of control. A correct balance lets project members feel involved, have a say in how the project is run, and have some influence over the final look of a new system or service. It does not give them the freedom to go their separate ways within the project. This particular bank project ran over the scheduled deadline slightly, but the system was delivered in good working order. It is better this way than delivering a poor working version or an unfinished product just to meet the deadline. The client should be convinced it is not worth jeopardizing the project simply to avoid minor delay, although a long delay is cause for worry. Full discussion and involvement of the client need not degenerate into arguments and project paralysis. Diplomacy and professionalism are the order of the day.

Mergers and acquisitions

Globalization brings the prospect of more mergers and buy-outs. We have already seen, for example, Citicorp-Travelers, BP-Amoco, Mercedes-Chrysler. Yet, according to the UK consultancy, Euro Business Management Ltd (EBM), M&A is risky. EBM says three-quarters of UK acquisitions fail to meet their financial targets. Reasons given include personality and culture clash, and a lack of leadership from the top.[24] When you go farther afield into emerging markets, such risks can have an even greater effect. See Risk management as a cultural issue, p. 136.

It is recommended that risk analysis, and thorough groundwork, is first carried out to see if both parties are compatible. It has become fashionable to go hunting for good targets or cheap deals. M&A has become more of an end in itself than a means. But it should be remembered that all that glitters is not necessary gold.[25]

> **CASE STUDY**

Cendant and the fraudulent accounts

Accounts are a valuable source of information for the project manager, especially when it comes to assessing the financial health of a company or investment project. Unfortunately, DSL experience in the emerging markets leads us to conclude that accounts and financial statements have to be taken with a fair pinch of salt. We may not believe religiously what we are told even in advanced western markets. A case in point is that of Cendant, known as CUC, which owned Avis Car Rentals. CUC was also involved in the attempted takeover of the Royal Automobile Club (RAC) and the National Car Parks (NCP) in the UK. CUC suffered a $20 billion market price implosion when facts came to light that contradicted the earlier rosy picture painted by their official accounts. Take a careful look at the true financial health of a company or investment before you sink money into your project.

Until Cendant's spectacular implosion in April 1998, investors believed America had the toughest accounting standards in the world. Evidence uncovered by Arthur Andersen at CUC '... suggests that 61 per cent of net income was simply made up. So much for US accounting standards ... accounting standards are only ever as tough as the accountants who are enforcing them.'[26]

Take-over procedures for corporations

A lack of proper communication, or finance, risks killing off fruitful corporate relationships. A firm that takes over a target company does not want to find that the best staff jump ship.

> *'In many companies, communication systems consist of relationships that have built up over time between customers and sales people or employees and management.'*[27]

There is a standard *modus operandi* in the take-over or merger process. Secrecy is paramount during search and negotiations before the official corporate marriage. Rumours or indiscreet revelations will be sufficient to raise the share price of the target company, perhaps to a level that makes the planned take-over no longer appear viable. If the merger or take-over still goes ahead, the loss of secrecy can cost the initiator millions in additional costs.

There are some obvious steps to running a sensitive project:

- keep the project team small
- limit the takeover-associated data on a need-to-know basis. Separate the groups involved as much as possible, so that outsiders cannot easily obtain a full picture of the impending take-over (see Chinese walls, p. 169)

● make sure your take-over activities, for example due diligence, are low-profile.

The clash of personalities in arguments over the split of company power is a serious threat to corporate success. The business world is strewn with the wreckage of failed corporate merger projects. The differences between the two chairmen, Jan Leschly at Smith-Kline Beecham and Sir Richard Sykes at Glaxo Wellcome, are well documented within the examples of merger failures. The personal and corporate cultural differences blew the proposed union apart. Smith-Kline Beecham stated the reasons as a dispute over top management and the allocation of responsibilities in the new combined company, plus 'corporate and philosophical differences'.[28]

There were serious risks to be faced when two tough and competitive chairmen have to decide who will be the new top man in the combined group. 'The main problem for corprorate mergers is deciding the management structure of the combined company and many have faltered on this primary point. Beyond that, merging two different corporate cultures successfully is very difficult and many mergers have not delivered the expected advantages.'[29]

Merger and acquisition projects may be attractive propositions, but they can also be fraught with potential risk.

The euro in business

The role of the euro in risk management is one that is evolving rapidly. The euro has the benefits of a bigger capitalized currency in that it has the backing of the reserves and might of the ECB rather than much smaller individual banks. We have seen the downside risk of currency turmoil where central banks such as the Banks of England, Italy, Sweden or France have felt compelled to defend their currencies by selling foreign reserves. The euro, at least until the disappearance of EMU member currencies in 2002, is the synthetic equivalent of investing in a basket of currencies and, thereby, spreading the risk. The aim is a fairly obvious one of safety in numbers.

The euro can act as a hedge when either side in a deal feels threatened by unfavourable currency risk. Settlement may be stipulated in a stable currency. Formerly, Swiss francs were a favourite; the US dollar is the front-runner for this role in Russia. Obviously, settling in euros is beneficial for companies in the EU, and also for many outside – as long as the euro proves to be a stable currency in the long term. A single-owner business might find that such trans-action arrangements are easy in theory, but a bit more expensive to set up. The amount of risk varies from country to country, but it is safe to say that in countries like Russia, traders may feel more secure when payment is made in the euro rather than in the rouble. Nevertheless, billing and settling in euros is not a full project risk management strategy in itself. The euro was looking weak after falling from $1.17 in January 1999, then approached parity at $1.02 in July 1999. EU exporters having to settle their obligations by buying US dollars in mid-1999 would have suffered a large knock to their account. Managing project risk entails having a clear idea of how long your exposure will be.

Within the EU, project owners will find that there are other factors apart from currency risk that affect how they do business with partners. Take retail banking. There is a whole range of cultural, legal and regulatory reasons why consumers are reluctant to buy their mortgages, life assurance and pensions outside their own countries. The arrival of the euro is not, by itself, expected to change this.

> *'The currency differential is the smallest one a bank faces in deciding whether to move across a border. There are other issues such as brand, access to customers and distribution ... The single currency doesn't make people more open-minded about using unknown brands.'*[30]

Quality of service, including local presence for point of contact, non-delivery risk and counter-party risk are main factors that affect how we do business in a foreign country, even a European one. A price may look good in terms of euros, but there are other considerations. We recommend that you examine these risk factors before you do business in another country.

The advent of the euro cuts down much of the perceived currency risk. It raises the degree of price transparency in Europe and enables people to shop around. This means that currency flows are considered more convenient and safer. The property market, for example, is well-placed to take advantage of the relaxed currency flow. One of the benefits is that people can shop around for the best buys. Another area is that of EU car prices, which the British government is investigating.[31] Prices are high in the UK compared to, say, Belgium, Ireland or Portugal. It also means that a French-made Peugeot can be more expensive in France than in other EU countries. This two-tier pricing will be reduced, although it may not disappear completely. Such a system means that project managers can shop farther afield for labour and materials, which can bring substantial project cost savings. However, project managers are also faced with the prospect of greater counter-party risk when going farther afield. This comes from operating in markets which are unfamiliar, particularly if they do not understand the language, nor have significant reliable agents and contacts there. (See Counter-party risk, p. 54.)

As regards the property market, instead of making large local investments in real estate, companies and individuals can transfer their funds to invest in a portfolio of international properties.

> *'Property investors are starting to think that European economic and monetary union will bring fundamental changes to the way property is bought and sold. And they reckon EMU will change the way occupiers own and manage their real estate assets.'*[32]

The euro lets property dealers invest in several countries. It certainly has a lot of significance for managers of projects that have a large percentage of property costs.

Notes and references

1 Chicken, J. C. and Posner (1994) *Managing Project Risks in Major Projects*, Chapman & Hall, p. 71.

2 *Financial Times*, 15 June 1998.

3 Carter, T., Project Finance Manager, Halliburton, Brown & Root, UK (1999).

4 *Financial Times*, 24 November 1998, p. 18.

5 *Financial Times*, 24 November 1998, p. 18.

6 *Financial Times*, 24 November 1998, p. 18.

7 *Financial Times*, 4 December 1998, p. 32.

8 Galitz, L. (1994) *Financial Engineering*, Financial Times Pitman Publishing and Holiwell, J. (1998) *The Financial Risk Manual*, Financial Times Pitman Publishing.

9 *Financial Times*, 2 October 1998, p. 14.

10 Barakat, Dr. M., personal correspondence, December 1998. Dr Barakat is a world expert on financial modelling and risk management analysis. He is the creator of the MBRM risk management software package.

11 *The Times*, 10 October 1998, Business News, p. 29.

12 *Financial Times*, 2 October 1998, p. 15.

13 Chong, Y. Y. (1997) *Risk Management in Russia and the Baltic States*, FT Publications, p. 122.

14 Chong, Y. Y. (1999) 'Long-term capital management and financial control', published on-line by Global Association of Risk Professionals (GARP) on www.garp.com

15 *The Times*, 17 October 1998, Business Section, p. 25.

16 *Financial Times*, 2 August 1998, p. 12.

17 The risk of unsatisfactory project performance can be mitigated by formulating a Service Level Agreement (SLA) with your contractor. The criteria may be defined in various ways, for example, all computers must be available on-line 99.5 per cent of the working year; 98 per cent of buses or trains to arrive within 8 minutes of published timetable times; 95 per cent of all meals to be delivered to customers within 20 minutes with fewer than 100 letters of complaint per year. The targets set in the SLA are performance gateways over which the contractors must successfully cross. Failing this, you as project manager or the client can refuse to pay them 100 per cent of fees or to renew their contract.

18 See, for example, *Constructor's Key Guide to PFI* (1998) Construction Industry Council, Thomas Telford, London.

19 RAMP, 1998, p. 46.

20 Prescott, J., Deputy Prime Minister, October 1998

21 The *Observer*, 11 October 1998, Business Section, p. 7.

22 *Computer Weekly*, 30 July 1998, p. 1.

23 *Financial Times*, 22 October 1998, p. 8.

24 Czarnecki, T., Euro Business Management, personal correspondence, January 1998.

25 See, for example, *The Economist*, 9 January 1999, 'How to make mergers work'.

26 *The Times*, 14 August 1998.

27 *Financial Times*, 16 October 1998, Mergers and Acquisitions, p. 6.

28 *Financial Times*, 24 February 1998, p. 1.

29 *The Herald*, UK, 25 February 1998.

30 *Financial Times*, 18 December 1998.

31 *Financial Times*, 18 March 1998, p. 1.

32 *Financial Times*, 22 October 1998, p. 21.

Technology platforms in risk management

Protection of intellectual property rights

Standards and risk management toolkits

Project management toolkits

Practical projects and IT developments for SMEs

" Vorschprung durch Technik "

Protection of intellectual property rights

One of the main aims of using risk management is to keep your operations running safely. Another goal is to keep one step ahead of your rivals through competitive advantage. This one step ahead may embody a technological innovation or invention. This invariably involves protection of intellectual property rights and, often, the application for patents or copyright.

Patents are usually in operation for a maximum of 15 years, depending on law and jurisdiction. Legal issues naturally arise over the drafting of the patent and to what extent it can be legally enforced. There are instances when the potential value of a technical asset has been lost. The jet engine, the ball-point pen and, more recently, Rubik's cube have been available to all and sundry. Dispute over the copyright of major books or software have been in the news regularly. There used to be a more laissez-faire attitude to patents and copyright in technological pioneering. Take aerospace for example.

> '*In the 1960s NASA patent policy was that any patent from contractual effort required a free licence for governmental use. Thus, there was no strong management interest in patents; rather, there was the prestige value for the individual engineer, which often led to patent activity.*'[1]

Patents and copyrights are now big business. There is less room for haphazard ways of protecting intellectual property. DSL experience of intellectual property rights for small businesses has found how difficult comparatively large projects can be for them. The steps that lead to granting a patent from the initial research are quite trying for small enterprises. Expenditure on registration, time and labour can be large for smaller firms. This can pose a budgetary risk for a project.

The key is to gear your company for silent running during the critical phases of research and development. You need to know the exact nature of what you want to patent, and in which country. Whatever it is you want protected must be novel;

i.e. you need to carry out a search to find out if it has already been created and patented. This may involve many patent applications in different countries, whereby your national patent office copies them and sends them to countries you have specified. Consult an expert or documentation.[2] You would be advised not to publicly disclose your invention or innovation until you are ready. Just before a patent is applied for, and before it is granted, is the crucial period when a product is most vulnerable. Yet venture capitalists and potential backers are unwilling to provide funding without evidence of a patent. For services, there is also the same period when an innovation is vulnerable. There is the same need to keep the lid on the project. Go public only when you know you are covered.

A project needs a consistent policy and resources to safeguard intellectual property. This should be done as a matter of course, and built into the business plan at the outset, rather than just as an afterthought. The sale of pirate software in shops in China or Russia, or internationally through the Internet, gives cause for concern. According to US figures, the country's international sales of software and entertainment products totalled $60.2 billion in 1996; this is more than any other US industry.[3] But these figures do not include the billions lost to illegal copies and unpaid copyright fees.

The extension of global trading brings nations together under trade blocs regulated by, for instance, GATT and its successor, the World Trade Organization. The WTO deals with the removal or reduction of tariffs, import quotas and other trade barriers. One condition for trade membership entails the subscription by countries to laws protecting copyright. Organizations such as FAST (Firms Against Software Theft) were set up to police the extensive use of pirated software. The threat of law suits has changed the tactics of some manufacturers in this multi-billion dollar industry as they adapt towards producing look alike and imitation goods rather than 100 per cent counterfeit items. This practice occurs, for example, on a large scale, e.g. in Mexico, and anti-pirating professionals in the US have their work cut out.[4]

Table 10.1 ● Pirating in practice

Product category	Amount lost through piracy ($m)	Per cent pirated
Software	$265	82%
Cassettes and CDs	$70	50%
Videotapes	$55	55%
University textbooks	$35	25%

Source: International Intellectual Property Alliance, 1998

The practice occurs particularly in Russia and China where firms operate outside western legal jurisdiction and local authorities are reluctant to crack down on culprits.[5] This is not something that will go away and it harms the revenue stream of any company that produces an easily-counterfeited article. Nevertheless Microsoft chief Bill Gates and others are on the prowl. Western companies have to keep up the pressure, and anti-piracy scouts are on patrol, but their costs should be factored into a project's budget if it is thought there is a piracy risk.

Standards and risk management toolkits

One of the keys to project success is to use the right people and the right tools for the job.

CASE STUDY

RAF Tornado aircraft

People still recollect the bravery of Allied armed forces during Operation Desert Storm in the Gulf War in 1991. Allied air forces had simply defined projects or goals – to fly over Iraqi territory and render targets out of action. Yet it is generally forgotten that the RAF lost four aircraft. These were designed for possible war in Europe against the former USSR. They were switched to roles in the desert against Iraq. Unfortunately, the RAF aircraft were brought down by anti-aircraft fire – pilots had to fly over Iraqi airfields to bomb them, as the RAF had no adequate remote stand-off missiles to bomb the enemy airfields from a distance. Conversely, the US F117A fighter-bombers suffered no losses, partly because of Stealth mechanisms and their low radar and heat signatures.

Why standards?

Companies may operate several projects at the same time. It is often difficult to see which ones return the highest profit if there is no project-specific accounting. Projects run under different conditions, and are not always deemed to be directly comparable. Thus, there will be different operating criteria, and few institutional standards for comparison. Many companies do not have a full picture of where their value is; i.e. which departments, staff or production processes really make the profits. Therefore, it is difficult to implement corporate-wide risk management where few standards for comparison exist. When you transfer staff, they will have to learn a whole new set of procedures. This is time-consuming and expensive. It is also essential that your company establish some standard on project performance. Sometimes forgotten in the rush into a project is the need to maintain competence in that particular field; i.e. the need to keep your company in a business that it understands.

Klaus Winkler, project manager with Telepassport, Germany, has views on the importance of effective risk management in maintaining good staff direction on a project and keeping good client relations.

> *'How important is it to set priorities and tell team members and customers where they stand and what the priorities for the project are? I can say: Very important! There are always a lot of good projects going on, but you have to concentrate on your core competence. That is why it is sometimes valuable to include a consultant in the group to get some know-how not available in the company.'*

Two key points raised here are:

- stick to what you know (i.e. your core skills and market competences)
- outsource the skills that your project really needs and cannot find in-house.

This has already been highlighted in a variety of case studies. At DSL we found that some firms we worked with on major projects did not pay sufficient attention to:

- establishing performance standards
- measuring standards
- remedial action or enforcement where failure had been diagnosed.

CASE STUDY

GTE and US army telecommunications

US military telecommunications were rather in disarray. The US Army used 5 000 different radio and telecoms units, with different hardware and software, and they did not talk too well to each other. Standards in telecommunications were called for. The Army specified that the winning contractor had to take responsibility for and therefore the risk in systems acquisition, production, implementation and testing. It was said that the Army was seeking developed working telecommunications systems; it was far less concerned with state-of-the-art R&D projects that carried high risk of non-delivery or under-performance.

GTE won its tender in the Army's sealed bid auction. GTE's bid had to satisfy 19 essential performance features, which it did. GTE met 69 of the 82 desired nice-to-have features too. The standardization programme was successfully implemented for the Army to test the system in the only place where it could be proved beyond doubt – war. During the Gulf War, GTE's system ran without major problems, except for 45 minutes of down-time.[6]

Standards and certification do not guarantee that the job will be done well, within budget, or on time. Some project practitioners may feel that the use of government quality standards will help ensure good quality projects. If only things were so simple. Risk management may be explicit in government standards and in PRINCE 2 project methodology. But PRINCE 2 is a methodology for project structure and control, it is not risk management per se. International standards will favour the bigger firms in the ITT process. This may be what the client wants. It may be that he or she wants a big firm for the comfort factor. You may believe big firms have the resources to pay out non-performance penalties or large damages in law suits. That is the theory.

Project management toolkits

Here we examine some of the various toolkits and IT packages. Some appropriate project solutions require a good mind and discipline. They all rely, to varying extents, upon the same set of basic project management principles. You have to select the right package for the job. Technology will not bring you success by itself. It is imperative that you:

● analyze the needs of your project

● have a good idea of what you are trying to do with toolkits

● have a good idea of how much you are prepared to pay

● understand what is available on the market

● be prepared to put effort into separating sales claims from real performance.

Project management and IT platforms

The importance of IT in project management means that the reliability and resilience of computer-based systems become essential for project success. The IT risk comes in the hardware and software (operating system and applications programmes); if your system fails then it could be your project's welfare that is on the line.

This poses questions about the risk impact of IT systems failure, or if your IT functions are not operating to your desired quality level. This is generally categorized within Operational Risk.

What we think of Microsoft Project Manager as a small toolkit does not constitute risk management in itself. If anything this is a project management documentation software package. It may be quite handy because it is portable and inexpensive and can run on a small desktop PC or laptop computer onsite. All project team staff can input their relevant information at their various project sites. What such toolkits do well is to help you document what project tasks are running, who is involved, how long they are working, how much you have spent, and approximately how much you have left to go on a project. You may choose to use Microsoft PM as main scheduler and budgeter for the project line workers. The benefits are that such software packages are easily available in computer stores and from IT dealers. There are lots of people experienced to some extent in using such packages, which also have relatively low per unit licence fees for tactical planning compared to larger packages such as ABT or Hoskyns PMW. If you already have, or plan to purchase, a risk management software toolkit, you can collect the raw data from your project team and dump it into your risk management toolkit for an overview and analysis. It may be the most cost-effective way of getting an overview. From it, you will be able to get a snap-shot of where project plan deviations and risk lie.

Some of the best-run projects use fairly simple computers and software. They are, however, backed up by good planning and administrative staff. For example: Company X uses ABT as a main number cruncher; the raw data is input at the project team leader level. He or she will put raw time sheets, schedules and budgets into Microsoft Project Manager, then drop them into a big ABT vat to scrunch into a more refined analysis. Why? When talking magnitudes of cost, a single-user licence can cost $5000–$10000 for a software package such as ABT's. Microsoft Project Manager is a fairly standard off-the-shelf box that costs about $150. It is not fancy, but then, project management is not a fancy-dress ball. A lot of project management and risk management is the strictly tedious checking and controlling of work and data flow. Microsoft Project Manager can handle these basic data types.

Project risk management is a reality check. It puts road-signs on the route, and an occasional toll-booth in the way. The signs point you to where you should go. The toll-booth tells you that you have to pay something at this appropriate point. You will need to pay attention, devote time, assign staff, deploy resources and raw materials. There will be considerable amounts of paperwork – it's not for fun.

Practical projects and IT developments for SMEs

There are many IT options or toolkits available for industry, with some attractively priced for small firms or self-employed businesses. The SoHo market (Small office, Home office) is a rapid growth sector that accounted for some 5 million PCs sold in Europe in 1997, representing some $8.5 billion in sales.[7] This represents a burgeoning sector of people gathered around their PC and printer with fax, Internet and other accessories to run a business. Nevertheless, the growth of the SoHo market does not seem to show any corresponding development in risk management for SMEs.

SMEs can try to manage their risk by buying an IT system or PC. Most SMEs do this already, and SoHos are no exception. Such enterprises may develop into a successful business partly due to a sound IT foundation. SoHos and SMEs have to consider essential cost-benefit analysis under strict budgets and tight schedules. This should apply irrespective of the nature of the project involved.

Questions that must be asked about an IT system are:

1 why do we need it?

2 what are we trying to achieve with it?

3 can we afford it?

4 who is going to use it?

5 how long will it take to obtain?

6 who will install it?

7 what do we do with it after she/he has finished?

The need to reassure the SME owner is paramount if he is to use IT successfully, or if he starts it at all. Hewlett-Packard created its Spotlight program to target SME operators.[8] It found that SMEs had three reasons that prevented the buying of IT:

● fear that buying IT equipment would not solve business problems

● fear that their IT system would soon be obsolete

● reluctance to deal with IT suppliers far away.

HP saw that people were being risk-averse, and for very good reasons. A SoHo that cannot type letters, invoices, tax returns and other correspondence is rather dead in the water. The fear is not simply whether they could afford $500. The real fear is whether:

● the business is hostage to an IT system that it does not understand

● it takes a lot of time and effort to install and use

● the business will fail if the IT system crashes.

Thus, for SMEs, and SoHos in particular, the relevance of project management and risk management toolkits starts becoming more of an academic question. There are few dedicated management systems that are aimed at the SME sector. Nevertheless, there are various IT packages that lessen the potential risk of project failure for the SME and SoHo sector.

Quicken, SAGE and other accounting packages help to reduce financial downside risk, if only as a basic tool to keep some track over accounts payable, accounts receivable and cash-flow. These budgeting tools can be written in basic spreadsheet packages such as Lotus 1-2-3, Excel or Corel WP2000

Office. Some free accounting software is also available on the Internet under the shareware facilities. Keisha can help with inflow and outflow of materials, plus use of money and staff within the SME hierarchy. Schedule+ or the newer Outlook can help to plan your time and organize important appointments. This system functionality can also be written in spreadsheet packages or listed in Word or WordPerfect or your other WP system. Once again software is available free of charge on the Internet in the shareware section.

The principle is that SMEs do not have to try to re-invent the wheel, nor do they have to spend huge sums on IT equipment and software that they cannot use. There is a lot of choice on the market that is low-priced or offered free of charge. One may be the one for you. The lesson for big and small firms is – shop around.

The Internet

We have taken a brief look at the market in project risk management products and services. One of the best ways to get information on what is available is through the Internet. Supplier information sites scanned with an appropriate browser make market research easier; some useful web addresses (URLs) are in the appendix. Computer networks and the Internet remain powerful tools to help accumulate data to manage projects, but they remain only tools. The web sites referred to in the appendix give contact Internet addresses for companies and experts. The downside to this usefulness is that ease of access through the Internet may pose security risks for a company. The Internet can be a Trojan Horse.

'The internet, with its direct, unregulated access to customers, is popular for financial scams.'[9]

A survey revealed that 73 per cent of companies had a security breach or computer data theft over one year.[10] Around 1600 IT staff in 50 countries were asked about security risk in relation to use of Internet/e-commerce. A majority of companies (60 per cent), suffered security breaches from their own staff (see Operational risk, p. 59). About the same proportion suffered security breaches from increased use of e-commerce, where customer details and even monetary transactions are transmitted over the Internet. The clear message is that the open Internet highway is double-edged: you benefit from access to market information, but you also leave the company open to greater risk of being a victim of commercial data abuse or theft. The danger comes partly from a poor risk attitude, and from the uncertainty that arises when security staff discover there has been a breach of IT security.

'While they know security is important, they have not been able to monitor the damage or pinpoint potential issues before they turn into substantial problems.'[11]

191

There can be a confusing chain of events:

1 senior staff are unaware of security lapses
2 senior staff are unaware who, or what, caused the security breach
3 even if they knew, they may not have a complete security procedure defined
4 if they wanted to apprehend or punish the offender, they may not have the funding, authority, resources or training to do so. This would be even more difficult if the guilty party had used another person's Internet name, or a made-up name, or lives in another country where there is no proper jurisdiction.

How useful is the Internet for project management? There is no doubt that the Internet raises the potential for it. It helps to make the project easier to manage in some ways, such as getting feedback, and monitoring in remote locations. Yet the openness of the Internet leaves projects vulnerable to penetration and to leaks in security on the internal company intranet.

Enterprise resource planning (ERP) and data warehousing

Companies have made strategic reviews of their use of resources over the past few years. Data warehousing in integrated databases can show the inefficiencies in flow of resources and work. The trend towards the accumulation of information in linked databases allows such useful information to be datamined. Questions can include: Where were the most important paying customers located over the past six months? Who tends to give us the lowest prices for our raw goods in NE Europe?

Large data warehouses extend the database concept, but do not change the overall IT principle. They aim to raise the chance of finding the desired answers through an intense process of data mining. Should it matter to you? Well, if your company or one of your clients has devoted itself to ERP, it would seem a good idea to keep tabs on what they are doing, and how well they are doing.

Companies have been given the chance to install Enterprise Resource Planning in the form of electronic supply chain management systems. These can be adept at pinpointing the answers to such pertinent questions. ERP systems such as SAP, Oracle, Baan or Peoplesoft can integrate supply chains in order to maximize useful data retained at the corporate headquarters, and to exercise greater cost control over resource flows. However, the integration process makes ERP companies particularly vulnerable.[12] They adopted ERP systems that allow people with IT access, authorized or unauthorized, to get massive amounts of data about customers, staff, goods and revenue flows. Yet there are benefits from ERP.

Klaus Winkler runs international projects using ERP.[13]

'Telepassport are using Navision. The cost benefits are that you have a standard tool for all the activities of the company and thus make them more compatible and comparable. The dangers to company security are no higher than the risk from all the other software.'

The key is that ERP is a tool, i.e. a means to an end. In many firms, however, the introduction of ERP constitutes a major project in itself, entailing large capital and training expenditure. Another point is that ERP can help to establish a standard for operations and data exchange; in this sense, it is more of a platform that can assist the project to run more smoothly and efficiently. Quite possibly, ERP can let your project run with less risk – if it is implemented correctly.

CASE STUDY

British Telecom and its data warehouse

This is essentially a large database of some four terabytes of optical disk storage; this amounts to something in the region of 1000 PCs of information on a single database. The BT data warehouse system was designed by Business Objects on Hewlett Packard UNIX computers. Data concerning up to 1000 calls per second is collated from various exchanges around the country and dropped down to the main computer centre at Ipswich. The data is automatically processed using an expert system to fit it into a common data format. The result enables the customer, BT, to make fast, flexible and intelligent queries and reports on its customer base.[14]

ERP and data warehousing do have their occasional disappointments and failures. They do not replace effective risk management in projects. Merely possessing more information on a central database does not necessarily mean that you are using data better. Inevitably, the company must be faced with the decision on whether to put in project risk management systems, hopefully before someone tries to penetrate corporate security. The security risk is down to the break in commitment between risk analysis and risk management implementation; it seems that many companies managing projects fall down in both camps.

There is also the risk that the IT project will not live up to expected performance levels, particularly if the expectations were too unrealistic. An enterprise should be driven by business needs, rather than being completely driven by technology. At the end of a project perhaps the question should be asked: 'It looks very nice, but what is it for, and why did we spend so much money?' Project risk management is not subordinate to, nor is it replaced by, technology. A company that wishes to have more technology does not control project risk per se, it makes the type and nature of the risks different.

Project risk management principles will never go out of fashion, nor will they become outdated, whatever the level of technology.

Notes and references

1 Kolker, M., personal correspondence, December 1998.
2 *Patent Protection* (1998) The Patent Office, UK or World Intellectual Property Organization www.wipo.int
3 US Commerce Department Statistics, 1998.
4 *Wall Street Journal*, 3 December 1998, p. 4.
5 *Financial Times*, 5 December 1998, p. 7.
6 *Project Management Network*, January 1992.
7 *Financial Times*, 2 December 1998, p. 13.
8 *Financial Times*, 2 December 1998, p. 13.
9 *Financial Times*, 2 October 1998, World Economy supplement, p. 8.
10 IT survey, Price Waterhouse Coopers/*Information Week*, 1 September 1998.
11 IT survey, Price Waterhouse Coopers/*Information Week*, 1 September 1998.
12 *Financial Times*, 1 September 1998, 'Security risk increased by e-commerce'.
13 Winkler, K., Project Manager Interconnection, TelePassport Service GmbH, Germany.
14 British Telecom and Business Objects, 1996.

11

Risk management – a hard choice for a soft science

" Enough of science and of art "

William Wordsworth

A lot of risk management in practice involves analysis but less implementation, i.e. more words and less action. Companies behave like living organisms in many respects; there are many concurrent projects running within the body. All these projects, and their requisite personnel, have individual characteristics and emotions. It is, therefore, difficult to come up with a homogeneous textbook to conduct corporate risk management.

The problem is that of a risk culture, or a management culture that is unwilling to embrace proper risk management. We have already seen this in western and eastern Europe for varying reasons. One major problem for project risk management is that it is viewed as a cost and not a profit. The perception is that risk management adds costs and detracts from the firm's profits. During a lean time or a recession, risk management staff and admin personnel will be among the first to be laid off. There is a tendency to select the lower-profile workers who do not seem to bring in profits. Sometimes, calling in the risk management experts is as welcome as calling in the rat-catcher. First, you have to accept that there might be a problem; second, you have to act. Some managers prefer to ignore the problem and the possible social stigma of calling in the 'rat-catcher'.

We have to try to ensure that risk management is an intrinsic and constant part of the project cycle. Risk management is, in many ways, a soft science, not a hard mix of number-crunching to a pre-set formula. If anything, business needs a more human view of risk management. Projects cannot operate in isolation from the other mainstream management skills. Hana Bishop's eagle's top view of information systems gives us this list of project success factors in the UK health service:

- chief executive commitment
- clinician's active involvement, enthusiasm and 'buy-in'
- clarity of purpose – well iterated objectives
- ability to change

- evidence of benefit
- good relationship with suppliers
- good project management
- realistic setting of expectations
- key performance indicators – clear, quantifiable and measurable
- well defined, structured contract
- managed expectations.

Risk management is meant to help your company operate more safely, or to evaluate risks better in order to make higher profits. It is not designed to slow your company to a dead pace. There are times when the process and those associated with it, such as due diligence, are not feasible. Piper Alpha is one example where risk management may be seen to have been a low priority. When secrecy, budgeting or expedience are the order of the day, even a slimmed-down risk management may get the desired results.[1]

Risk modelling and simulation

There are fundamental desirable properties for any project management modelling product or exercise. It must be:

1 **Realistic,** that is to say accurately mirroring the aims of the company and the project team. It must apply to the situation being studied without the need for unrealistic assumptions. A model has to get away from the 'in an ideal world' or 'all other things being equal' premises that dog unrealistic economic models;

2 **Capable,** i.e. it can handle different time horizons, events such as currency devaluation, interest rate changes, strikes, non-delivery of materials, etc.

3 **Modifiable,** i.e. it can be altered readily to cope with new operating regulations or other desired risk levels;

4 **Easy to use** – it should not tie up too many people in training, and should be simple for the end-user to implement and understand;

5 **Economical,** i.e. it should not cost a great deal in relation to the whole project. The cost of collecting data, creating the model, testing and demonstrating it should be a low proportion of the total project cost;

6 **Computable** in some format; most companies would require the results duplicated, transmitted or processed in computer-ready format.

Elementary risk modelling for computers

With the growing trend for PC-based modelling, it is tempting to put the above into a machine-ready format. Thus, we need to sum the above risk elements:

Sum [(political risk × its probability) + (market risk × its probability) + (credit risk × its probability) + (operational risk × its probability) + a residual factor or other unspecified or unknown risk]

Total Risk = Σ R_i × $Prob_i$

where

R_i is the risk exposure and $Prob_i$ is the likelihood of the outcome happening.

This tends to assume that all risks are discrete and independent variables. Unfortunately, to add to the difficulties of computer modelling, the risk factors can be difficult to enumerate and can be very subjective. It is difficult to ascribe mathematical values to the prediction of the elements, such as the weather or a natural disaster; these are usually calculated on an extrapolation of past data. The elements of incompetence or corruption are very important but are difficult to ascribe with any objectivity. They exist, but it is difficult to enter them in hard data form.

Then again, you can come up with an objective solution to mathematical problem, e.g. the four-colour map puzzle. This postulates that you can colour in any 2-D map using only four colours such that no two contiguous countries have the same colour. But we could ask some pertinent questions:

1 What use is this theory?

2 What mathematical proof is there?

3 Is this mathematical proof really provable?

Of these, the last one is the most pithy, and it is certainly of great relevance to all of those who are less numerate. But then, even the most numerate Nobel prize-winner may be a party to a great modelling botch too.

'Black box' risk management

One might reasonably ask, where was risk management in this operation? Merton and Scholes (of the renowned Black-Scholes model for options pricing) and their mathematical models seemed to have the answers to price bonds and derivatives. Much of this advanced modelling is more like rocket science. The use of squiggly and unfamiliar symbols reflects the use of Greek letters α, β, γ, τ etc. to denote various mathematical values.

Because of its arcane and obscure origins, such models are sometimes called 'black boxes'. This means you put in raw data to extract a value of risk or return at the other end. It is sometimes difficult to question exactly where the model could go wrong because this requires specific skills and quite a lot of time.

Risk management in any project should use models that can be understood.

> *'Models after all are just a tool. Taking a speedometer as an analogy, if it shows you are doing 40, that in itself does not indicate if you are too fast or too slow. You need to know what is happening in the street around you (i.e. are you on a fast moving highway, or in rush hour city centre traffic?).'*[2]

This school of thought favours the use of complex mathematical formulae, and the input of extensive computer power and technical skills, where the subject matter is very specialized. Sometimes (more often than not) we get a conclusion or advice from this modelling that is difficult to understand. It is not so much than we do not comprehend the conclusion, it may be very straightforward, e.g. *'It's a great product – buy it now!'* Rather, we are unable to follow the derivation of the recommendation, i.e. 'How on earth did you arrive at this conclusion?' This, as much, is the essence of the arcane art of Black Box risk management.

Most projects offer the choice of presenting the prevailing risk factors in a more 'human' format. For example, Analytic Hierarchy Process (AHP)[3] presents the factors in such a way that they can be read easily, and can be assigned weights and values for easy calculation and simulation by computer models. The AHP basic model can be used to select from a series of options for a company faced with three project choices:

1 Continue with basic existing system
2 Work on an upgrade of the present system
3 Initiate a new system.

The AHP computation will be along the lines of those shown in Fig. 11.1.

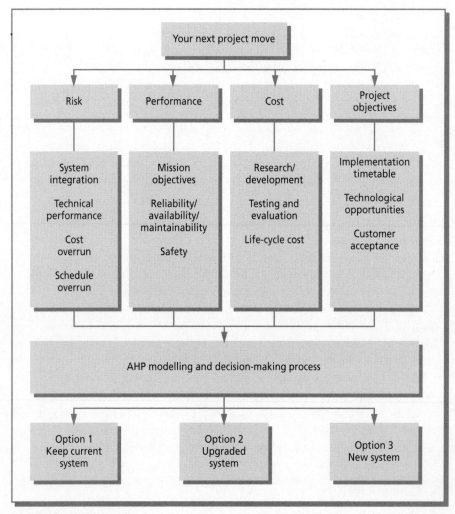

Fig 11.1 ● Project options

AHP presents the data in human-ready and computer-ready data format. The weighting and interaction of the project components is generally easier to understand, and the overall model logic can be grasped. However, a computer-based model may over-simplify project risk to come up with evaluations, e.g. 'you have a low risk' or 'the likelihood of failure is 0.05 per cent'. Modelling is poor or open to question where unsuitable assumptions or weak reasoning can be shown. We cannot ignore the overwhelming need for sharpness of human thought and judgement backed by hard proof. Mathematical models should be only assistants or tools in the decision-making process.

Deterministic versus Stochastic models

These are sometimes construed as the two great opposing schools of theory. Deterministic models take a set of inter-linked variables, outline some assumptions, then conclude that there will be some end result. For example, economic theory can take factors of $120 billion fixed capital formation, a 3.5 per cent GDP government budget deficit, 10.5 per cent interest rates and assume *ceteris paribus* (everything else being equal) to postulate a 2.8 per cent economic growth rate and 9.2 per cent unemployment. 'Chartist' analysts who extrapolate price movements to predict future prices are classic students of the determinist school. They have many tools in their box to define moving averages, trends, support levels and plateaus. Then again, we have to remember the small writing at the bottom of a packet of shares: *'Past performance is not guarantee of future results. The share price can go down as well as up.'*

Stochastic models take a very different approach. These are less fixed in assuming 'this is what will happen (B) from a given premise (A)'. Instead, they use a variety of simulations of real life to obtain data which they believe have some predictive powers for their model. Thus they can use some random data to simulate activities such as trading of shares on a stock exchange, or use laboratory mice running around a maze to predict what human beings would do in a closed space.

Monte Carlo simulation comes from the school of trial, run once and run many times. Daniel Bernouilli examined the nature of probability and human rationality 260 years ago. Once again, dice crept into the analysis as the guinea pig for his experimentation, now called Bernouilli trials. His analysis was based on the theoretical model of a variable behaving in certain ways over a time series. To prove that his example was not random, he came from a family in which eight remarkable mathematicians sprang up over two centuries. Bernouilli trials are a model for real-life projects. An extensive set of data is obtained by using a technique such as random simulation (e.g. dice). The results of the simulation run are reviewed or evaluated, then stored for future use. These results end up as a large computer database that requires a lot of technical expertise and resources to build up and analyze. Daniel Bernouilli's uncle, Jacob, was able to define what we might reasonably expect from our modern-day business behaviour, even when writing three centuries ago: *'The value of our expectation always signifies something in the middle between the best we can hope for and the worst we can fear.'*[4]

Modern business projects still trouble us with the fundamental question: 'What is the expected return from this project?' Perhaps we should rephrase the question: 'What is the reasonable expected return from this project?' Numbers have troubled mathematicians through the ages, even when using the 'advanced' decimal notation. Thus, numbers such as Pi, or the square root of two or three were described as 'irrational'. Our modern understanding of numbers is fine, except possibly when trying to evaluate probability and profit in business. There is a whole raft of models that can be used to moderate the exuberance of entrepreneurs in business projects. These can be tailored to fit the needs of your project. We look to rational mathematical and accountancy techniques to provide us with such useful tools. This is a small sample of possible techniques.

Estimated monetary value

EMV looks at your expected risk result as an absolute value, e.g. $1 million expectation of damage coming from two events:
a) 0.1 per cent chance of $1 billion disaster, or
b) 10 per cent chance of $10 million disaster.

But whereas the latter could be absorbed or suffered by most large firms, the first event would be enough to put many large companies out of business. Experts' evaluation of probability can be wrong by a factor of ten, or a firm may be genuinely unlucky. Therefore risk management expert counsel in the first event is likely to involve sharing of risk, or some form of insurance to externalize the potential damage to the company.

Risk-adjusted discount rate

This is a return to Fig. 3.4 'Factoring in risk: discounted returns' set out in Chapter 3. The RADR process can take risk exposure and risk attitude into account for the project. Thus, the revenue stream is first discounted to give us a net present value (NPV) number for the future worth of our money. Then, we discount it further by the RADR to derive an idea of how much that money is really worth to us bearing in mind that we took various risks to get it. The RADR approach can try to separate the risk component from our business project. Thus, the discount rate on Government Treasury bonds can be held as the nominal interest rate of 'risk-free' ventures (Rf); any additional interest above this rate is assumed to be because of risks taken. The risks can be broken down into various stages, e.g. project initiation, design, procurement, production and testing. We can also break down the risk factor into two elements, R1 and R2, where R1 is the going rate for projects in our normal line of business, and R2 is an additional risk premium for undertaking this particular project.

Therefore, RADR = Rf + R1 + R2.

Value at risk

This has come to the fore in the 1990s, particularly in banking and portfolio management. VaR is a measure of the value of the loss from the potential market risk when you are holding a particular position, e.g. a portfolio of bonds held in various currency denominations. Thus, for a company holding a market position x in US dollars:

$$VaRx = Vx \times dV/dP \times \Delta Pi$$

where VaRx is the value at risk of position x, Vx is the market value of position x, dV/dP is the price sensitivity per $ market value, ΔPi is the adverse change in price over time period i.

The VaR model has various assumptions over the normal probability distribution used – the skewness and the nature of long tails (see BSE case study, p. 10). It has also assumptions over standard deviation (volatility), the interrelationship between different price movements and the time series data being used. If these assumptions cannot be proven to hold in your case, then there are grounds to say that the VaR model is not robust for your given situation. Nevertheless, VaR has proven to be a valuable tool and an industry standard, provided its limitations are realized for each specific application.

Multiple estimating risk analysis

You can update your risk management plan, and rank the risk options that you studied. List the:

- base risk estimate
- average risk estimate
- most likely estimate.

Multiple estimating using risk analysis creates such an analytical structure.[5] Risk will entail both likelihood and gain (or loss). However, if you cannot easily quantify the benefits, or there are considerable 'social' gains, then MERA and EMV might kill off your project prematurely.

Criticism of 'hard' risk models

Put the 'hard' risk models into action. You may find them:

- mechanical and unrealistic
- difficult for obtaining accurate objective measures
- inflexible and not creative for businesses
- strait-jacket judgements, i.e. do not encourage pro-active risk management actions
- pessimistic about business – some opportunities are good but long-shots.

According the Air Marshal Sir John Curtiss, Chief Executive of the medical relief charity, Pathfinders:

'Projects for charities such as ours face the twin challenges of raising funds to save victims of natural disasters, and the considerable risk in sending skilled staff and supplies out to remote areas that have experienced recent devastation. We feel that the problems posed can be solved by experienced and brave staff backed by well planned logistics support operations. Furthermore, the satisfaction gained from saving lives and helping others through disasters is considerable, and exceeds what can be expressed by profits from normal business decision-making.'[6]

One valid criticism is that monetary models can kill project ideas too easily. Where monetary profits become hazy and difficult to predict, the hard models will be first to put the ideas in the wastepaper basket. Inventions that take a long time in gestation, or projects that take a lot of capital investment before taking in revenue, would tend to be among the first to be shot. This is particularly so in longer-term or high-tech industries, and is certainly true in non-profit projects.

CASE STUDY

Beijing–Paris classic car rally

The 1998 Beijing–Paris classic car rally followed in the time-honoured tradition of journeys and adventures around the world. All contestants were willing to invest time, effort and money into a physically gruelling, and at times life-threatening, race. It would have been difficult, if not impossible, to justify on cost-benefits analysis alone.

Planning meant rebuilding the 1932 Ford Model B, and stress-testing to help make it over China and the Himalayas. Modifications to strengthen the chassis, together with modern tools (e.g. satellite telephone), were necessary to lessen the chance of getting stranded. All this required project finance. Besides sponsorship by Hard Rock Asia and Carlsberg et al, and the favourable publicity, this was simply good fun. This was the real project success. The majority of the project owners (sponsors and drivers), plus the supporting team managers and mechanics, were more than happy to participate. They reached their goal (fourth in their class), and for the most part this goal was not a monetary one. It was a successful project.

Richard Curtis and Prince Idris Shah provide an account of the rally in *From Peking to Paris*. One contestant remarked:

'We're old boys with old toys. Our aim is to have a bloody good time, enjoy the experience, the scenery and the journey of a lifetime.'[7]

Scenario analysis

This is a 'softer' modelling technique, but one that is extremely subjective. We are going back to parts of the Delphi group (see Risk Analysis, Chapter 3). Modellers can choose various outcomes or scenarios as a basis for their plan of action. This technique is very useful where there is no adequate past data upon which to base accurate predictions or where outcomes are based on factors which are difficult to forecast, e.g. the weather.

CASE STUDY

Building a Venetian dam

Historical data show that floods in Venice occurred five times annually over 50 years; yet that figure has now risen to 80 times a year. The water rose 80cm 787 times over ten years, and came up up 1000cm high 137 times – a normal distribution.

One of the essential skills needed in managing project risk is that of project termination. A flood hazard may be either too difficult to protect against, or too expensive to justify in a politically-charged atmosphere. The Italian government's decision to scrap the proposed $2.5 billion flood barriers in Venice after ten years of discussion is an example of this.[8]

There is still the possibility of encountering the long tails of probability distribution that can occur with historic data (see BSE case study, p. 10). Or with the risk of floods in Venice, we could adopt the 'worst case scenario'. Let's say the waters rose by a maximum 1.4m in 1957, so we put an extra 20 per cent on top as our safety margin. Our risk analysis would lead us to build the flood barriers to block a possible 1.68m rise in the water level.

Stress testing or sensitivity analysis

There are ways in which we run simulations to test the operation of a project. The use of variations in the input factors can be reflected in major changes to the results. Thus, we can play 'what if' games to see how our project would behave. For example, raising inflation rates (or profit deflators) by 3 per cent, 4 per cent, 5 per cent, 10 per cent would tell you how profitable (or sensitive) your project would be under different conditions. You can raise the rate to a level which you believe is realistic, or where you think you have enough data to make a decision, e.g. to go ahead with the project or not.

CASE STUDY

Stress testing on London's telephone system

You might like to take a system as far as it will go, that is, take it and load it so much that the system breaks or stops functioning under the strain. Thus, you can put (or computer simulate) an excessive load of 50 000 cars and articulated lorries on the highway per hour to discover the point where everything just freezes up. You may also use automatic testing equipment to call into the Private Branch eXchange (PABX) telephone exchange and see when the whole system stops working, or when the PABX has an unacceptably high proportion of un-answered or rejected calls to your company. This service disruption is increased when it concerns a whole city. In London, for example, the telephone dialling code had to be changed to cope with the growing demand because the risks of increasing telecommunications usage had not been properly analyzed. Another change, in April 1999, meant new codes had to be announced worldwide, clients and personal contacts advised, letterhead paper changed, signs re-ordered. Each change represents millions of pounds for the greater London area which has a population of about 12 million people.

The considerable disruption could be minimized by adequate forecasting of future usage. Take a look at the DSL postcode for instance. London started with:

Mrs E. Brown
London →
London East Central →
London EC2 → then with the 'new postcodes'
London EC2M 5PP → then in 1999
London EC2M 5UU

Let your project platform have room to grow.

CASE STUDY

Big company simulation business from DSL

A common project in companies is to build the foundations of a suitable corporate telecommunications backbone. DSL experience shows us that many companies fix their telecommunications expansion limits too low, providing little room for growth. This means that their telecommunications system stand a higher risk of meeting failure of chronic system constraints because:

1 The system will not stand peaks of high usage, i.e. faxes, phone calls or Internet phone calls are blocked in queues.

2 The system may fail completely under higher loads – hence the need for '*stress testing*'.

3 The system will need to be upgraded, which can be disruptive.

4 The system will have to be replaced with a completely new one – very expensive indeed.

In very simple terms, a system capacity chart, incorporating future expansion, is needed for any telecommunications project, basically on the lines of:

Question	Number	Number of dial-up lines needed	Number of direct digital links
a) number of phone users now	250	25	4
b) number of phone users in three years	300		5
c) additional telephone sets	100	30	1
d) additional faxes	2	2	
e) other equipment, e.g. PC Internet modems to be used	50	15	1
Total = a+b+c+d+e		72	11

Project planning needs a good view of balancing the technology and business constraints. The principle is that the telecommunications system is not just a success now, it will also still be a success in three years' time. We never know the exact future needs, but we make estimates that cater for the risk of unexpected demand.

Risk modelling for the 21st century

There are myriad offers coming on the market for project management and risk management tools. Yet what many project managers crave is a clear vision through the project issues. We can see from previous mistakes that an over-abundance of technology does not solve fundamental problems. The London Stock Exchange Taurus system, a £500 million IT project cancelled in March 1993 after five years work, illustrates this point. A case of the mañana syndrome working overtime perhaps.[9]

Project control requires a deep-rooted understanding of how to handle human expectations and work flows. We have the technology, but we don't necessarily have the management. There is a need to control and also to bind a team of people working together. War is the supreme occasion when teams are bound together in extreme conditions. There is no short-cut to training good soldiers, given adequate raw material. The nature of war is a project that puts men to the ultimate test.

CASE STUDY

War against the communists post-world war II

US-led efforts in the Korean and Vietnam wars ended up as open-ended projects, with the western forces unable to triumph over opposing troops, despite their rather basic technology. The Korean conflict emphasized the problems in project logistics when US-dominated ground forces were being held at a standstill by the vastly technologically inferior Chinese, Vietnamese and Korean armies. The US found it impossible to destroy all communist transport and logistical operations, despite its superiority in the air and the fact that the communists were often resorting to primitive man, mule and oxen transport systems. The US forces had unclear project goals and were left wondering why they were in the country at all.

The Communists' Vo Nguyen Giap goes on record as one of the greatest modern-day generals. He conducted a lengthy battle against the French and Americans and beat them in Vietnam – which surely ranks as one of the worst conducted western wartime 'projects'. Giap identified one decisive factor in warfare – manpower (both male and female). A team without good quality soldiers has lost the war.

'In war there are two factors – human beings and weapons. Ultimately, though, human beings are the decisive factor. Human beings! Human beings!'[10]

A project that tries to replace the unharnessed resources of a human being entirely with technology is probably doomed.

The tools that we need to manage projects are generally very basic. They include a clear vision of what you are trying to achieve, with a structure that is geared towards control and monitoring. Open-ended projects are almost doomed because of the lack of control.

CASE STUDY

The Starr inquiry and 'Clintongate'

The Starr investigation of President Bill Clinton was a prime example of an open-ended project. This was given no clear mandate, and was allowed a free rein. Thus, improprieties over irregular property dealings in the Clintons' White-water, Arkansas, experience were expanded to a much wider field. Paula Jones's sexual harassment lawsuit to the much-heralded 'Monicagate' Lewinsky testimony meant that Special Prosecutor Starr could broaden the investigative project to cover many subjects that were not envisaged at the outset.

'... Vincent Foster's death, Filegate, Travelgate. A normal CEO, having spent his shareholders' capital and failed to produce a marketable product, would have been fired, but Starr was never a normal business-man. The fault doesn't lie with him; it lies with a statute that provides no incentive for special prosecutors to act in the interests of the people who employ them.'[11]

It also meant that the schedule, milestones, self-checking and project budgeting became alien notions.

It can be said that political and personal aims took over in many respects as the allegations of sexual misconduct dominated news headlines. Clinton aides were exasperated that an estimated four years and $40 million[12] study could be conducted in such a case, as opposed to the 1997 TWA plane crash off New York's Kennedy airport when over 200 people were killed. That investigation led by the Federal Aviation Authority, was reckoned to have cost the US taxpayer some $20 million, and had implications for the safety of air passengers around the world. No one was killed in Clintongate. Clearly, open-ended projects are something to avoid if you are worried about footing the bill.

'Though this was vastly too long and vastly too expensive, serious inquiry requires much more effort from Congress. Instead, the committee called Mr Starr as first witness in a clear attempt to cut the process short; and, by failing to question him with any incisiveness, showed that its chief interest was to score what political points it could, and then to shut up shop.'[13]

Clinton was acquitted in his impeachment on 12 February 1999. The 13-month 'Monica case' is a classic example of an open-ended project with poor aims definition, and unending budget that was bound to try the patience of the taxpayer.

Proper methodology and tools

Control and monitoring processes are essential for projects. These require a template or methodology such as RAMP or PRINCE, which would help to delineate the responsibilities of the project members. Adequate attention should be paid to the current and potential political risk and any likely effects upon the project. You will need a clear definition (goals) of what you are trying to achieve, and how you can measure success. Then you need a project team made up of people who work well together. The questions that arise come from understanding not just who is involved but who should be involved? Take a private company winning a bid for a scientific project.

CASE STUDY

NASA scientific project – task responsibilities

The company organization was a matrix of interconnected project roles: marketing and programme management in one organization with financial control and different functional departments. The programme manager acted as system engineer and purchased the technical expertise from the relevant departments, funding them with fixed dollar tasks. The technical experts were encouraged to be competitive with each technology and attempt to win the choice of technology for their department for follow-on effort in developing the satellite. The system requirements were defined flexibly enough to permit each technology to emphasize its strengths.[14]

A project success overall in technological, business and political terms.

SMEs and those dealing with smaller projects should be advised to adopt a more suitably-sized and cost-effective, slimmed-down project management package. A mini-RAMP, Spoce or Spocette are possible choices when the projects are deemed to be too small to undertake with the standard methodologies, and would not tie up as many resources in labour, paperwork and time as the mainstream project management packages. Once again, the choice is yours; you might care to select a different package for your needs.

A clear vision of a project structure should come out:

- goals
- key personnel
- milestones
- schedule
- budget.

These should all be obtained as soon as possible.

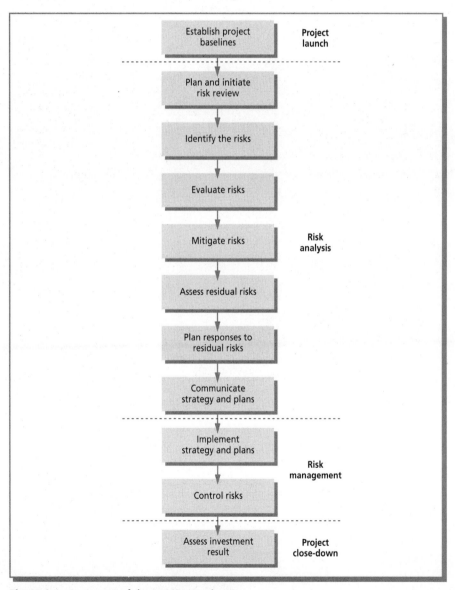

Fig 11.2 ● **An extract of the RAMP overview**[15]

The RAMP methodology can be suitable for handling risk issues in many projects. An extract of the RAMP overview is shown in Fig. 11.2.

A risk-managed project can be plotted on one of the range of industry-standard tools and packages and can be outlined at the beginning using software such as spreadsheets on Excel or Lotus 1-2-3. This sort of planning on basic software is particularly useful in SMEs or in small projects that cannot justify the purchase and implementation of larger-scale risk management toolkits. A big picture of where we are trying to get to would help everyone.

A Gantt chart is often used because it is easy to understand – it is preferable to prove the validity of the project by tried-and-trusted means first, without using unfamiliar techniques. The project manager can bring in state-of-the-art technological tools later to impress the message on his/her audience. Nevertheless, the traditional tools do require some modification in order to analyze and manage project risk effectively. Take the old-fashioned Waterfall project life cycle. See Fig. 11.3. Notable features are the inclusion of:

1 multi-stage concurrent task process to reflect real life

2 contingency or buffer of added time for getting each stage completed

3 evaluation of pessimistic and optimistic views of budget and schedule

4 accounting by 'trigger' mechanism to instigate more project control.

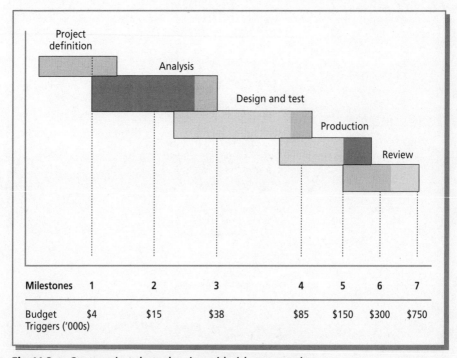

Fig 11.3 ● Gantt project chart planning with risk status review

These are refinements on tried-and-trusted techniques and would work for both small and large projects. They have the additional benefit of being easy to understand and to implement. The key phrase is 'tried and trusted' – they are not state-of-the-art 'black-box' scientific techniques of project management.

The revised Gantt chart takes into account a contingency for each stage of the project, such as a buffer of extra time needed to finish each stage. The varying subjective estimations of time required can be refined by the use of the Delphi group to assess the pessimistic and optimistic values. These are usually derived in the PERT-CPA analysis. The traditional Waterfall project development rarely occurs in real life; usually project constituent stages have started before their preceding activities have finished.

A milestone is erected at each critical stage to monitor progress. Associated performance parameters are given for a project to have reached such a stage. This will be the quality assurance matrix of criteria to judge the project quality at that particular milestone. When the budget runs above certain trigger levels, automatic reporting and investigating procedures should commence. Serious project controllers should examine why the project has gone over budget, and how to get it back on track as soon as possible. This sort of monitoring will help to guard against the risk of runaway projects or 'project creep', where things get out of hand, then get caught up in a vicious circle. At some point essential project features will have to be separated from the optional extras. The contractor and project manager will have to negotiate and agree on which functions and products were listed in the contract and which are additional and have to be paid for outside the budget.

The project owner will have to do all he can to deliver the most suitable project. He will have to decide which functions are vital and delete those that are redundant, making amendments where required. At a critical time in the project he will have to freeze changes or the process will become never-ending.

Risk analysis follows on naturally when making a realistic assessment of the project and which factors can influence it. A natural consequence is a clear listing of relative probabilities and their impacts. Risk analysis must be understandable and actionable.

Barry Riley, writing a column for the *Financial Times*, looked at the actions of WM Company, a UK investment consultancy specializing in fund performance measurement. WM's risk measurement service provides an interpretation that is designed to be fairly easy to understand.

> *'Risk analysis … is "too mathematical, too esoteric". Investment professionals would mostly lap the subject up, but WM is clearly worried about baffling and alienating its clients.'*[16]

Summary of scheduling and budgeting

We can use standard risk management techniques such as the Monte Carlo model to derive predicted project elapsed schedules or cost patterns to build up a database of simulated outcomes. Or we could look up an historical database of records (if one exists) to establish project results. Either method will give us a probability distribution that points to likely trends. Our model shows that your project has an average (median) outcome of 48 weeks' duration, or total costs of £48 million. Thus, any directive or desire to drive the project at high speed or low cost could be an extremely risky option. Our modelling of the data leads us to conclude that any proposal to complete the project within 48 weeks or with project costs of £48 million is very optimistic. The chances of this occurring are almost zero, so your project or you as project manager are probably going to end up with a problem.

We can get a good picture of how risk will appear by looking at how the probability is distributed (see Fig. 11.4). Looking at the nature of the project, what is the likely progression? Let's take a two-year project with a DM86 million budget. Some project managers might assume that there will be fairly straight-line progress, as in Line A. In fact, the nature of the project industry, or the way you manage a project, could mean that you will either:

1 start rapidly on the project, as in Line B, and spend a lot of money in the early stages, then slow down in the final phases. This could be due to a lack of the relevant personnel, waiting for parts or suitable operating conditions, or favourable testing and approval;

2 commence slowly, spend rapidly in the middle project stages, then curb expenditure towards the end. This is a more usual operating manner, as depicted in Line C.

You will need to be aware of the style and inertia you are likely to experience during the project, which will have considerable impact on how the risk factors will affect your project.

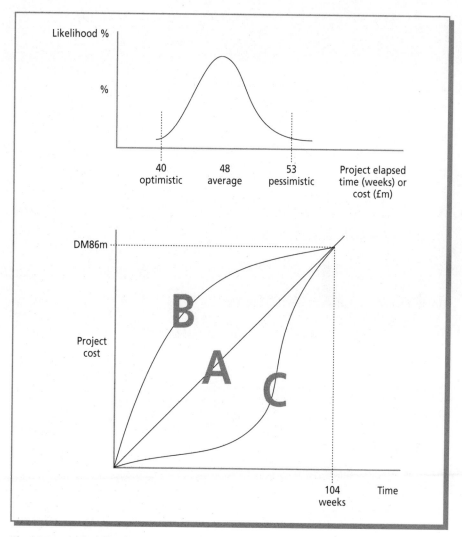

Fig 11.4 ● Probability factors

One of the key points is to understand what type of probability distribution we are faced with. This directly affects how the average mean project cost (or completion time) is calculated. Project managers can be under the wrong assumptions about how their data is distributed.

We can look at this somewhat mechanistic triangular distribution as an A-shaped data curve.

215

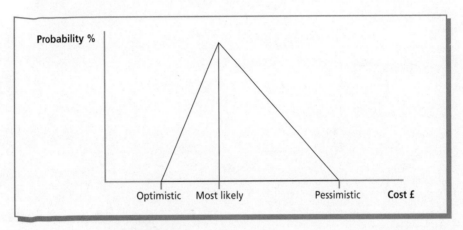

Fig 11.5 ● Triangular distribution

Table 11.1 ● Triangular distribution task costs

Task	Low value a (£)	Most likely m (£)	High value b (£)	Mean X £	Standard Deviation	Variance
Task A	550	600	740	630		1616.67
Task B	650	750	790	730		866.71
Task C	900	1090	1130	1040		2517.02
Total estimate	2100	2440	2660	2400	70.71	$\sqrt{5000.57}$

Thus, a group of experts such as economists or bankers would be assembled to determine the likely GDP or interest rates for the next few years, or for the life of the project. They would present scenarios for, let's say, three years. For example:

3-4.99 per cent interest rates (10 per cent sure)
5-6 per cent interest rates (60 per cent sure) – most likely
above 6 per cent interest rates (30 per cent sure)

Beta distributions using PERT-derived values as from our experts on the Delphi group give us an evaluation of pessimistic (a), most likely (m), optimistic (b) outcomes. We can adopt different calculations when dealing with Beta distributions.

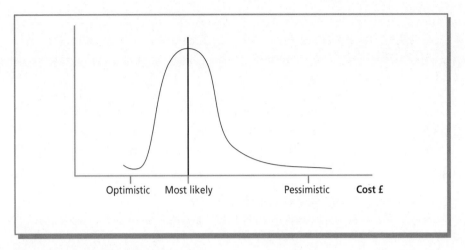

Optimistic   Most likely   Pessimistic   **Cost £**

Fig 11.6 ● The Beta distribution

Table 11.2 ● Beta distribution task costs

Task	Low value a (£)	Most likely m (£)	High value b (£)	Mean X £	Standard Deviation	Variance
Task A	550	600	740	615		1002.78
Task B	650	750	790	740		544.44
Task C	900	1090	1130	1065		1469.44
Total estimate	2100	2440	2660	2420	54.92	$\sqrt{3016.66}$

What does this mean? A low variance, such as the weather around San Diego, California, makes us more comfortable because we know that outdoor events are less vulnerable to freak weather conditions there. You can generally bet on the sun shining and the outdoor temperature being around 25°C, good enough for a picnic. But New York or Chicago run the gamut of weather that could plunge to –15°C or lower. There might also be snow. Chicago-O'Hare airport was closed during the snow storms of early 1999. High variance results in higher unpredictability, and higher risk. Don't plan an outdoor picnic all year round.

People often choose to refer to historical logs to forecast the risk to their project, such as warm weather during a skiing holiday. In this respect, places like Aviemore in Scotland cannot hope to compete with Switzerland and

Austria, which tend to be blessed with snow-filled ski slopes and sunny weather. In this decision-making process, tourists can regard the bottom (pessimistic view) and the top (optimistic opinion) as being wildcats, and focus on the middle section. Thus, they can lend a deaf ear to friends who advise them with their expert opinion: *'It'll be sunny and brilliant weather the whole two weeks!'* Or, *'It always pours down the whole time you're there!'* People going on holiday, it should be noted, tend to be more risk-ignorant, and thinking of sunshine can shut out the glum reality of prevailing weather conditions. The perceived conditions form a more optimistic Beta distribution, even though the existing risk remains the same. Put yourself on the right side of the curve.

Conversely, the ranking of assessments can play an effective part in eliminating some of the risk-averse and risk-seeking views to form a more balanced judgement. Then the company can use the remaining views to take an average. You can try to reduce project bias, not so much eliminate it entirely. Expert opinions generally differ in types of risk which are subjective and for which there is not an established hard set of data.

Notes and references

1 Refer to, for example, Spocette, a mini risk management package for small projects.

2 Barakat, M., personnel correspondence, December 1998.

3 Shtub, A. et al. (1994) *Project Management*, Prentice Hall, p. 196.

4 Hacking, I. (1975) *The Emergence of Probability*, Cambridge University Press, p. 144.

5 Refer to Raftery, J. (1996) *Risk Analysis in Project Management*, by Chapman & Hall; *Riskmetrics*, J.P. Morgan at www.jpmorgan.com

6 Personal correspondence with Air Marshal Sir John Curtiss, Chief Executive of Pathfinders, London.

7 Shah, Prince I. and Curtis, R. (1998) *From Peking to Paris*, Jugra Publications, p. 45.

8 *Financial Times*, 11 December 1998, p. 2.

9 Drummond, H., 'Are we closer to the end? Escalation and the case of Taurus', pp. 17–28, IPMA vol. 17, nr. 1, February 1999.

10 Karnow, S. (1994) *Vietnam: A History*, Penguin USA, p. 206.

11 The *New Yorker*, 21 September 1998, 'Monicanomics 101'.

12 *The Economist*, 28 November 1998, p. 19.

13 *The Economist*, 28 November 1998, p. 19.

14 Kolker, M., personnel correspondence, December 1998.

15 RAMP (1998), p. 98, Thomas Telford Books (London).

16 *Financial Times*, 2 December 1998, p. 19.

12

Summary

66 'The time has come,' the Walrus said,
'to talk of many things.' **99**

Lewis Carroll: *Alice Through the Looking-Glass*

Projects, such as those in the field of architecture, sometimes involve conflicting factors. The practice of architecture has to include finance, engineering, construction and project management. At the outset it is not so much an exercise in art expression, but, particularly where there is a budget and time constraint as there always is on large projects, architecture becomes a strenuous exercise in both business and project management. Creating Berlin's Potsdamer Platz from just a waste-ground in six years is a real success story, but where there is such a rush, true art should not necessarily be expected.[1] Where the architect is in dispute with the project owner, true art and architectural merit tend to be compromised first in order to meet deadlines.

Projects are collective enterprises involving a combination of resources to be used towards achieving a stated goal or set of objectives. This invariably involves putting people together in a joint effort; they may never have worked together, and need a lot of controlling and monitoring. The structured project with risk management runs along the lines of:

- risk analysis
- identify project players, risks and their probabilities and impact
- identify project risk partners and risk management through means of either:
  (a) risk sharing
  (b) risk mitigation
  (c) risk avoidance
  (d) risk absorption;
- risk re-assessment
  – use milestones and project review
  – look for new risks, or analyze new data to evaluate risks
  – amend plan if necessary;
- prototype (where necessary or advised)
  – get a better conceptual view of the project and product
  – encourage the client/project owner to give input
  – put new data into changes to design where feasible;

- test
  - possibly go into production
  - look at maintenance and post-sales service.

We can summarize many project risk management factors with an example involving a letter copied to DSL.

CASE STUDY

Z construction project, London 1999

Dear X

With reference to the Z construction project, we attach the following details.

We estimate that the site is worth £4 million. (See note A)

Our quantity survey has made a preliminary examination and estimates that £12 million of work will be required. (Note B)

We believe, from our experience of similar complex projects, that an extra 15 per cent worth of work will be needed. (C)

We estimate that the project would take 22 months to complete. (D)

We would be prepared to commence the project for an initial down-payment of 20 per cent, cleared into our bank account. (E)

Our associates will be willing to grant you a loan at a rate of LIBOR +3 per cent should you require it. (F)

They will grant you the loan based on the security of 51 per cent of your company shares. (G)

The terms in this offer are valid up to 15 April 1999. (H)

Please reply by return of registered post. (I)

Yours truly

Note A: intrinsic worth or initial value of project/collateral
Note B: use of outside expert or Delphi to assist in project estimates
Note C: bench-marking to create a contingency fund
Note D: schedule estimate, sometimes the hardest part
Note E: reduce risk by taking first payment up-front
Note F: structured finance to help the project happen
Note G: collateral on the loan; gain control of the company if loan problems arise
Note H: make the project time-sensitive to reduce risk exposure
Note I: use reliable and secure correspondence.

Project leadership

Project management has often been affected by risk. This has been attributed to:

(a) improper risk perception

(b) poorly funded or inadequately staffed risk analysis

(c) a risk group or staff with no power to take effective action

(d) too much emphasis on mechanical risk factors

(e) a failure to account for political or social risk factors

(f) too rigid an adherence to an out-of-date view of the business and risk

(g) no methodology or procedure for handling risk.

Project risk-management can:

- reduce the element of perceived 'bad luck'
- reduce the likely loss
- be used to maximize the likely profit
- improve the quality of planning
- lead to the most efficient use of personnel and capital
- help to differentiate betwen good management and bad
- be an intrinsic part of good business procedure.

We have distinguished between likelihood and luck. Good project management is able to remove or reduce some of the elements attributed to bad luck. You have to examine the practicality and benefits of risk operations for your project. Risk management is not an afterthought in a project; it needs to be built into the project design at the start. One way to introduce risk management is as part of a consistent methodology. There is no one-size-fits-all methodology – all toolkits and procedures generally have to be amended in some way to suit a particular project. For small projects, research points to tailored procedures having a success rate of 80 per cent. This is compared to a lower 59 per cent for 'untailored' standard procedures. Conversely, when we look at the failure rate, standard procedures fared worse in small projects with a high failure rate of 16 per cent. This was much worse than the 2 per cent failure rate when using tailored procedures.[2] Adapt to the project in question!

The cost of implementing and operating risk management should not outweigh the benefits, particularly for small and medium size enterprises, which are cost-sensitive. SME managers can use risk analysis/management, though probably a slimmed-down version.

Project risk methodology

A methodology such as RAMP can use risk analysis/management, but methodologies should be evaluated to determine whether they suit a customer's or project manager's needs. Deployment of risk management services can be outsourced, bearing in mind the issues and caveats already listed. Risk management services provided by outside parties have to be compared in a benchmarking process and investigated for value for money. Official standards in themselves are not a guard against project risk, although you are still encouraged to adopt these standards for your business operations within a wider project risk management methodology. The direction of future risk management will most likely see standards develop as a bigger and more fundamental part of normal project management.

Project management technology

Scientific and technological advances are bringing a host of welcome benefits. These form a platform or foundation on which you can run a project. This will involve a greater degree of IT within the project, for example use of the internet, ERP and risk modelling. One of the keys to a successful project is a good IT platform. This should be viewed as a flexible base for managing the project. Technology involves an element of risk, and it should not be seen as a solution to fundamental business problems. Throwing manpower at a project does not necessarily create better results; in fact, it may slow down the project.[3] Spending more money does not always solve deep-rooted problems. For instance, the UK Audit Commission has compiled figures on the performance of local services. It finds that, with the country's police forces, better results are not necessarily the result of increased spending.

> *'In some forces, there were increases in the number of police officers ... but the percentage of crimes solved either stayed the same or fell ... simply deploying more police officers does not reduce the amount of crime occurring in an area.'*[4]

Technology tends to make the business community more open – this can be an advantage in both cutting costs and increasing choice, but it can also be a disadvantage in posing a potential security threat. It has to be implemented on a proper timescale, with control over user requirements and budget. Otherwise, things will go wrong because everyone wants to pull the project in his or her own direction.

The direction of future risk management will most likely see it develop as a bigger and more fundamental part of normal project management. Tools and toolkits will become more commonplace. As we have shown, many of the techniques and tools in project risk management do not involve rocket science, nor are they astronomically expensive. Some data and tools are available free of charge or at low cost on the internet (see Appendix 2), and are within the reach of small organizations too if they want to use them.

Conclusions

We have identified various categories and characteristics of risk to gain a brief overview of what they entail. Bad luck in a project can be a smokescreen for risk magnets – those projects that are designed to attract risk. This risk comes from different sources and will have different effects on your business. The first thing needed is an appreciation of project risk. Organizations should be neither risk-ignorant nor risk-seeking.

Risk analysis is used to evaluate which types of risk exist and how they may affect your project. Many projects do not dedicate enough time and resources to this. The initial focus should be on evaluation and risk modelling: a thinking stage, if you like. Risk management is the next essential stage. It is all about action to reduce potential negative impact on your project. Projects that make use of risk analysis should follow it through into risk management. This is the doing part of our understanding of risk. Companies that have risk management teams without adequate resources or authority to make use of them are likely to suffer in some way. Token risk management offers little or no protection.

Risk analysis and risk management are nearly always desirable because potential damage can cancel out potential profits. They should not be considered a luxury or an unnecessary cost. Too often, organizations do not devote enough resources to risk analysis and risk management. Technology alone will not handle project risk. Humans do.

It is also necessary to evaluate a project's costs and benefits, plus its risk management measures. There are three important stages in which to examine risk or cost-benefits:

1 project initiation
2 during the project execution
3 at project close-down.

One vital skill is judging project termination. This is deciding on and carrying out termination of projects that have little benefit, too high costs, unacceptable risks, or goals that are no longer achievable. Projects that pass evaluation of cost-benefit and risk should be allowed to continue to their logical conclusion.

The great value of risk management is having trained staff who know what to do. Companies may not wish to get involved in training either because they do not believe things will go wrong or because they think such precautions are too expensive. The reasons for the damage that projects all too often suffer may be apparent only with the benefit of hindsight. The need for risk management exists from the outset. It should not be an afterthought.

Not all projects fail by any means. Successful projects do occur in real life, but they are nurtured throughout, rather than left out in isolation. People live and work in buildings that are constructed to withstand stresses from usage and the weather. Sailors ride the waves and weather the troughs – while their boats may sustain occasional damage. Projects have a life of their own and they are designed to survive a reasonable amount of shock or damage, even to thrive, but they succeed through constant supervision and checks. Managing project risk is through design and proper utilization of resources and not by accident. This is basic human effort, not arcane rocket science, and it is the essence of good project risk management.

Project risk and risk management are with us to stay. Good luck!

Notes and references

1 The World Today, BBC World, 24 December 1998.
2 IPMA, February 1999, vol. 17, no. 1, p. 56.
3 Brookes, F. (1995) The Mythical Man-Month: Essays on Software Engineering, Addison-Wesley.
4 The *Independent*, 28 January 1999, p. 11.

Assignments

Here are some issues and questions which might arise during a project.

Assignment 1
Introducing a hospital's IT-based diagnostic system

A new computer system is being installed in a hospital at Wardbrookes Healthcare. This system is reputed to use the latest technology to assist the doctors in diagnosing symptoms and prescribing the necessary drugs. It has been tested in a South-East Asian hospital, where we are told it was successful, and is making its debut in a western European healthcare environment. There is a lot of pressure to ensure that this pilot project is a success.

You are told to assess its performance for use in your hospital. You have also been called in to address some key issues, including medical ethics, responsibility for installation, responsibility when litigation arises, user support and training.

Questions:

How effective is it in helping to treat patients?
What do you think of the use of computer diagnoses in treating patients?
Will the computer diagnoses be put to practical use?
Can we mix and match from the doctor's diagnoses and the computer's diagnoses?
What are the possible outcomes if some diagnoses prove to be incorrect?
What if some diagnoses prove fatal?
What are the likely legal damages both in money and in staff terms?
Is the doctor covered by insurance for diagnosis and prescription errors?
Is the hospital covered by insurance for diagnosis and prescription errors?
Can the computer system supplier be sued for diagnosis and prescription errors?
Are there any instances of similar law suits?
Are there any other cases of diagnostic error involving the computer system supplier?
What other cases of diagnostic error have been handled by the insurance company?

What do you know of the legal framework for computer system diagnoses in treating patients in South-East Asia?
Who will operate the system in the hospital?
How will your hospital staff be trained to operate this system?
What training and back-up will the computer supplier give?
What back-up facilities are there for the staff?
What back-up facilities will there be for the computer?

Assignment 2
Constructing a new school in an emerging market

An unnamed Muslim country asks you and your company to build a large schooling complex for them. It is hoping that the project can be completed very quickly, so there is unlikely to be an international call for tenders.

Is this a good market? You have a short time to complete a detailed reply to their request.

Questions

What are the prospects over the next five (or so) years?
Can I get an acceptable return within this time?
Who are the main project players?
Is the political climate going to be favourable?

Assignment 3
Building an airport in Africa

General Siswe-Banze of the Equatorial African Republic (EAR) has invited your company to bid for this contract in the capital, Benzoso. You will have to put down $1 million as a deposit to bid. Decisions are due at the end of 12 months.

Questions

Is there political stability?
What is the likelihood of war or of the general's regime toppling?
What is the likelihood of securing the contract?
How much work (man-weeks and dollars) is needed to prepare the bid?
How great is the risk of losing your deposit?
How many sweeteners are likely to be needed for this bid?
What is the likelihood of them annulling the contract?

Assignment 4
Opening a traffic management system

You have won a contract to open a new traffic management system but your former contractor in technological signalling systems is going out of business. Plus, you have to find contractors to install the systems on site.

Questions

What are the technologies available for this system?
What are their relative merits and disadvantages?
Who are the contractors for these systems?
How do the contractors' performance records look?
What is your probable back-up system?
Who will accept liability for accidents caused by faulty traffic signals?

Assignment 5
Installing a bank's IT-based dealing system

The world-famous Dudley's Bank Corp has invited your company to design and install a large and complex dealing system. They want the project completed before 31 December 1999. There will be a wide invitation to tender. You have a short time to prepare your tender.

Questions

What are the prospects of us winning this tender?
What is our probable winning price?
How much surety do we have to put up in order to bid?
What is our probable performance bond for this contract?
What will be our performance limits?
Can we get an acceptable profit at this price?
Who are the main competing project bidders?
Will the bank be in a position to honour its commitments to us?
What measures are already in place to handle Year 2000 problems?
Who will guarantee/insure against Year 2000 compliance for the client?

Assignment 6
Opening a restaurant

You have decided to open a restaurant. You have to prepare a business plan for backers at short notice.

Questions

Who are your backers?
Do you have an adequate history for each of them?
How will you finance the project?
Is this secure?
What do you need to consider, for instance interest rates offered?
Do you have 100 per cent planning permission?
Are there any planning restrictions?
What is the health and safety policy here?
What are the sanitary standards necessary?
Are there sufficient restaurants in the area?
What is the local council's policy for new restaurants?

Assignment 7

Opening a department store

You and your partners are opening a new department store. You estimate that your reserves will stand at $12 million at the start of the project.

Questions

How do you forecast your cash flow over 12, 24, 36 months?
What are the terms of your borrowings?
What kind of cash modelling have you used: NPV, DCF, IRR, MERA or other?
How resilient and applicable is your cash modelling?
Do you have a contingency if sales drop 10 per cent next year?
What have you done to minimize theft from a) outside parties, b) staff?
Have you installed closed-circuit cameras?
Are there enough guards on the door?
Do you have plain-clothes surveillance staff?

Assignment 8

Opening a network of stores

You have decided to open a network of video and media stores.

Questions

Who have you chosen as your project manager?
How did you select him/her?
Who are their construction sub-contractors?
What is their record on previous construction jobs?
How do you ensure your franchise holders maintain good operational quality?

What contingencies do you have if they fail to pay you?
What have you done to protect against leakage on deliveries?
What have you done to ensure that tapes and discs are not damaged in use?
What have you done to protect against shoplifting?

Assignment 9
Introducing a new line of pharmaceutical products

Questions
Has this drug been thoroughly tested?
What results and assumptions underlined the test plan?
What is the current FDA regulatory status on your testing?
Have you determined the significance of the long probability tails on testing?
What if there are side-effects?
What other similar products are there on the market?
Is any one product of the same formula?
Can you be successfully sued for copying any formula?

Assignment 10
Designing and installing a jewellery store abroad

You are called in as the sub-contractor to the project manager. He has asked you to implement the security measures.

Questions
What are the physical design characteristics of the premises?
What are the constraints on placing and positioning equipment and staff?
Is there closed-circuit CCTV?
Are there zoned areas of security?
Is there a security room and vaults in most central and secure locations?
Are there infra-red or photoelectric eyes for motion detectors?
Are there metal scanners in special sections?
Have you placed armed guards on the front door?
Is there fire and smoke detector equipment?
Is there a back-up electricity supply?
Do you keep a log of your staff to sign in?
Are there coded doors or door keys/cards?
Are wires concealed or buried in concrete?
Is there a back-up telephone system?
Have you carried out a vetting procedure of staff on their career and social background?
Central Computer & Telecoms Agency, info@ccta.gov.uk

APPENDIX 2

Further information

Bibliography

Chicken, J. C. (1994) *Managing Project Risks in Major Projects*, Chapman & Hall.
Construction Industry Council (1998) *Constructor's Key Guide to PFI*, Telford.
CCTA, the Central Computer & Telecommunications Agency, UK (1997) *Instruction to SSADM 4+*.
Karnow, S. (1994) *Vietnam: A History*, Random House.
Institute of Civil Engineers and Institute of Actuaries, *RAMP: Risk Analysis*.
Institute of Civil Engineers (1991) *Guidance on Tenders for Civil Engineering Contracts*.
Institute of Civil Engineers (1997) *Adjudication Procedure*.
Institute of Civil Engineers (1997) *Arbitration Practice*.
Institute of Civil Engineers (1994) *Conciliation Procedure*.
The International Project Management Association, *International Journal of Project Management*, Elsevier, UK, February 1999.
(1998) *Management for Projects*, Thomas Telford.
Meredith, J. & Mantel, S. (1997) *Project Management*, John Wiley.
Morris, P., *The Management of Projects* (1997) Thomas Telford.
Project Management Institute, *Project Management Book of Knowledge*, USA.
Raftery, J. (1996) *Risk Analysis in Project Management*, E&F.N. Spon (Chapman & Hall).
Soros, G. (1998) *The Crisis of Global Capitalism*, Little, Brown & Co.
Wallace, J. (1997) *Overdrive*, John Wiley.

Further contacts

American National Standards Institute, www.ansi.org
Association of Pathfinders, pathfinder_association@email.msn.com
British Standards Institute, London, www.bsi.org.uk
Central Computer & Telecoms Agency, info@ccta.gov.uk
DSL Consultants Ltd, www.dslconsultants.com
Euro Business Management (M&A), www.ebml.co.uk
Federation Internationale des Ingenieurs-Conseils (International Federation of Consulting Engineers), www.fidic.org
GARP (Global Association of Risk Management Professionals), www.garp.org
IBM Project Manager, www.europe.ibm.com/pmdirect
Institute of Actuaries, www.actuaries.org.uk
Institute of Civil Engineers, www.ice.org.uk
International Standards Organisation, Switzerland, www.iso.ch
Mamdouh Barakat Risk Management, www.mbrm.com
JP Morgan, www.jpmorgan.com
Newsbase, UK, www.newsbase.co.uk
Project Management Institute, USA, www.pmi.org

Index